CW00779066

Muslim Saints and Mystics

Muslim Saints and Mystics

Episodes from
the Tadhkirah al-Awliyā'
of Farīd al-Dīn 'Aṭṭār

Translated
A.J. Arberry

IBT
Islamic Book Trust
Kuala Lumpur

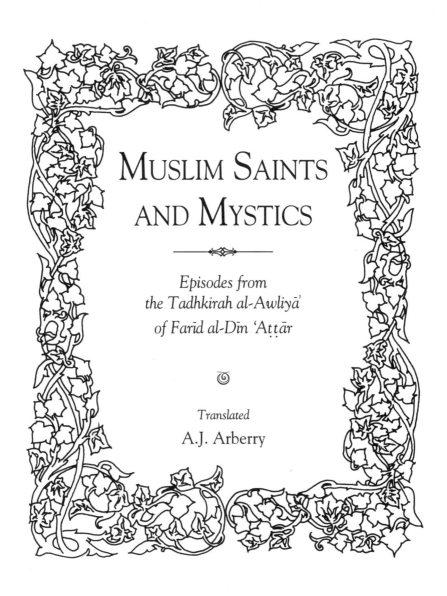

© Islamic Book Trust 2008

This new edition 2008 by
Islamic Book Trust
607 Mutiara Majestic
Jalan Othman
46000 Petaling Jaya
Malaysia
www.ibtbooks.com

Islamic Book Trust is affiliated to The Other Press.

Perpustakan Negara Malaysia Cataloguing-in-Publication Data

Attar, Farid al-Din
Muslim saints and mystics : episodes from tadhkirah al-awliya (memorial of the saints) / by Farid al-Din Attar ; translated by A. J. Arberry.
ISBN 978-967-5062-09-4
ISBN 978-967-5062-13-1 (Hard Cover)
1. Sufism--Iran. 2. Muslim saints. I. Arberry, A.J. (Arthur John).
II. Title.
297.40922

Printed by
Academe Art & Printing Services

Publisher's Note

This book is intended to introduce to the readers such names whose lives reflected the light of the true spirit of Islam.

Sufism is said to be the cultivation of perfect human beings who are mirrors reflecting the Divine Names and Attributes. In Sufism, a perfected human being is also called a *walī* (saint), a word that literally means 'sincere friend'. All prophets have also been *walīs* of Allah. The mission of Muḥammad, peace be upon him, was both absolute sainthood and prophethood.

The saints, each according to his or her own capacity, have drunk from the fountain of Truth. Because they are known only by God, only God can truly know the differences between their spiritual stations. In a *ḥadīth qudsī*, God says, "My friends (saints) are under my banner; no one knows them but me."

Most people do not have the patience necessary to know the saints, whose deep spiritual experience provided the foundation of their devotional life in Islam. The present work by Farīd al-Dīn ʻAṭṭār, the great sufi poet of Iran, is undoubtedly an important one in that it throws much light on the teachings and practices of Sufism.

This book follows our earlier book *Men Around the Messenger*, and is part of a series of books Islamic Book Trust has started on great Muslims whose lives and teachings would inspire young Muslims to seek guidance from Islam.

Islamic Book Trust,
Kuala Lumpur,

Contents

Introduction

Farīd al-Dīn 'Aṭṭār, author of the book here presented in an abridged translation, is to be accounted amongst the greatest poets of Persia; his dimensions as a literary genius increase with the further investigation of his writings, which are still far from completely explored, though welcome progress has been made of late in their publication. The existence of a number of remarkable studies of 'Aṭṭār, listed in the Bibliography below, absolves the present writer from the necessity of going into lengthy detail about the keenly disputed details of his life and works. Here it will suffice to state that he appears to have died between AD 1220 and 1230 at an advanced age, possibly at the hands of the Mongol invaders of Persia; the traditional account that he was born in 1119 and murdered precisely in 1230 is now generally rejected. Of the very numerous epics and idylls ascribed to 'Aṭṭār perhaps nine may be recognised as authentic of these the most famous is the *Manṭiq al-Ṭayr,* that subtle and charming allegory of the soul's progress towards God, familiar, (though still not familiar enough) to English readers through Edward Fitzgerald's summary *Bird-Parliament.*

The origins of Sufism

Sufism is the name given to the mystical movement within Islam; a Sufi is a Muslim who dedicates himself to the quest after mystical union (or, better said, reunion) with his Creator The name is Arabic in origin, being derived from the word *ṣūf* meaning "wool"; the Sufis were distinguishable from their fellows by wearing a habit of coarse woollen cloth, in time when silks and brocades had become the fashion of the wealthy and mundane-minded, symbolic of their renunciation of worldly values and their abhorrence for physical comforts.

Mystical awareness was certainly present in the Prophet Muḥammad's attitude to Allah, and "mystical" is an entirely appropriate adjective to describe his many experiences of supernatural Presence making contact through him with a message to mankind. The Qur'an, the book of Allah's revelations to Muḥammad, contains numerous passages of a mystical character which the Sufis seized upon eagerly to buttress their own claims to personal trafficking with God.

> And when My servants question thee
> concerning Me—I am near to answer
> the call of the caller, when he calls
> to Me; so let them respond to Me,
> and let them believe in Me: haply so they will go aright.
>
> (Qur'an, 2: 182)

> We indeed created man; and We know
> what his soul whispers within him,
> and We are nearer to him than the jugular vein.
>
> (Qur'an, 50: 51)

> All that dwells upon the earth is perishing, yet still
> abides the Face of thy Lord, majestic, splendid.
>
> (Qur'an, 55: 26)

One pregnant context was taken to refer to a pre-eternal covenant between God and man, the re-enactment of which became the earnest aspiration of the enthusiastic Sufi.

> And when thy Lord took from the Children of Adam,
> from their loins, their seed, and made them testify
> touching themselves, "Am I not your Lord?"
> They said, "Yes, we testify."
>
> (Qur'an, 7: 171)

The ascetic outlook and practice, an indispensable preparation to mystical communion, characterised the life not only of Muḥammad himself but of many of his earliest followers. Even when the rapid spread of Islam and the astonishing military conquests of neighbouring ancient kingdoms brought undreamed-of riches to the public exchequer, not a few of the leading men in the new commonwealth withstood all temptation to abandon the austere life of the desert, and their example was admired and emulated by multitudes of humbler rank. Nevertheless with the passage of time, and as Islam became increasingly secularised consequent upon further victories and rapidly augmenting complications of statecraft, the original ascetic impulse tended to be overwhelmed in the flood of worldly preoccupation.

Towards the end of the eighth century AD pious Muslims who remained faithful, through all trials and temptations, to the high ideals of the fathers began to form themselves into little groups for mutual encouragement and the pursuit of common aims; these men and women (for there were women amongst them of a like mind), opting out of the race for worldly advancement, took to wearing wool to proclaim their other-worldliness and were therefore nicknamed Sufis. These circles of devotees, and many isolated anchorites besides, appeared simultaneously in various parts of the Muslim empire; anecdotes from their lives and conversations, such as are told in the following pages, constitute the hagiography of Islam. A strong tradition connects the growth of this movement with the Prophet through his cousin and son-in-law 'Alī ibn Abī Ṭālib, the fourth caliph whose abdication led to the greatest schism in the history of the faith, the separation between Sunni and Shiite. According to this version, the Prophet invested 'Alī with a cloak or *khirqah* on initiating him into the esoteric mysteries, imparting to him therewith the heavenly wisdom which transcends all formal learning. In his turn 'Alī invested his own initiates, and through them the *silsilahs* or chains of affiliation passed on the inner lore of mystical truth to succeeding generations. Another prominent figure in some versions of early Sufism is the Persian convert Salmān, who is said to have taken part in the great siege of Madīnah. If any credence can be attached to this legend, Salmān would certainly be the first Persian Muslim to become a Sufi; he was the forerunner of a great multitude of Persian Sufis.

Sufism and Persia

The cities of Basra, Kūfah, Damascus, Cairo, Baghdad feature, along with the desert wastes of Arabia, Sinai, and Mesopotamia, as centres where the Sufi movement took root and flourished. At the same time a "school" of mysticism of extraordinary vitality and influence came into being in the distant province of Khurasan, the bridgehead between the Middle East and the Far East. The earliest semi-historical figure in this gallery of Persian saints is Ibrāhīm ibn Adham, "Prince of Balkh", whose conversion to the mystical life has been not inaptly compared with the legend of Gautama Buddha. It may be noted in this connection that in pre-Muslim times Balkh was the centre of a large Buddhist community, and the ruins of the massive Buddhist monastery called Naubahar were still pointed out centuries after the coming of Islam. Ibrāhīm travelled from Balkh to Syria in quest of "honest toil" and is said to have died fighting at sea against Byzantium in about 780; he had made personal contact with many Sufis of Syria and Iraq.

However spectacular the example of Ibrāhīm ibn Adham may have been, his influence upon the history of Sufism was soon overshadowed by the emergence in Khurasan of a mystical genius of the first order, Abū Yazīd of Bisṭām, who died about 875. His recorded acts and sayings ("Glory be to Me!" he ejaculated memorably in the fervour of mystical ecstasy) reveal him as a man of profound spirituality, who through long austerity and meditation reached a state of compelling awareness of the merging of his human individuality into the Individuality of God; a long and graphic description of his "flight of the alone to the Alone", a psychical journey performed in emulation of the Ascension of Muḥammad, will be found in due place in this book. To him is attributed the introduction of "intoxication" into Sufi doctrine, and in this respect he is contrasted with the "sober" school of Baghdad, headed by the great Junayd (d. 910). The latter, who studied and commented on Abū Yazīd's ecstatic sayings, reached indeed the same conclusions regarding the supreme mystical experience, the passing away of the temporal ego into the Eternal Ego; but he expressed the matter much more cautiously, supporting his argument by adroit "Neo-Platonic" interpretation of certain key quotations from the Qur'an and the sayings of the Prophet.

The early years of the tenth century witnessed the climax of a sharp orthodox Muslim reaction against the individualistic transcendentalism of the Sufis (some of whom deliberately flouted the proprieties to prove their contempt for human judgements), when the Persian-born al-Ḥallāj, who declared himself to be the Truth, was executed for blasphemy in Baghdad in 922. Thereafter the majority of vocal Sufis laboured to effect a reconciliation with traditionalism and accepted theology; and Persians played a notable part in this ironic endeavour. Textbooks aiming to prove the essential conformity of Sufi claims within the framework of strict Islamic doctrine were compiled by Sarrāj al-Ṭūsī (d. 988), Abū Bakr al-Kalābādhī (d. *circa* 995), and, most famous of all, al-Qushayrī of Nishapur (d. 1072). To Nishapur (whose most famous son to the world at large was of course 'Umar al-Khayyām) belonged also al-Sulamī (d. 1021), author of the oldest surviving collection of Sufi biographies; whilst Isfahan produced Abū Nu'aym (d. 1038) whose encyclopaedic *Ornament of the Saints* is our chief sourcebook on Muslim hagiology.

These men all wrote in Arabic, the learned and prestige language of Islam. Meanwhile the political renaissance of Persia under the virtually independent tenth-century dynasties of Saffarids and Samanids led to a revival of the Persian language, transformed as dramatically out of the old Pahlavi as English out of Anglo-Saxon, both phenomena the results of foreign conquest; and the eleventh century produced the first Sufi compositions in that tongue. On the formal side, we have in the *Kashf al-Maḥjūb* of Hujwīrī the earliest Persian textbook of Sufi doctrine, in its own way fully the equal of al-Qushayrī's celebrated *Risālah.* Then al-Anṣārī of Herat, an eminent Ḥanbalī lawyer (d. 1088) who wrote notable works in Arabic including the classic *Stages of the Mystic Travellers,* chose Persian, and a remarkably beautiful Persian at that, as the medium of his mystical meditations and prayers (*Munājāt*); he also produced in Herati Persian an enhanced edition of al-Sulamī's *Classes of the Sufis.* The following extract from the *Munājāt,* made into rhyming and rhythmical prose in imitation of the original, shows how closely Anṣārī adhered to the thought and expression of the earlier Sufis.

O my friend, behold yon cemetery, and see
how many tombs and graves there be;
how many hundred thousand delicate ones there sleep
in slumber deep.

Much toiled they every one and strove,
and feverishly burned with barren hope and selfish love,
and shining garments jewel-sprinkled wove.

Jars of gold and silver fashioned they,
and from the people profit bore away,
much trickery revealing, and great moneys stealing;
but, at the end, with a full regretful sigh
they laid them down to die.

Their treasuries they filled,
and in their hearts well-tilled
planted the seed
of lustful greed;
but, at the last,
from all these things they passed.

So burdened, suddenly
at the door of death they sank,
and there the cup of destiny
they drank.

O my friend, ponder well thy dissolution,
and get thee betimes thine absolution;
or, know it full well,
thou shalt in torment dwell.

In this same period Abū Sa'īd ibn Abī al-Khayr of Mayhanah (Khurasan), a man of great saintliness who met and corresponded with the masterphilosopher Avicenna, is credited with having used the newly invented and popular *rubā'ī* (quatrain) as his medium for expressing mystical ideas and experiences. His contemporary Bābā Ṭāhir, a wandering dervish, composed dialect verses in a somewhat similar quatrain form to court the Heavenly Beloved, pictured as coy and cruelly reluctant as any rustic maiden.

Like hyacinths on roses
Thy tangled locks are strung;
Shake out those gleaming tresses,
And lo, a lover young
On every hair is hung.

The breeze that fans thy tresses
Surpasseth fragrant posies.
In sleep I press thine image,
And as mine eye uncloses
I breathe the scent of roses.

Give me thy two soft tresses,
Therewith my lute I will string;
Since thou wilt never love me,
Why dost thou nightly bring
Soft dreams, my heart to wring?

Two eyes with surmeh languid,
Two curls that idly stray,
A body slim, seductive—
And dost thou truly say,

"Why art thou troubled, pray?"

Thou hast me, soul and body,
My darling, sweet and pure;
I cannot tell what ails me,
But this I know for sure,
Thou only art my cure.

The rise of Persian Sufi literature

The central theme of this ecstatic literature of early Persia Sufism was the yearning of the lover (the mystic) for the Beloved (God), and for a renewal of that intimate union which existed between the two before the dawn of creation. The language and imagery of old Arab erotic poetry became transformed into a rich and highly symbolical vocabulary mystical aspiration. This theme was taken up again by Aḥmad al-Ghazālī of Ṭūs, brother of the more famous Ḥujjah al-Islām whose learned and eloquent Arabic writings completed the reconciliation between Sufism and orthodoxy. The *Savaneh* of Aḥmad al-Ghazālī (d. 1123), a series of short and very subtle meditations in prose and verse upon the trinity of Beloved, Love, and Lover, set a fashion which was followed by, amongst others, 'Ayn al-Quẓāt of Hamadan (executed in 1131), the poet 'Īrāqī (d. 1289), and the great Jāmī (d. 1492).

By the beginning of the twelfth century, the *ghazal* (lyric) had also, like the *rubā'ī,* been taken over for Sufi use by the mystical lovers of God, who combined with its erotic symbolism a bacchanalian imagery deriving from the profane songs of Abū Nuwās and his school. The *qaṣīdah* (formal ode), the ancient creation of the pagan bards of Arabia and originally confined to panegyric and satire, had been converted to religious purposes by Nāṣir Khusrū, the Ismaili propagandist (d. 1060). The way was thus prepared for the emergence of the first major mystical poet of Persia, Sanā'ī, who devoted a long life (ending about 1140) and great talent to preaching in verse the Sufi discipline and doctrine.

The nightingale hath no repose
For joy that ruby blooms the rose;
Long time it is that Philomel
Hath loved like me the rosy dell.

'Tis sure no wonder if I sing
Both night and day my fair sweeting:
Let me be slave to that bird's tongue
Who late the rose's praise hath sung!

O *sāqī*, when the days commence
Of ruby roses, abstinence
By none is charged; then pour me wine
Like yonder rose incarnadine.

Not content with using *qaṣīdah, ghazal,* and *rubā'ī* in masterly fashion, Sanā'ī broke new ground in taking over the *mathnavi* (the rhyming couplet perfected and immortalised by Firdawsī in his *Epic of Kings)* as the medium par excellence for mystical instruction, an example presently followed by Niẓāmī (once in his *Treasury of Secrets). '*Aṭṭār, Rūmī, and thereafter by a host of notable emulators. His *Ḥadīqah al-Ḥaqīqah* ("Garden of Truth"), divided into ten graduated chapters in which the doctrine is kindly interspersed with illustrative anecdotes, is in effect an adaptation in verse of the prose treatises of al-Qushayrī and Hujwīrī. As a poet Sanā'ī perhaps did not reach the topmost heights; as a pioneer of what was to prove the mainspring of poetic inspiration in Persia (and without his example, we might never have enjoyed the masterpieces of Rūmī, Sa'dī, Ḥāfiẓ, Jāmī, and how many more) he fully merit the fame which he has secured.

To historical or semi-historical anecdote, the raw material of Sufi hagiography, now came to be added the apologue, the invented parable. Credit for the perfecting of this genre in Persian Sufi literature belongs to Suhrawardī Maqtūl (executed at Aleppo in 1191), a rigorous philosopher turned mystic whose beautiful myths (in which animal symbolism is freely used, harking-back to the *Fables of Bidpai* mediated through the *Kalila va-Demna* which the Persian Ibn al-Muqaffa' in about 75 put into Arabic from the Pahlavi) mount back via Avicenna to Plato. Thus, the Neo-Platonist doctrine of the descent of the soul into the body, which had been accepted by the Sufis as a prefiguration of the Qur'anic concept of a Primordial Covenant and which found eloquent expression in Avicenna's famous *Poem of the Soul,* is built by Suhrawardī into a very striking an graphic myth.

> A certain king possessed a garden which through all the four seasons never lacked for fragrant herbs, verdant grasses and joyous pleasances; great waters therein flowed, and all manner of birds sitting in the branches poured forth songs of every kind. Indeed, every melody that could enter the mind

and every beauty that imagination might conceive, all was to be found in that garden. Moreover a company of peacocks, exceedingly graceful, elegant and fair, had there made their abode and dwelling-place.

One day the king laid hold of one of the peacocks and gave orders that he should be sewn up in a leather jacket, in such wise that naught of the colours of his wings remained visible, and however much he tried he could not look upon his own beauty. He also commanded that over his head a basket should be placed having only one aperture, through which a few grains of millet might be dropped, sufficient to keep him alive.

Some time passed, and the peacock forgot himself, the garden-kingdom and the other peacocks. Whenever he looked at himself he saw nothing but a filthy, ugly sack of leather and a very dark and disagreeable dwelling-place. To that he reconciled himself, and it became fixed in his mind that no land could exist larger than the basket in which he was. He firmly believed that if anyone should pretend that there was a pleasurable life or an abode of perfection beyond it, it would be rank heresy and utter nonsense and stupidity. For all that, whenever a breeze blew and the scent of the flowers and trees, the roses and violets and jasmine and fragrant herbs was wafted to him through the hole, he experienced a strange delight and was curiously moved, so that the joy of flight filled his heart. He felt a mighty yearning within him, but knew not the source of that yearning, for he had no idea that he was anything but a piece of leather, having forgotten everything beyond his basket-world and fare of millet. Again, if ever he heard the modulations of the peacocks and the songs of the other birds he was likewise transported with yearning and longing; yet he was not wakened out of his trance by the voices of the birds and the breath of the zephyr.

The rest of this myth, with its subtle use of quotations from ancient Arabic poetry and the Qur'an, may be read in my *Classical Persian Literature.* It recalls a greater animal fable with a spiritual meaning, the sublime *Manṭiq al-Ṭayr* of 'Aṭṭār which Edward Fitzgerald epitomised in his *Bird-Parliament.* Meanwhile, within the field of hagiography (with which this present book is primarily concerned), full-length biographies of individual Sufi saints had begun to appear. The life and sayings of Abū Yazīd of Bisṭām provided al-Sahlajī with very rich materials. Ibn Khafīf of Shiraz found a Boswell in his pupil al-Daylamī. The poet-mystic Abū Sa'īd ibn Abī al-Khayr was commemorated by two biographers of his own descendants. The fashion was thus established for countless disciples to collect the acts and words of their Sufi masters; a very famous later instance is the *Fīhi mā fīhi* in which one of Rūmī's circle published the *Discourses* of that great man. Mention may be made in this context of the *Ma'ārif* ("Gnoses") of Rūmī's father, a lengthy autobiography recording in a wealth of detail the spiritual experiences of the author.

Such in brief is the background against which we may assess the works and achievements of the author of the book here translated.

'Aṭṭār and his *Memorial of the Saints*

In addition to the poetical writings, we possess from 'Aṭṭār's pen one work in prose, this *Memorial of the Saints* (the *Tadhkirah al-Awliyā'*) whose genuineness, certainly over a very substantial part (I refer to the edition by R.A. Nicholson from which all the following references are taken), is beyond reasonable doubt. It seems probable that this book was completed and made public somewhat late in 'Aṭṭār's life, but that large sections existed in draft when he was writing his poems; for many apologues in these were clearly based on materials assembled in the *Memorial.* In the preface to the *Memorial* 'Aṭṭār lists his reasons for writing the book, but not the sources used by him. His declared motives, as summarised by R.A. Nicholson, were as follows:

1. He was begged to do so by his religious brethren.
2. He hoped that some of those who read the work would bless the author and thus, possibly, secure his welfare beyond the grave.
3. He believes that the words of the Saints are profitable even to those who cannot put them into practice, inasmuch as they strengthen aspiration and destroy self-conceit.
4. Junayd said, "Their sayings are one of the armies of Almighty God whereby He confirms and reinforces the disciple, if his heart be dejected."
5. According to the Prophet, "Mercy descends at the mention of the pious": peradventure, if one spreads a table on which Mercy falls like rain, he will not be turned away portionless.
6. 'Aṭṭār trusts that the blessed influence of the Saints may be vouchsafed to him and bring him into happiness before he dies.
7. He busied himself with their sayings in the hope that he might make himself to resemble them.

8. The Qur'an and the Traditions cannot be understood without knowledge of Arabic, wherefore most people are unable to profit by them; and the Sayings of the Saints, which form a commentary on the Qur'an and the Traditions, were likewise uttered, for the most part, in Arabic. Consequently the author has translated them into Persian, in order that they may become accessible to all.
9. Since an idle word often excites keen resentment, the word of Truth is capable of having a thousandfold effect even though you are unconscious thereof. Similarly, 'Abd al-Raḥmān Iskāfī said that the reading of the Qur'an was effectual, although the reader might not understand it, just as a potion of which the ingredients are unknown.
10. Spiritual words alone appeal to the author. Hence he composed this "daily task" for his contemporaries, hoping to find some persons to share the meal which he has provided.
11. The Imam Yūsuf al-Hamadhānī advised some people, who asked him what they should do when the Saints had passed away from the earth, to read eight pages of their Sayings every day. 'Aṭṭār felt that it was incumbent upon him to supply this desideratum.
12. From his childhood he had a predilection for the Sufis and took delight in their sayings. Now, when such words are spoken only by impostors and when true spiritualists have become as rare as the philosopher's stone, he is resolved to popularise literature of this kind so far as lies in his power'
13. In the present age the best men are bad, and holy men have been forgotten. The *Memorial* is designed to remedy this state of things.
14. The Sayings of the Saints dispose men to renounce the world, meditate on the future life, love God, and set about preparing for their last journey. "One may say that there

does not exist in all creation a better book than this, for their words are a commentary on the Qur'an and Traditions, which are the best of all words. Any one who reads it properly will perceive what passion must have been in the souls of those men to bring forth such deeds and words as they have done and said."

15. A further motive was the hope of obtaining their intercession hereafter and of being pardoned, like the dog of the Seven Sleepers which, though it be all skin and bone, will nevertheless be admitted to Paradise.

In his preface 'Aṭṭār mentions three books which he recommends for those ambitious to attain a full understanding of the pronouncement of the Sufis. These he entitles: *Kitāb Sharḥ al-Qalb* ("The Exposition of the Heart"), *Kitāb Kashf al-Asrār* ("The Revelation of the Secrets"), and *Kitāb Ma'rifah al-Nafs wa al-Rabb* ("The Knowledge of the Self and of the Lord"). No clue is given here to the authorship of these works, but 'Aṭṭār refers in one other context (II, 99) to the *Sharḥ al-Qalb* as a book of his own composition; see also 'Aṭṭār's introduction to his own *Mokhtar-nama.* It may therefore be deduced that 'Aṭṭār was the author of the other two titles. No copy of any of the three has so far been recovered.

Sources of 'Aṭṭār's *Memorial*

Since 'Aṭṭār did not trouble to specify the precise sources upon which he drew in compiling the *Memorial,* these are to be identified on the basis of internal evidence. It cannot be claimed that anything like a complete analysis has been attempted, for such a task (wanting direct clues) is obviously very intricate and laborious, requiring a prolonged research. So far, however, it has been established as certain that 'Aṭṭār consulted the authors and texts here listed.

1. *Ḥikāyah al-Mashāyikh* of Abū Muḥammad Ja'far ibn Muḥammad al-Khuldī (d. 348/959). 'Aṭṭār quotes from al-Khuldī once directly (II, 51); in the supplementary section of the *Memorial* his biography is briefly given (II, 284-285), but that part of the text is of very doubtful authenticity. For further information on al-Khuldī, described by Hujwīrī *(Kashf al-Mahjub,* trans. R.A. Nicholson, p. 156) as "the well-known biographer of the Saints", see C. Brockelmann, *Geschichte der arabischen Litteratur*, Suppl. I, p. 358.
2. *Kitāb al-Luma'* of Abū Naṣr 'Abdullah ibn 'Alī al-Sarrāj (d. 378/988). Mentioned specifically in the supplement (II, 182-183) where a biographical notice is given; though this reference is of questionable value, the section in which it occurs being very likely a later addition, 'Aṭṭār's use of this fundamental text can be deduced from many contexts.
3. *Ṭabaqāt al-Ṣūfiyyah* of Abū 'Abd al-Raḥman Muḥammad ibn al-Ḥusayn al-Sulamī (d. 412/1021). This celebrated author, whose biographies of the Sufis 'Aṭṭār undoubtedly used, is cited thrice in the supplement (II, 263, 308, 326).
4. *Ḥilyah al-Awliyā'* of Abū Nu'aym Aḥmad ibn 'Abdullah al-Aṣbaḥānī (d. 430/1038). Though Abū Nu'aym is not

specifically named, it is clear that 'Aṭṭār knew and used this encyclopaedic work.

5. *Al-Risālah* of Abū al-Qāsim al-Qushayrī (d. 465/1072). Cited by name in the main text (II, 135) and the supplement (II, 200, 207, 309, 332, 333), it is abundantly evident that 'Aṭṭar leaned very heavily on this authoritative exposition of Sufi doctrine.
6. *Kashf al-Mahjūb* of Abū al-Ḥasan al-Hujwīrī (d. *circa* 467/1075. Named once in the main text (II, 68), Hujwīrī is verbally cited without acknowledgment in a number of passages. This was the easier to contrive, since Hujwīrī himself wrote in Persian

When dealing with certain individual Sufis, 'Aṭṭār appears to have had access to some of their own writings, either direct or through quotation by others, as well as to special monographs on their lives and acts. Two obvious instances are al-Sahlajī's biography of Abū Yazīd al-Bisṭāmī, and al-Daylamī's biography of Ibn Khafīf. Further reference to these two books will be found in my notes on the relevant texts.

Though in his prefatory remarks 'Aṭṭār lays much weight upon the "words" of the Sufis as his overriding preoccupation, in fact he put at least equal stress on their "acts" or the legends of their preternatural powers. In setting out his materials he took as his model the *Ṭabaqāt al-Ṣūfiyyah* of al-Sulamī, in which the Sufis are treated more or less in chronological order; he may well also have known al-Anṣārī's Persian version of this book, which Jāmī later used as the foundation of his *Nafaḥāt al-Uns.* It is to be noticed, however, that ʻAṭṭār abandoned al-Sulamī's arrangement of the Sufis by "classes"; he also found the *Ṭabaqāt* inadequate on the human side. For valuable as that work undoubtedly is as an anthology of Sufi dicta, to ʻAṭṭār, who was interested at least as much in the personalities of the Sufis as in what they said and wrote, it needed to be supplemented with biographical details. So to eke out al-Sulamī's somewhat austere fare, he combined with the *Ṭabaqāt* the human and superhuman materials contained in the *Ḥikāyāt* of al-Khuldī, the *Risālah* of al-Qushayrī, and the *Kashf al-Maḥjūb* of Hujwīrī. The following table is self-explanatory in establishing the relationship between the *Memorial* and its forerunners.

Comparative table of Sufi biographies

ʻAṭṭār	**Sulamī**	**Qushayrī**	**Hujwīrī**
1. Jaʻfar al-Ṣādiq	—	—	9
2. Uways al-Qaranī	—	—	10
3. Ḥasan al-Baṣrī	—	—	12
4. Mālik ibn Dīnār	—	—	15
5. Muḥammad ibn Wāsiʻ	—	—	18
6. Ḥabīb al-ʻAjamī	—	—	14
7. Abū Ḥāzim al-Makkī	—	—	19
8. ʻUtbah al-Ghulām	—	—	—
9. Rābiʻah al-ʻAdawiyah	—	—	—
10. Fuḍayl ibn ʻIyāḍ	1	3	22
11. Ibrāhīm ibn Adham	3	1	24
12. Bishr ibn al-Ḥārith	4	6	25
13. Dhū al-Nūn al-Miṣrī	2	2	23

14. Abū Yazīd al-Bisṭāmī	8	10	26
15. ‘Abdullah ibn al-Mubārak	—	—	21
16. Sufyān al-Thawrī	—	—	—
17. Shaqīq al-Balkhī	7	9	30
18. Abū Ḥanīfah	—	—	20
19. Al-Shāfi‘ī	—	—	34
20. Aḥmad ibn Ḥanbal	—	—	35
21. Dāwūd al-Ṭā’ī	—	8	28
22. Al-Muḥāsibī	6	7	27
23. Abū Sulaymān al-Dara’ī	9	12	31
24. Muḥammad ibn al-Sammāk	—	—	—
25. Aslam al-Ṭūsī	—	—	—
26. Aḥmad ibn Ḥarb	—	—	—
27. Ḥātim al-Aṣamm	11	13	33
28. Sahl ibn ‘Abdullah al-Tustarī	30	11	54
29. Ma‘rūf al-Karkhī	10	4	32
30. Sarī al-Saqaṭī	5	5	29
31. Fatḥ al-Mūṣilī	—	—	—
32. Aḥmad ibn Abī al-Hawārī	18	16	36
33. Aḥmad ibn Khiḍrūyah	13	15	37
34. Abū Turāb al-Nakhshabī	20	18	38
35. Yaḥyā ibn Mu‘ādh	14	14	39
36. Shāh ibn Shujā‘	27	33	52
37. Yūsuf ibn al-Ḥusayn	26	34	50
38. Abū Ḥafṣ al-Ḥaddād	15	17	40
39. Ḥamdūn al-Qaṣṣār	16	22	41
40. Manṣūr ibn ‘Ammār	17	21	42
41. Al-Anṭākī	18	20	43
42. ‘Abdullah ibn Khubayq	19	19	44

43. Abū al-Qāsim al-Junayd	21	23	45
44. ‘Amr ibn ‘Uthmān	29	30	53
45. Abū Sa‘īd al-Kharrāz	34	37	58
46. Abū al-Ḥusayn al-Nūrī	22	25	46
47. Abū ‘Uthmān al-Ḥīrī	23	24	47
48. Ibn al-Jallā’	24	26	48
49. Ruwaym	25	27	49
50. Ibn ‘Aṭā’	42	42	—
51. Ibrāhīm al-Raqqī	—	—	—
52. Yūsuf ibn al-Asbaṭ	—	—	—
53. Al-Nahrajūrī	48	60	—
54. Samnūn	28	31	51
55. Al-Murta‘ish	42	54	—
56. Muḥammad ibn al-Faḍl	31	28	55
57. Al-Būshanjī	58	74	—
58. Al-Tirmidhī	32	35	56
59. Abū al-Khayr al-Aqṭa‘	66	58	—
60. ‘Abdullah al-Tarughbadī	—	—	—
61. Abū Bakr al-Warrāq	33	36	57
62. ‘Abdullah ibn Munāḍil	—	56	—
63. ‘Alī ibn Sahl al-Aṣfahānī	35	40	59
64. Khayr al-Nassāj	57	51	60
65. Abū Ḥamzah al-Khurasānī	58	52	61
66. Aḥmad ibn Masrūq	36	39	62
67. ‘Abdullah al-Maghribī	37	38	63
68. Abū ‘Alī al-Jūzajānī	38	—	64
69. Abū Bakr al-Kattānī	67	59	—
70. Ibn Khafīf	—	75	75
71. Abū Muḥammad al-Jurayrī	41	41	65

72. Al-Ḥallāj	53	—	67
73. Ibrāhīm al-Khawwāṣ	57	43	68
74. Mimshād al-Dīnawarī	55	50	—
75. Al-Shiblī	61	53	71

In making the present selection, attention has been concentrated on the biographical sections of each entry, leaving aside the much-prized dicta perhaps for future treatment. The original edition of the *Memorial* terminated with the entry on al-Ḥallāj, whom 'Aṭṭār appears to have regarded—and with historical as well as artistic justification—as forming the climax and supreme crisis of the early Sufi movement. (The inclusion of Ibn Khafīf is eccentric.) Some manuscripts contain an extensive supplement which Nicholson accepted as authentic and included in his text; it seems possible that part of this supplement, though by no means all I think, was added by the original author. In my selection I have drawn on the additional material to include al-Shiblī, whose death marks the end of the formative period of Sufism. I have furnished brief biographies and bibliographies for each entry, and notes which are intended rather as specimens than as exhaustive commentaries.

1

Ḥasan al-Baṣrī

Al-Ḥasan ibn Abī al-Ḥasan al-Baṣrī was born at Madīnah in 21 (642), the son of a slave captured in Maisan who afterwards became a client of the Prophet Muḥammad's secretary Zayd ibn Thābit. Brought up in Basra, he met many Companions of the Prophet including, it is said, seventy of those who fought at the Battle of Badr. He grew up to become one of the most prominent figures of his generation, being famous for his uncompromising piety and outspoken condemnation of worldliness in high places. Whilst the Mu'tazilite theologians claim him as the founder of their movement (and 'Amr ibn 'Ubayd and Wāṣil ibn 'Aṭā' are counted amongst his pupils), in Sufi hagiography he is revered as one of the greatest saints of early Islam. He died at Basra in 110 (728). Many of his speeches—he was a brilliant orator—and sayings are quoted by Arab authors and not a few of his letters have been preserved.

The conversion of Ḥasan al-Baṣrī

The beginning of Ḥasan al-Baṣrī's conversion was as follows. He was a jewel merchant and was called Ḥasan of the Pearls. He traded with Byzantium, and had to do with the generals and ministers of Caesar. On one occasion, going to Byzantium he called on the prime minister and conversed with him a while.

"We will go to a certain place," the minister told him, "if you are agreeable."

"It is for you to say," Ḥasan replied. "I agree."

So the minister commanded a horse to be brought for Ḥasan. He mounted with the minister, and they set out. When they reached the desert Ḥasan perceived a tent of Byzantine brocade, fastened with ropes of silk and golden pegs, set firm in the ground. He stood to one side. Then a mighty army, all accoutred in the panoply of war, came out; they circled the tent, said a few words, and departed. Philosophers and scholars to the number of nigh four hundred arrived on the scene; they circled the tent, said a few words, and departed. After that three hundred illumined elders with white beards approached the tent, circled it, said a few words, and departed. Thereafter more than two hundred moon-fair maidens, each bearing a plate of gold and silver and precious stones, circled the tent, said a few words, and departed.

Ḥasan relates that, astonished and filled with wonder, he asked himself what this might be.

"When we alighted," he went on, "I asked the minister. He said that the Caesar had a son of unsurpassable beauty, perfect in all the branches of learning and unrivalled in the arena of manly prowess. His father loved him with all his heart."

Suddenly he fell ill—so Ḥasan related on the authority of the minister. All the skilled physicians proved powerless to cure him. Finally he died, and was buried in that tent. Once every year people come out to visit him. First an immense army circles the tent, and they say: "O prince, if this circumstance that has befallen thee had come about in war, we would have all sacrificed our lives for thee, to ransom thee back. But the circumstance that has befallen thee is at the hand of one against whom we cannot fight, whom we cannot challenge." This they say, and then return.

The philosophers and the scholars come forward, and say: "This circumstance has been brought about by one against whom we cannot do anything by means of learning and philosophy, science and sophistry. For all the philosophers of the world are powerless before him, and all the learned are ignorant beside his knowledge. Otherwise we would have contrived devices and spoken words which all in creation could not have withstood." This they say, and then return.

Next the venerable elders advance, and say: "O prince, if this circumstance that has befallen thee could have been set right by the intercession of elders, we would all have interceded with humble petitions, and would not have abandoned thee there. But this circumstance has been brought upon thee by one against whom no mortal man's intercession profits anything." This they say, and depart.

Now the moon-fair maidens with their plates of gold and precious stones advance, circle the tent, and say: "Son of Caesar, if this circumstance that has befallen thee could have been set right by wealth and beauty, we would have sacrificed ourselves and given great moneys, and would not have abandoned thee. But this circumstance has been brought upon thee by one on whom wealth and beauty have no effect." This they say, and return.

Then Caesar himself with his chief minister enters the tent, and says: "O eye and lamp of thy father, O fruit of the heart of thy father, O dearest beloved of thy father, what is in thy father's hand to perform? Thy father brought a mighty army, he brought philosophers and scholars, intercessors and advisers, beautiful maidens, wealth and all manner of luxuries; and he came himself. If all this could have been of avail, thy father would have done all that lay in his power. But this circumstance has been brought about by one before whom thy father, with all this apparatus, this army and retinue, this luxury and wealth and treasure, is powerless. Peace be upon you, till next year!" This he says, and returns.

These words of the minister so affected Ḥasan that he was beside himself. At once he made arrangements to return. Coming to Basra, he took an oath never to laugh again in this world, till his ultimate destiny became clear to him. He flung himself into all manner of devotions and austerities, such that no man in his time could exceed that discipline.

Ḥasan al-Baṣrī and Abū 'Amr

It is related that Abū 'Amr, the leading authority on the reading of the Qur'an, was teaching the Qur'an one day when suddenly a handsome boy arrived to join his class. Abū 'Amr gazed at the child improperly, and immediately he forgot the whole Qur'an, from the *p* of "Praise" to the *n* of "jinn and men". A fire possessed him, and he lost all self-control. In this state he called on Ḥasan al-Baṣrī and described to him his predicament.

"Master," he wept bitterly, "such is the situation. I have forgotten the whole Qur'an."

Ḥasan was most distressed to hear of his situation.

"Now is the season of the pilgrimage," he said. "Go and perform the pilgrimage. When you have done that, repair to the mosque of Khayf. There you will see an old man seated in the prayer-niche. Do not spoil his time, but let him be until he is disengaged. Then ask him to say a prayer for you."

Abū 'Amr acted accordingly. Seated in a corner of the mosque, he observed a venerable elder and about him a circle of people seated. Some time passed; then a man entered, clad in spotless white robes. The people made way before him, greeted him, and conversed together.

When the hour of prayer arrived, the man departed and the people departed with him, so that the elder remained alone.

Abū 'Amr then approached and saluted him.

"In Allah's name, help me," he cried.

And he described his predicament. The elder, much concerned, raised his eyes to heaven.

"He had not yet lowered his head," Abū 'Amr recounted, "when the Qur'an came back to me. I fell down before him for joy."

"Who recommended me to you?" the elder asked.

"Ḥasan al-Baṣrī," Abū 'Amr replied.

"Anyone who has an imam like Ḥasan," the old man commented, "what need has he of another? Well, Ḥasan has exposed me. Now I will expose him. He rent my veil, and I will rend his as well. That man," he went on, "in the white robes who entered after the afternoon prayer and left before the rest, and the others did him reverence—that man was Ḥasan. Every day he prays the afternoon prayer in Basra and then comes here, converses with me, and returns to Basra for the evening prayer. Anyone who has an imam like Ḥasan, why should he ask me for a prayer?"

Ḥasan al-Baṣrī and the fire-worshipper

Ḥasan had a neighbour named Simeon who was a fire-worshipper. Simeon fell ill and was at death's door. Friends begged Ḥasan to visit him; he called, to find him in bed, blackened with fire and smoke.

"Fear God," Ḥasan counselled him. "You have passed all your life amid fire and smoke. Accept Islam, that God may have mercy on you."

"Three things hold me back from becoming a Muslim," the fire-worshipper replied. "The first is, that you speak ill of the world, yet night and day you pursue worldly things. Secondly, you say that death is a fact to be faced, yet you make no preparation for death. In the third place, you say that God's face shall be seen, yet today you do everything contrary to His good pleasure."

"This is the token of those who know truly," Ḥasan commented. "Now if believers act as you describe, what have you to say? They acknowledge the unity of God; whereas you have spent your life in the worship of fire. You who have worshipped fire for seventy years, and I who have never worshipped fire—we are both carried off to Hell. Hell will consume you and me. God will pay no regard to you; but if God so wills, the fire will not dare so much as to burn one hair of my body. For fire is a thing created by God; and the creature is subject to the Creator's command. Come now, you who have worshipped fire for seventy years; let us both put our hands into the fire, then you will see with your own eyes the impotence of fire and the omnipotence of God."

So saying, Ḥasan thrust his hand into the fire and held it there. Not a particle of his body was affected or burnt. When Simeon saw this he was amazed. The dawn of true knowledge began to break.

"For seventy years I have worshipped fire," he groaned. "Now only a breath or two remains to me. What am I to do?"

"Become a Muslim," was Ḥasan's reply.

"If you give it me in writing that God will not punish me," said Simeon, "then I will believe. But until I have it in writing, I will not believe."

Ḥasan wrote it down.

"Now order just witnesses of Basra to append their testimony."

The witnesses endorsed the document. Then Simeon wept many tears and proclaimed the faith. He spoke his last testament to Ḥasan.

"When I die, bid them wash me, then commit me to the earth with your own hands, and place this document in my hand. This document will be my proof."

Having charged Ḥasan thus, he spoke the attestation of faith and died. They washed his body, said the prayer over him, and buried him with the document in his hand. That night Ḥasan went to sleep pondering what he had done.

"How could I help a drowning man, seeing that I am drowning myself? Since I have no control over my own fate, why did I venture to prescribe how God should act?"

With this thought he fell asleep. He saw Simeon in a dream glowing like a candle; on his head a crown, robed in fine raiment, he was walking with a smile in the garden of Paradise.

"How are you, Simeon?" Ḥasan enquired.

"Why do you ask? You can see for yourself," Simeon answered. "God Almighty of His bounty brought me nigh His presence and graciously showed me His face. The favours He showered upon me surpass all description. You have honoured your guarantee; so take your document. I have no further need of it."

When Ḥasan awoke, he saw that parchment in his hand. "Lord God," he cried, "I know well that what Thou doest is without cause, save of Thy bounty. Who shall suffer loss at Thy door? Thou grantest a Guebre of seventy years to come into Thy near presence because of a single utterance. How then wilt Thou exclude a believer of seventy years?"

2

Mālik ibn Dīnār

Mālik ibn Dīnār al-Sāmī was the son of a Persian slave from Sejestan (or Kabul) and became a disciple of Ḥasan al-Baṣrī. He is mentioned as a reliable traditionist, transmitting from such early authorities as Anas ibn Mālik and Ibn Sīrīn. A noted early calligrapher of the Qur'an, he died c. 130 (748).

How Mālik ibn Dīnār came to be so named, and the story of his repentance

When Mālik was born his father was a slave; yet though he was a slave's son, he was free from bondage to both worlds.

Some say that Mālik ibn Dīnār once embarked in a ship. When the ship was far out to sea the mariners demanded,

"Produce your fare!" "I do not have it," he answered.

They beat him till he was senseless. When he recovered, they shouted again.

"Produce your fare!"

"I do not have it," he repeated.

They beat him unconscious a second time. When he came to his senses, they demanded a third time.

"Produce your fare!"

"I do not have it."

"Let us seize him by the feet and throw him overboard," the sailors shouted.

All the fish in the water at that moment put up their heads. Each one held two golden dinars in its mouth. Mālik reached down his hand and, taking two dinars from one of the fish, gave it to them. Seeing this, the crew fell at his feet. He walked on the face of the waters and vanished.

That is why he was called Mālik ibn Dīnār.

Now his conversion came about as follows. He was a very handsome man and fond of worldly things, and he possessed great wealth. He lived in Damascus, where Mu'āwiyah had built the cathedral mosque, endowing it liberally. Mālik was very eager to be appointed in charge of that mosque. So he went and threw his prayer rug down in the corner of the mosque, and there for a whole year continued in devotion, hoping that whoever saw him would find him at prayer.

"What a hypocrite for you!" he would say to himself.

A year passed in this way. By night he would leave the mosque and take his amusement. One night he was enjoying music, and all his companions had fallen asleep. Suddenly a voice came from the lute he was playing.

"Mālik, what ails thee that thou repentest not?"

Hearing these words, Mālik dropped the instrument and ran to the mosque in great confusion.

"For a whole year I have worshipped God hypocritically," he communed with himself. "Is it not better that I should worship God in sincerity? Yet I am ashamed. What am I to do? Even if they offer me this appointment, I will not accept it."

So he resolved, and he put his conscience right with God.

That night he worshipped with a truthful heart. Next day people assembled as usual before the mosque.

"Why, there are cracks in the mosque," they exclaimed. "A superintendent ought to be appointed to keep it in order."

They reached the unanimous view that no one was better fitted for the post than Mālik. So they came to him. He was at prayer, so they waited patiently until he was finished.

"We have come to plead with you to accept this appointment," they said.

"O God," cried Mālik, "I served Thee hypocritically for a whole year, and no one looked at me. Now that I have given my heart to Thee and firmly resolved that I do not want the appointment, Thou hast sent twenty men to me to place this task on my neck. By Thy glory, I do not want it."

And he ran out of the mosque and applied himself to the Lord's work, taking up the life of austerity and discipline. So respected did he become, and of such excellence of life, that when a certain wealthy citizen of Basra died, leaving behind a lovely daughter, the latter approached Thābit al-Bunānī.

"I wish to become the wife of Mālik," she announced, "so that he may help me in the labour of obedience to God." Thābit informed Mālik.

"I have divorced the world," Mālik replied. "This woman belongs to the world I have divorced. I cannot marry her."

Mālik and his licentious neighbour

There was a certain youth living in Mālik's neighbourhood who was extremely depraved and dissolute in his ways. Mālik was constantly pained on account of his bad behaviour, but he endured patiently waiting for someone else to speak. To be brief, in due course others came forward to complain about the young man. Mālik then arose and went to him to bid him mend his ways. The youth reacted in a very headstrong and overbearing manner.

"I am the Sultan's favourite," he told Mālik. "No one has the power to check me or restrain me from doing as I please."

"I will talk to the Sultan," Mālik threatened.

"The Sultan will never swerve from his approval of me," the youth retorted. "Whatever I do, he will approve."

"Well, if the Sultan cannot do anything," Mālik proceeded, "I will tell the All-merciful."

And he pointed to heaven.

"Ah," the youth replied. "He is too generous to take me to task."

This floored Mālik, and he left him. Some days went by, and the youth's depravity surpassed all bounds. People came again to complain. Mālik rose up to rebuke him; but on the way he heard a voice.

"Keep your hands off My friend!"

Amazed, Mālik went in to the youth.

"What has happened," the youth demanded on seeing him, "that you have come a second time?"

"I have not come this time to chide you," Mālik answered. "I have come simply to inform you that I heard such a voice."

"Ah," the youth exclaimed. "Since things are like that, I dedicate my palace wholly to His service. I care nothing for all my possessions."

So saying, he cast everything aside and set out to wander the world.

Mālik relates that after a certain time he saw the youth in Makkah, utterly destitute and at his last breath.

"He is my friend," he gasped. "I went to see my friend." And with that he expired.

Mālik and his abstinence

Years passed without anything sour or sweet passing Mālik's lips. Every night he would repair to the baker's and buy two round loaves on which he broke his fast. From time to time it happened that the bread was warm; he found consolation in that, taking it as an appetizer.

Once he fell sick, and a craving for meat entered his heart. For ten days he controlled himself; then, unable to restrain himself any longer, he went to a delicatessen and bought two or three sheep's trotters and put them in his sleeve. The shopkeeper sent his apprentice after him to see what he would do. After a little while the boy returned in tears.

"From here he went to a desolate spot," he reported. "There he took the trotters out of his sleeve, kissed them twice or thrice, then he said, 'My soul, more than this is not meet for you.' Then he gave the bread and trotters to a beggar, saying, 'Weak body of mine, do not think that all this pain I impose on you is out of enmity. It is so that on the resurrection morn you may not burn in Hell. Be patient for a few days, and it may be that this trial will come to an end, and you will fall into bliss that shall never pass away.'"

Once Mālik said, "I do not know the meaning of the statement that if a man does not eat meat for forty days, his intelligence is diminished. I have not eaten meat for twenty years, and my intelligence increases every day."

For forty years he lived in Basra and never ate fresh dates. When the season of ripe dates came round he would say, "People of Basra, behold, my belly has not shrunk from not eating them, and you who eat them daily—your bellies have not become any larger."

After forty years he was assailed by a mood of restlessness. However hard he tried, he could not withstand the craving for fresh dates. Finally after some days, during which the desire daily increased whilst he constantly denied his appetite, he could resist no more the importunity of his carnal soul.

"I *will* not eat fresh dates," he protested. "Either kill me, or die!"

That night a heavenly voice spoke.

"You must eat some dates. Free your carnal soul from bondage."

At this response his carnal soul, finding the opportunity, began to shout.

"If you want dates," Mālik said, "fast for a week without breakfasting once, and pray all night. Then I will give you some."

This contented his carnal soul. For a whole week he prayed all night and fasted all day. Then he went to the market and bought some dates, and betook himself to the mosque to eat them. A boy shouted from the rooftop.

"Father! A Jew has bought dates and is going to the mosque to eat them."

"What business has a Jew in the mosque?" the man exclaimed. And he ran to see who the Jew might be. Beholding Mālik, he fell at his feet.

"What were those words the boy uttered?" Mālik demanded.

"Excuse him, master," the boy's father pleaded. "He is only a child, and does not understand. In our quarter many Jews live. We are constantly fasting, and our children see the Jews eating by day. So they suppose that everyone who eats anything by day is a Jew. What he said he said in ignorance. Forgive him!"

When Mālik heard this, a fire consumed his soul. He realised that the child was inspired to speak as he had.
"Lord God," he cried, "I had not eaten any dates, and Thou didst call me a Jew by the tongue of an innocent child. If I eat the dates, Thou wilt proclaim me an unbeliever. By Thy glory, if I ever eat any dates!"

3

Ḥabīb al-ʻAjamī

Ḥabīb ibn Muḥammad al-ʻAjamī al-Baṣrī, a Persian settled at Basra, was a noted traditionist who transmitted from Ḥasan al-Baṣrī, Ibn Sīrīn, and other authorities. His conversion from a life of ease and self-indulgence was brought about by Ḥasan's eloquence; he was a frequent attendant at his lectures, and became one of his closest associates.

The story of Ḥabīb the Persian

Ḥabīb to begin with was a man of property and a usurer. He dwelt in Basra, and every day he made the rounds to dun his clients. If he got no money, he would demand payment for his shoe leather. In this manner he covered his daily expenditure. One day he had gone to look for a certain debtor. The man was not at home; so failing to find him, he demanded shoe leather payment.

"My husband is not at home," the debtor's wife told him. "I myself have nothing to give you. We had killed a sheep, but only the neck is left. If you like I will give you that."

"That is something," the usurer replied, thinking that he might at least take the sheep's neck off her and carry it home. "Put a pot on the fire."

"I have neither bread nor fuel," the woman answered.

"Very well," the man said. "I will go and fetch fuel and bread, and it can be charged to shoe leather."

So he went off and fetched these things, and the woman set the pot. When the pot was cooked the woman was about to pour its contents into a bowl when a beggar knocked at the door.

"If we give you what we have got," Ḥabīb shouted at him, "you will not become rich, and we will become poor ourselves."

The beggar, despairing, petitioned the woman to put something in the bowl. She lifted the lid of the saucepan, and found that its contents had all turned to black blood. Turning pale she hurried back and taking Ḥabīb by the hand, led him towards the pot.

"Look what has happened to us because of your cursed usury, and your shouting at the beggar!" she cried. "What will become of us now in this world, not to mention the next?"

On seeing this, Ḥabīb felt a fire within him which never afterwards subsided.

"Woman," he said, "I repent of all I have done."

Next day he went out to look for his clients. It happened to be a Friday, and the children were playing in the street. When they sighted Ḥabīb they started to shout.

"Here comes Ḥabīb the usurer. Run away, lest his dust settles on us and we become as cursed as he!"

These words hurt Ḥabīb very much. He took his way to the meeting hall, and there certain phrases passed Ḥasan al-Baṣrī's lips which struck Ḥabīb straight to the heart, so that he fainted. Then he repented. Realising what had happened, Ḥasan al-Baṣrī took him by the hand and calmed him.

As he returned from the meeting he was spotted by one of his debtors, who made to run away.

"Do not run away," Ḥabīb called to him. "Till now it was for you to flee from me; now I must run away from you."

He passed on. The children were still playing. When they sighted Ḥabīb they shouted again.

"Here comes Ḥabīb the penitent. Run away, lest our dust settles on him, for we are sinners against God."

"My God and Master!" cried Ḥabīb. "Because of this one day that I have made my peace with Thee, Thou hast beaten the drums of men's hearts for me and noised my name abroad for virtue."

Then he issued a proclamation:

"Whoever wants anything from Ḥabīb, come and take it!"

The people gathered together, and he gave away all his possessions so that he was left penniless. Another man came with a demand. Having nothing left, Ḥabīb gave him his wife's chaddur. To another claimant he gave his own shirt, and remained naked. He repaired to a hermitage on the banks of the Euphrates, and there gave himself up to the worship of God. Every night and day he studied under Ḥasan, but he could not learn the Qur'an, for which reason he was nicknamed the Barbarian.

Time passed, and he was completely destitute. His wife asked him for housekeeping money constantly. So Ḥabīb left his house and made for the hermitage to resume his devotions. When night came he returned to his wife.

"Where have you been working, not to bring anything home?" his wife demanded.

"The one I have been working for is extremely generous," Ḥabīb replied. "He is so generous that I am ashamed to ask him for anything. When the proper time comes, he will give. For he says, 'Every ten days I pay the wages.'"

So Ḥabīb repaired daily to the hermitage to worship, till ten days were up. On the tenth day at the time of the midday prayer a thought entered his mind.

"What can I take home tonight, and what am I to tell my wife?"

And he pondered this deeply. Straightway Almighty God sent a porter to the door of his house with an assload of flour, another with a skinned sheep, and another with oil, honey, herbs, and seasonings. The porters loaded up all this. A handsome young man accompanied them with a purse of three hundred silver dirhams. Coming to Ḥabīb's house, he knocked on the door.

"What do you want?" asked Ḥabīb's wife, opening the door.

"The Master has sent all this," the handsome youth replied. "Tell Ḥabīb, 'You increase your output, and we will increase your wages.'"

So saying, he departed. At nightfall Ḥabīb proceeded homeward, ashamed and sorrowful. As he approached his house, the aroma of bread and cooking assailed his nostrils. His wife ran to greet him and wiped his face and was gentle with him as she had never been before.

"Husband," she cried, "the man you are working for is a very fine gentleman, generous and full of loving kindness. See what he sent by the hand of a handsome young man! And the young man said, 'When Ḥabīb comes home, tell him, You increase your output, and we will increase your wages.'"

Ḥabīb was amazed.

"Wonderful!" he exclaimed. "I worked for ten days, and he did me all this kindness. If I work harder, who knows what he will do?"

And he turned his face wholly away from worldly things and gave himself up to God's service.

The miracles of Ḥabīb

One day an old woman came to Ḥabīb and, falling at his feet, wept bitterly.

"I have a son who has been absent from me a long time. I can no longer endure to be parted from him. Say a prayer to God," she begged Ḥabīb. "It may be that by the blessing of your prayer God will send him back to me."

"Have you any money?" Ḥabīb asked her.

"Yes, two dirhams," she replied.

"Bring them, and give them to the poor."

And Ḥabīb recited a prayer, then he said to the old woman,

"Be gone. Your son has returned to you."

The old woman had not yet reached the door of her house, when she beheld her son.

"Why, here is my son!" she shouted, and she brought him to Ḥabīb.

"What happened?" Ḥabīb enquired of him.

"I was in Kirmān," the son replied. "My teacher had sent me to look for some meat. I obtained the meat and was just returning to him, when the wind seized hold of me. I heard a voice saying,

"'Wind, carry him to his own home, by the blessing of Ḥabīb's prayer and the two dirhams given in alms.'"

One year on the eighth day of Dhū al-Ḥijjah, Ḥabīb was seen in Basra and on the ninth day at 'Arafāt.

Once a famine was raging in Basra. Ḥabīb purchased many provisions on credit and gave them away as alms. He fastened his purse and placed it under his pillow. When the tradesmen came to demand payment, he would take out his purse and it was full of dirhams, which he gave away as loans.

Ḥabīb had a house in Basra on the crossroads. He also had a fur coat which he wore summer and winter. Once, needing to perform the ritual washing, he arose and left his coat on the ground. Ḥasan al-Baṣrī, happening on the scene, perceived the coat flung in the road.

"This 'barbarian' does not know its value," he commented. "This fur coat ought not to be left here. It may get lost."

So he stood there watching over it. Presently Ḥabīb returned.

"Imam of the Muslims," he cried after saluting Ḥasan, "why are you standing here?"

"Do you not know," Ḥasan replied, "that this coat ought not to be left here? It may get lost. Say, in whose charge did you leave it?"

"In His charge," Ḥabīb answered, "who appointed you to watch over it."

One day Ḥasan came to call on Ḥabīb. Ḥabīb placed two rounds of barley bread and a little salt before Ḥasan. Ḥasan began to eat. A beggar came to the door, and Ḥabīb gave the two rounds and the salt to him.

"Ḥabīb," remarked the astonished Ḥasan, "you are a worthy man. If only you had some knowledge, it would be better. You took the bread from under the nose of your guest and gave it all to the beggar. You ought to have given a part to the beggar and a part to the guest."

Ḥabīb said nothing. Presently a slave entered with a tray on his head. A roast lamb was on the tray, together with sweetmeat and fine bread, and five hundred silver dirhams. He set the tray before Ḥabīb. Ḥabīb gave the money to the poor, and placed the tray before Ḥasan.

"Master," he said when Ḥasan had eaten some of the roast, "you are a good man. If only you had a little faith, it would be better. Knowledge must be accompanied by faith."

One day officers of Ḥajjāj were searching for Ḥasan. He was hiding in Ḥabīb's hermitage.

"Have you seen Ḥasan today?" the officers demanded of Ḥabīb.

"I have seen him," he answered.

"Where was he?"

"In this hermitage."

The officers entered the hermitage, but for all their searching they did not find Ḥasan. ("Seven times they laid their hands on me," Ḥasan afterwards related, "but they did not see me.")

"Ḥabīb," Ḥasan remarked on leaving the hermitage, "you did not observe your duty to your master. You pointed me out."

"Master," Ḥabīb replied, "it was because I told the truth that you escaped. If I had lied, we would both have been arrested."

"What did you recite, that they did not see me?" Ḥasan asked.

I recited the Throne-verse ten times," Ḥabīb answered. "Ten times I recited The Messenger believes, and ten times Say, He is God, One. Then I said, 'O God, I have committed Ḥasan to Thee. Watch over him.'"

Ḥasan once wished to go to a certain place. He came down to the bank of the Tigris, and was pondering something to himself when Ḥabīb arrived on the scene.

"Imam, why are you standing here?" he asked.

"I wish to go to a certain place. The boat is late," Ḥasan replied.

"Master, what has happened to you?" Ḥabīb demanded. "I learned all that I know from you. Expel from your heart all envy of other men. Close your heart against worldly things. Know that suffering is a precious prize, and see that all affairs are of God. Then set foot on the water and walk."

With that Ḥabīb stepped on to the water and departed. Ḥasan swooned. When he recovered, the people asked him,

"Imam of the Muslims, what happened to you?"

"My pupil Ḥabīb just now reprimanded me," he replied. "Then he stepped on the water and departed, whilst I remained impotent. If tomorrow a voice cries, 'Pass over the fiery pathway'—if I remain impotent like this, what can I do?"

"Ḥabīb," Ḥasan asked later, "how did you discover this power?"

"Because I make my heart white, whereas you make paper black," Ḥabīb replied.

"My learning profited another, but it did not profit me," Ḥasan commented.

4

Rābi‘ah al-‘Adawiyah

Rābi‘ah bint Ismā‘īl al-‘Adawiyah, born in humble circumstances and sold into slavery as a child, later settled in Basra where she attained great fame as a saint and a preacher and was highly esteemed by many of her pious contemporaries. The date of her death is given variously as 135 (752) and 185 (801). To her, a lifelong celibate, is attributed a large share in the introduction into Islamic mysticism of the theme of Divine love. Her tomb used to be pointed out near Jerusalem.

Rābi‘ah, her birth and early life

If anyone says, "Why have you included Rābi‘ah in the rank of men?" my answer is, that the Prophet himself said, "God does not regard your outward forms." The root of the matter is not form, but intention, as the Prophet said, "Mankind will be raised up according to their intentions."

Moreover, if it is proper to derive two-thirds of our religion from 'Ā'ishah, surely it is permissible to take religious instruction from a handmaid of 'Ā'ishah. When a woman becomes a "man" in the path of God, she is a man and one cannot any more call her a woman.

The night when Rābi'ah came to earth, there was nothing whatsoever in her father's house; for her father lived in very poor circumstances. He did not possess even one drop of oil to anoint her navel; there was no lamp, and not a rag to swaddle her in. He already had three daughters, and Rābi'ah was his fourth; that is why she was called by that name.

"Go to neighbour So-and-so and beg for a drop of oil, so that I can light the lamp," his wife said to him.

Now the man had entered into a covenant that he would never ask any mortal for anything. So he went out and just laid his hand on the neighbour's door, and returned.

"They will not open the door," he reported.

The poor woman wept bitterly. In that anxious state the man placed his head on his knees and went to sleep. He dreamed that he saw the Prophet.

"Be not sorrowful," the Prophet bade him. "The girl child who has just come to earth is a queen among women, who shall be the intercessor for seventy thousand of my community Tomorrow," the Prophet continued, "go to 'Īsā Zādān the governor of Baṣra. Write on a piece of paper to the following effect. 'Every night you send upon me a hundred blessings, an on Friday night four hundred. Last night was Friday night, and you forgot me. In expiation for that, give this man four hundred dinars lawfully acquired.'"

Rābi'ah's father on awaking burst into tears. He rose up and wrote as the Prophet had bidden him, and sent the message to the governor by the hand of a chamberlain.

"Give two thousand dinars to the poor," the governor commanded when he saw the missive, "as a thanksgiving for the Master remembering me. Give four hundred dinars also to the shaykh, and tell him, 'I wish you to come to me so that I may see you. But I do not hold it proper for a man like you to come to me. I would rather come and rub my beard in you threshold. However, I adjure you by God, whatever you may need, pray let me know.'"

The man took the gold and purchased all that was necessary

When Rābi'ah had become a little older, and her mother and father were dead, a famine came upon Basra, and her sisters were scattered. Rābi'ah ventured out and was seen by a wicked man who seized her and then sold her for six dirhams. This purchaser put her to hard labour.

One day she was passing along the road when a stranger approached. Rābi'ah fled. As she ran, she fell headlong and her hand was dislocated.

"Lord God," she cried, bowing her face to the ground, "I am a stranger, orphaned of mother and father, a helpless prisoner fallen into captivity, my hand broken. Yet for all this I do not grieve; all I need is Thy good pleasure, to know whether Thou art well-pleased or no."

"Do not grieve," she heard a voice say. "Tomorrow a station shall be thine such that the cherubim in heaven will envy thee."

So Rābi'ah returned to her master's house. By day she continually fasted and served God, and by night she worshipped standing until day. One night her master awoke from sleep and, looking through the window of his apartment, saw Rābi'ah bowing prostrate and praying.

"O God, Thou knowest that the desire of my heart is in conformity with Thy command, and that the light of my eye is in serving Thy court. If the affair lay with me, I would not rest one hour from serving Thee, but Thou Thyself hast set me under the hand of a creature."

Such was her litany. Her master perceived a lantern suspended without any chain above her head, the light whereof filled the whole house. Seeing this, he was afraid. Rising up he returned to his bedroom and sat pondering till dawn. When day broke he summoned Rābi'ah, was gentle with her and set her free.

"Give me permission to depart," Rābi'ah said.

He gave her leave, and she left the house and went into the desert. From the desert she proceeded to a hermitage where she served God for a while. Then she determined to perform the pilgrimage, and set her face towards the desert. She bound her bundle on an ass. In the heart of the desert the ass died.

"Let us carry your load," the men in the party said.

"You go on," she replied. "I have not come putting my trust in you."

So the men departed, and Rābi'ah remained alone.

"O God," she cried, lifting her head, "do kings so treat a woman who is a stranger and powerless? Thou hast invited me unto Thy house, then in the midst of the way Thou hast suffered my ass to die, leaving me alone in the desert."

Hardly had she completed this orison when her ass stirred and rose up. Rābi'ah placed her load on its back, and continued on her way. (The narrator of this story reports that some while afterwards he saw that little donkey being sold in the market.) She travelled on through the desert for some days, then she halted.

"O God," she cried, "my heart is weary. Whither am I going? I a lump of clay, and Thy house a stone! I need Thee here."

God spoke unmediated in her heart.

"Rābi'ah, thou art faring in the life-blood of eighteen thousand worlds. Hast thou not seen how Mūsā prayed for the vision of Me? And I cast a few motes of revelation upon the mountain, and the mountain shivered into forty pieces. Be content here with My name!"

Anecdotes of Rābi'ah

One night Rābi'ah was praying in the hermitage when she was overcome by weariness and fell asleep. So deeply was she absorbed that, when a reed from the reed-mat she was lying on broke in her eye so that the blood flowed, she was quite unaware of the fact.

A thief entered and seized her chaddur. He then made to leave, but the way was barred to him. He dropped the chaddur and departed, finding the way now open. He seized the chaddur again and returned to discover the way blocked. Once more he dropped the chaddur. This he repeated seven times over; then he heard a voice proceeding from a corner of the hermitage.

"Man, do not put yourself to such pains. It is so many years now that she has committed herself to Us. The Devil himself has not the boldness to slink round her. How should a thief have the boldness to slink round her chaddur? Be gone, scoundrel! Do not put yourself to such pains. If one friend has fallen asleep, one Friend is awake and keeping watch."

Two notables of the Faith came to visit Rābi'ah, and both were hungry.

"It may be that she will give us food," they said to each other. "Her food is bound to come from a lawful source."

When they sat down there was a napkin with two loaves laid before them. They were well content. A beggar arrived just then, and Rābi'ah gave him the two loaves. The two men of religion were much upset, but said nothing. After a while a maidservant entered with a handful of warm bread.

"My mistress sent these," she explained.

Rābi'ah counted the loaves. There were eighteen.

"Perhaps it was not this that she sent me," Rābi'ah remarked.

For all that the maidservant assured her, it profited nothing. So she took back the loaves and carried them away. Now it so happened that she had taken two of the loaves for herself. She asked her mistress, and she added the two to the pile and returned with them. Rābi'ah counted again, and found there were twenty loaves. She now accepted them.

"This is what your mistress sent me," she said.

She set the loaves before the two men and they ate, marveling.

"What is the secret behind this?" they asked her. "We had an appetite for your own bread, but you took it away from us and gave it to the beggar. Then you said that the eighteen loaves did not belong to you. When they were twenty, you accepted them."

"I knew when you arrived that you were hungry," Rābi'ah replied. "I said to myself, How can I offer two loaves to two such notables? So when the beggar came to the door I gave them to him and said to Almighty God, 'O God, Thou hast said that Thou repayest tenfold, and this I firmly believed. Now I have given two loaves to please Thee, so that Thou mayest give twenty in return for them.' When eighteen were brought me, I knew that either there had been some misappropriation, or that they were not meant for me."

One day Rābi'ah's servant girl was making an onion stew; for it was some days since they had cooked any food. Finding that she needed some onions, she said,

"I will ask of next door."

"Forty years now," Rābi'ah replied, "I have had a covenant with Almighty God not to ask for aught of any but He. Nevermind the onions."

Immediately a bird swooped down from the air with peeled onions in its beak and dropped them into the pan.

"I am not sure this is not a trick," Rābi'ah commented.

And she left the onion pulp alone, and ate nothing but bread.

Rābi'ah had gone one day into the mountains. She was soon surrounded by a flock of deer and mountain goats, ibexes and wild asses which stared at her and made to approach her. Suddenly Ḥasan al-Baṣrī came on the scene and, seeing Rābi'ah, moved in her direction. As soon as the animals sighted Ḥasan, they made off all together, so that Rābi'ah remained alone. This dismayed Ḥasan.

"Why did they run away from me, and associated so tamely with you?" he asked Rābi'ah.

"What have you eaten today?" Rābi'ah countered.

"A little onion pulp."

"You eat their fat," Rābi'ah remarked. "Why then should they not flee from you?"

Once Rābi'ah passed by Ḥasan's house. Ḥasan had his head out of the window and was weeping, and his tears fell on Rābi'ah's dress. Looking up, she thought at first that it was rain; then, realising that it was Ḥasan's tears, she turned to him and addressed him.

"Master, this weeping is a sign of spiritual languor. Guard your tears, so that there may surge within you such a sea that, seeking the heart therein, you shall not find it save in the keeping of a King Omnipotent'."

These words distressed Ḥasan, but he kept his peace. Then one day he saw Rābi'ah when she was near a lake. Throwing his prayer rug on the surface of the water, he called,

"Rābi'ah, come! Let us pray two *rak'ahs* here!"

"Ḥasan," Rābi'ah replied, "when you are showing off your spiritual goods in this worldly market, it should be things that your fellow-men are incapable of displaying."

And she flung her prayer rug into the air, and flew up on it.

"Come up here, Ḥasan, where people can see us!" she cried.

Ḥasan, who had not attained that station, said nothing. Rābi'ah sought to console him.

"Ḥasan," she said, "what you did fishes also do, and what I did flies also do. The real business is outside both these tricks. One must apply one's self to the real business."

One night Ḥasan with two or three friends went to visit Rābi'ah. Rābi'ah had no lantern. Their hearts yearned for light.

Rābi'ah blew on her finger, and that night till dawn her finger shone like a lantern, and they sat in its radiance.

If anyone says, "How could this be?" I answer, "The same as Mūsā's hand." If it is objected, "But Mūsā was a prophet," I reply, "Whoever follows in the footsteps of the Prophet can possess a grain of prophethood, as the Prophet says, 'Whoever rejects a farthing's worth of unlawful things has attained a degree of prophethood.' He also said, 'A true dream is one-fortieth part of prophethood.'"

Once Rābi'ah sent Ḥasan three things—a piece of wax, a needle, and a hair.

"Be like wax," she said. "Illumine the world, and yourself burn. Be like a needle, always be working naked. When you have done these two things, a thousand years will be for you as a hair."

"Do you desire for us to get married?" Ḥasan asked Rābi'ah.

"The tie of marriage applies to those who have being," Rābi'ah replied. "Here being has disappeared, for I have become naughted to self and exist only through Him. I belong wholly to Him. I live in the shadow of His control. You must ask my hand of Him, not of me."

"How did you find this secret, Rābi'ah?" Ḥasan asked.

"I lost all 'found' things in Him," Rābi'ah answered.

"How do you know Him?" Ḥasan enquired.

"You know the 'how'; I know the 'howless'," Rābi'ah said.

Once Rābi'ah saw a man with a bandage tied round his head.

"Why have you tied the bandage?" she asked.

"Because my head aches," the man replied.

"How old are you?" she demanded.

"Thirty," he replied.

"Have you been in pain and anguish the greater part of your life?" she enquired.

"No," the man answered.

"For thirty years you have enjoyed good health," she remarked, "and you never tied about you the bandage of thankfulness. Now because of this one night that you have a headache you tie the bandage of complaint!"

Once Rābi'ah gave four silver dirhams to a man.

"Buy me a blanket," she said, "for I am naked."

The man departed. Presently he returned.

"Mistress," he said, "what colour shall I buy?"

"How did 'colour' come into the business?" Rābi'ah demanded. "Give me back the money."

And she took the dirhams and flung them into the Tigris.

One spring day Rābi'ah entered her apartment and put out her head.

"Mistress," her servant said, "come out and see what the Maker has wrought."

"Do you rather come in," Rābi'ah replied, "and see the Maker. The contemplation of the Maker pre-occupies me, so that I do not care to look upon what He has made."

A party visited her, and saw her tearing a morsel of meat with her teeth.

"Do you not have a knife to cut up the meat?" they asked.

"I have never kept a knife in my house for fear of being cut off," she replied.

Once Rābi'ah fasted for a whole week, neither eating nor sleeping. All night she was occupied with praying. Her hunger passed all bounds. A visitor entered her house bringing a bowl of food. Rābi'ah accepted it and went to fetch a lamp. She returned to find that the cat had spilled the bowl.

"I will go and fetch a jug, and break my fast," she said.

By the time she had brought the jug, the lamp had gone out. She aimed to drink the water in the dark, but the jug slipped from her hand and was broken. She uttered lamentation and sighed so ardently that there was fear that half of the house would be consumed with fire.

"O God," she cried, "what is this that Thou art doing with Thy helpless servant?"

"Have a care," a voice came to her ears, "lest thou desire Me to bestow on thee all worldly blessings, but eradicate from thy heart the care for Me. Care for Me and worldly blessings can never be associated together in a single heart. Rābi'ah, thou desirest one thing, and I desire another; My desire and thy desire can never be joined in one heart."

"When I heard this admonition," Rābi'ah related, "I so cut off my heart from the world and curtailed my desires that whenever I have prayed during the last thirty years, I have assumed it to be my last prayer."

A party of men once visited her to put her to the test, desiring to catch her out in an unguarded utterance.

"All the virtues have been scattered upon the heads of men," they said. "The crown of prophethood has been placed on men's heads. The belt of nobility has been fastened around men's waists. No woman has ever been a prophet."

"All that is true," Rābi'ah replied. "But egoism and self-worship and 'I am your Lord, the Most High' have never sprung from a woman's breast. No woman has ever been a hermaphrodite. All these things have been the specialty of men."

Once Rābi'ah fell grievously sick. She was asked what the cause might be.

"I gazed upon Paradise," she replied, "and my Lord disciplined me."

Then Ḥasan al-Baṣrī went to visit her.

"I saw one of the notables of Basra standing at the door of Rābi'ah's hermitage offering her a purse of gold and weeping," he reported. "I said, 'Sir, why are you weeping?' 'On account of this saintly woman of the age,' he replied. 'For if the blessing of her presence departs from among mankind, mankind will surely perish. I brought something for her tending,' he added, 'and I am afraid that she will not accept it. Do you intercede with her to take it.'"

So Ḥasan entered and spoke. Rābi'ah glanced up at him and said,

"He provides for those who insult Him, and shall He not provide for those who love Him? Ever since I knew Him, I have turned my back upon His creatures. I know not whether any man's property is lawful or not; how then can I take it? I stitched together by the light of a worldly lamp a shirt which I had torn. For a while my heart was obstructed, until I remembered. Then I tore the shirt in the place where I had stitched it, and my heart became dilated. Ask the gentleman pray not to keep my heart obstructed."

'Abd al-Wāḥid 'Āmir relates as follows.

I went with Sufyān al-Thawrī to visit Rābi'ah when she was sick, but out of awe for her I could not begin to address her.

"You say something," I said to Sufyān.

"If you will say a prayer," Sufyān said to Rābi'ah, "your pain will be eased."

"Do you not know who has willed that I should suffer? Was it not God?" Rābi'ah demanded.

"Yes," Sufyān agreed.

"How is it that you know that," Rābi'ah went on, "and yet you bid me to request from Him the contrary of His will? It is not right to oppose one's Friend."

"What thing do you desire, Rābi'ah?" Sufyān asked.

"Sufyān, you are a learned man. Why do you speak like that? 'What thing do you desire?' By the glory of God," Rābi'ah asseverated, "for twelve years now I have been desiring fresh dates. You know that in Basra dates are of no consequence. Yet till now I have not eaten any; for I am His servant, and what business has a servant to desire? If I wish, and my Lord does not wish, this would be infidelity. You must want only what He wishes, to be a true servant of God. If God himself gives, that is a different matter."

Sufyān was reduced to silence. Then he said,

"Since one cannot speak about your situation, do you say something about mine."

"You are a good man, but for the fact you love the world," Rābi'ah replied. "You love reciting Traditions."

This she said, implying that that was a high position.

"Lord God," cried Sufyān, deeply moved, "be content with me!"

"Are you not ashamed," broke in Rābi'ah, "to seek the contentment of One with whom you yourself are not content?"

Mālik ibn Dīnār relates as follows.

I went to visit Rābi'ah, and saw her with a broken

pitcher out of which she drank and made her ritual ablutions, an old reed-mat, and a brick which she occasionally used as a pillow. I was grieved.

"I have rich friends," I told her. "If you wish, I will get something from them for you."

"Mālik, you have committed a grievous error," she answered. "Is not my Provider and theirs one and the same?"

"Yes," I replied.

"And has the Provider of the poor forgotten the poor on account of their poverty? And does He remember the rich because of their riches?" she asked.

"No," I replied.

"Then," she went on, "since He knows my estate, how should I remind Him? Such is His will, and I too wish as He wills."

One day Ḥasan al-Baṣrī, Mālik ibn Dīnār and Shaqīq al-Balkhī went to visit Rābi'ah on her sickbed.

"He is not truthful in his claim," Ḥasan began, "who does not bear with fortitude the lash of his Lord."

"These words stink of egoism," Rābi'ah commented.

"He is not truthful in his claim," Shaqīq tried, "who is not grateful for the lash of his Lord."

"We need something better than that," Rābi'ah observed.

"He is not truthful in his claim," Mālik ibn Dīnār offered, "who does not take delight in the lash of his Lord."

"We need something better than that," Rābi'ah repeated.

"Then you say," they urged.

"He is not truthful in his claim," Rābi'ah pronounced, "who does not forget the lash in contemplation of his Master."

A leading scholar of Basra visited Rābi'ah on her sickbed. Sitting beside her pillow, he reviled the world.

"You love the world very dearly," Rābi'ah commented. "If you did not love the world, you would not make mention of it so much. It is always the purchaser who disparages the wares. If you were done with the world, you would not mention it either for good or evil. As it is, you keep mentioning it because as the proverb says, whoever loves a thing mentions it frequently."

When the time came that Rābi'ah should die, those attending her deathbed left the room and closed the door. Then a voice was heard saying, O soul at peace, return unto thy Lord, well-pleased! A time passed and no sound came from the room, so they opened the door and found that she had given up the ghost. After her death she was seen in a dream. She was asked "How did you fare with Munkar and Nakīr?" She replied "Those youths came to me and said, 'Who is thy Lord?' I answered, 'Return and say to God, with so many thousand thousand creatures Thou didst not forget one feeble old woman. I, who have only Thee in the whole world, I shall never, forget Thee, that Thou shouldst sent one to ask me, Who is thy, God?'"

Prayers of Rābi'ah

O God, whatsoever Thou hast apportioned to me of worldly, things, do Thou give that to Thy enemies; and whatsoever, Thou hast apportioned to me in the world to come, give that to Thy friends; for Thou sufficest me.

O God, if I worship Thee for fear of Hell, burn me in Hell and if I worship Thee in hope of Paradise, exclude me from Paradise; but if I worship Thee for Thy own sake, grudge me not Thy everlasting beauty.

O God, my whole occupation and all my desire in this world of all worldly things, is to remember Thee, and in the world to come, of all things of the world to come, is to meet Thee. This is on my side, as I have stated; now do Thou whatsoever Thou wilt.

5

Fuḍayl ibn ‘Iyāḍ

Abū ‘Alī al-Fuḍayl ibn ‘Iyāḍ al-Ṭalaqānī was born in Khurasan, and in the beginning of his career he is said to have been a highwayman. After conversion he went to Kūfah and later to Makkah, where he resided for many years and died in 187 (803). He achieved considerable repute as an authority on Traditions, and his boldness in preaching before Hārūn al-Rashīd is widely reported.

Fuḍayl the highwayman and how he repented

At the beginning of his career, Fuḍayl ibn ‘Iyāḍ pitched his tent in the heart of the desert between Merv and Bavard. He wore sackcloth and a woollen cap, and hung a rosary around his neck. He had many companions who were all of them thieves and highwaymen. Night and day they robbed and pillaged, and always brought the proceeds to

Fuḍayl since he was the senior of them. He would divide the loot among the bandits, keeping for himself what he fancied. He kept an inventory of everything, and never absented himself from the meetings of the gang. Any apprentice who failed to attend a meeting he expelled from the gang.

One day a great caravan was passing that way, and Fuḍayl's confederates were on the alert for it. A certain man was travelling in the convoy who had heard rumour of the brigands. Sighting them, he took counsel with himself how he might conceal his bag of gold.

"I will hide this bag," he said to himself. "Then if they waylay the caravan, I will have this capital to fall back on."

Going aside from the road, he saw Fuḍayl's tent and Fuḍayl himself close by it, an ascetic by his looks and the clothes he wore. So he entrusted the bag of gold to him.

"Go and put it in the corner of the tent," Fuḍayl told him.

The man did as he was bidden, and returned to the caravan halt, to find that it had been pillaged. All the luggage had been carried out, and the travellers bound hand and foot. The man released them, and collecting the little that remained they took their departure. The man returned to Fuḍayl to recover his bag of gold. He saw him squatting with the robbers, as they divided up the spoil.

"Ah, I gave my bag of gold to a thief!" the man exclaimed.

Seeing him afar off, Fuḍayl hailed the man, who came to him.

"What do you want?" he asked.

"Take it from where you deposited it," Fuḍayl bade him. "Then go."

The man ran into the tent, picked up his bag, and departed.

"Why," cried Fuḍayl's companions, "in the whole caravan we did not find so much as one dirham in cash, and you give back ten thousand dirhams!"

"The man had a good opinion of me, and I have always had a good opinion of God, that He will grant me repentance," Fuḍayl replied. "I justified his good opinion, so that God may justify my good opinion."

One day later they waylaid another caravan and carried off the baggage. As they sat eating, a traveller from the caravan approached them.

"Who is your chief?" he asked.

"He is not with us," the brigands replied. "He is the other side of the tree by the river bank, praying."

"But it is not the hour of prayer," the man exclaimed.

"He is performing a work of supererogation," one of the thieves explained.

"And he is not eating with you," the man went on.

"He is fasting," the thief replied.

"But it is not Ramaḍān."

"Supererogation again," the thief retorted.

Greatly astonished, the traveller drew near Fuḍayl who was praying with great humility. He waited until he had finished, then he remarked.

"Opposites do not mingle, they say. How can one fast and rob, pray and at the same time murder Muslims?"

"Do you know the Qur'an?" Fuḍayl asked the man.

"I know it," the man replied.

"Well then, does not Almighty God say *And others have confessed their sins; they have mixed a righteous deed with another evil?*"

The man was speechless with astonishment.

It is said that by nature he was chivalrous and high-minded, so that if a woman was travelling in a caravan he never took her goods; in the same way, he would not pillage the property of anyone with slender capital. He always left each victim with a due proportion of his belongings. All his inclination was towards right doing.

At the beginning of his exploits Fuḍayl was passionately in love with a certain woman, and he always brought her the proceeds of his brigandage. In season and out of season he climbed walls in the infatuation of his passion for the woman, weeping all the while.

One night a caravan was passing, and in the midst of the caravan a man was chanting the Qur'an. The following verse reached Fuḍayl's ears: *Is it not time that the hearts of those who believe should be humbled to the remembrance of God?* It was as though an arrow pierced his soul, as though that verse had come out to challenge Fuḍayl and say, "O Fuḍayl, how long will you waylay travellers? The time has come when We shall waylay you!"

Fuḍayl fell from the wall, crying, "It is high time indeed, and past high time!"

Bewildered and shamefaced, he fled headlong to a ruin. There a party of travellers was encamped. They said, "Let us go!" One of them interjected, "We cannot go. Fuḍayl is on the road."

"Good tidings!" Fuḍayl cried. "He has repented."

With that he set out and all day went on his way weeping, satisfying his adversaries. Finally there remained only a Jew in Bavard. He sought quittance of him, but the Jew would not be reconciled.

"Today we can make light of these Muḥammadans," he chuckled to his fellows.

"If you want me to grant you quittance," he told Fuḍayl, "clear this heap."

He pointed to a mound of sand, to remove which would tax all the strength of a man except perhaps over a long period. The hapless Fuḍayl shovelled away the sand little by little, but how should the task ever be completed? Then one morning, when Fuḍayl was utterly exhausted, a wind sprang up and blew the heap clean away. When the Jew saw what had happened he was amazed.

"I have sworn," he told Fuḍayl, "that until you give me money I will not grant you quittance. Now put your hand under this rug and take up a fistful of gold and give it to me. My oath will then be fulfilled, and I will give you quittance."

Fuḍayl entered the Jew's house. Now the Jew had put some earth under the rug. Fuḍayl thrust his hand under, and brought forth a fistful of dinars which he gave to the Jew.

"Offer me Islam!" cried the latter.

Fuḍayl offered him Islam, and the Jew became a Muslim.

"Do you know why I have become a Muslim?" he then said. "It is because until today I was not certain which was the true religion. Today it has become clear to me that Islam is the true religion; for I have read in the Torah that if any man repents sincerely and then places his hand on earth, the earth turns to gold. I had put earth under the rug to prove you. When you laid your hand on the earth and it turned to gold, I knew for sure that your repentance was a reality and that your religion is true."

"For God's sake," Fuḍayl begged a man, "bind me hand and foot and bring me before the Sultan, that he may exercise judgement against me for the many crimes I have committed."

The man did as he requested. When the Sultan beheld Fuḍayl, he observed in him the marks of righteous folk.

"I cannot do this," he said. And he ordered him to be returned to his apartment with honour. When he reached the door of the apartment he uttered a loud cry.

"Hark at him shouting!" people remarked. "Perchance he is being beaten."

"Indeed, I have been sorely beaten," Fuḍayl replied.

"In what part?" they asked.

"In my soul," he answered.

Then he went in to his wife.

"Wife," he announced, 'I would visit God's House. If you wish, I will set you free."

"I will never go apart from you," his wife replied. "Wherever you may be, I will be with you."

So they set out and in due time came to Makkah, Almighty God making the road easy for them. There he took up residence near the Ka'bah, and met some of the Saints. He companioned Imam Abū Ḥanīfah for a while, and many stories are told of his extreme discipline. In Makkah the gates of oratory were opened to him, and the Makkans thronged to hear him preach. Soon all the world was talking about him, so that his family and kinsmen set forth from Bavard and came to look upon him. They knocked at his door, but he would not open it. They for their part would not depart, so Fuḍayl mounted the roof of his house.

"What idlers you are!" he cried to them. "God give you employment!"

He spoke many such words, till they all wept and were beside themselves. Finally, despairing of enjoying his society, they went away. He still remained on the roof and did not open the door.

Fuḍayl and Hārūn al-Rashīd

One night Hārūn al-Rashīd summoned Faḍl the Barmecide, who was one of his favourite courtiers.

"Take me to a man this night who will reveal me to myself," he bade him. "My heart is grown weary of pomp and pride."

Faḍl brought Hārūn to the door of the house of Sufyān ibn 'Uyaynah. They knocked at the door.

"Who is it?" Sufyān asked.

"The Commander of the Faithful," Faḍl replied.

"Why did he trouble himself so?" Sufyān said. "I ought to have been informed, then I could have come myself to him."

"This is not the man I am seeking," Hārūn commented "He fawns upon me like the rest."

Hearing of what had happened, Sufyān said, "Fuḍayl ibn 'Iyāḍ is such a man as you are seeking. You must go to him." And he recited this verse: *Or do those who commit evil deeds think that We shall make them as those who believe and do righteous deeds?*

"If I am seeking good counsel, this is sufficient," remarked Hārūn.

They knocked at Fuḍayl's door.

"Who is it?" Fuḍayl asked.

"The Commander of the Faithful," Faḍl replied.

"What business has he with me, and what have I to do with him?" Fuḍayl demanded.

"Is it not a duty to obey those in authority?" countered Faḍl.

"Do not disturb me," cried Fuḍayl.

"Shall I enter with an authority or a command?" said Faḍl.

"There is no such thing as authority," replied Fuḍayl. "If you enter by force, you know what you are doing."

Hārūn entered. As he approached Fuḍayl, the latter blew out the lamp so as not to see his face. Hārūn stretched out his hand, and Fuḍayl's hand met it.

"How smooth and soft this palm is, if only it could escape from Hell-fire!" Fuḍayl remarked.

So saying, he arose and stood in prayer. Hārūn was much affected and weeping overcame him.

"Say something to me," he begged. Fuḍayl saluted him and then spoke.

"Your ancestor, the Prophet's uncle, once demanded of the Prophet, 'Make me commander over some people.' The Prophet replied, 'Uncle, for one moment I have made you commander over yourself.' By this he meant, 'For you to obey God for one moment is better than a thousand years of people obeying you.' The Prophet added, 'Command shall be a cause of regretting on the Day of Resurrection.'"

"Say more," Hārūn pleaded.

"When 'Umar ibn 'Abd al-'Azīz was appointed caliph," Fuḍayl related, "he summoned Sālim ibn 'Abdullah, Rajā' ibn Ḥayāt, and Muḥammad ibn Ka'b. 'I have been afflicted with this trial,' he told them. 'What am I to do? For I know this high office to be a trial, even though men count it for a blessing.' One of the three said, 'If you wish tomorrow to escape from God's punishment, look upon aged Muslims as though each were your father, and regard youthful Muslims as your brothers, Muslim children as your own sons, treating them in all respects as one does one's father, brother, and son.'"

"Say more," Hārūn repeated.

"The lands of Islam are as your own house, and their inhabitants your family," Fuḍayl said. "Visit your father, honour your brother, and be good to your son. I fear," he added, "that your handsome face will be sorely tried by the fire of Hell. Fear God, and obey His command. And be watchful and prudent; for on the Resurrection Day God will question you concerning every single Muslim, and He will exact justice from you in respect of every one. If one night an old woman has gone to sleep in a house without provisions, she will pluck your skirt on that Day and will give evidence against you."

Hārūn wept bitterly, so that his consciousness was like to fail.

"Enough! You have slain the Commander of the Faithful," chided Faḍl the vizier.

"Be silent, Hāmān," cried Fuḍayl. "It is you and your creatures who are destroying him, and then you tell me that I have killed him. Is this murder?"

At these words Hārūn wept even more copiously.

"He calls you Hāmān," he said, turning to Faḍl, "because he equates me with Pharaoh." Then, addressing Fuḍayl, he asked,

"Have you a debt outstanding?"

"Yes," replied Fuḍayl. "A debt of obedience to God. If He takes me to task over this, then woe is me!"

"I am speaking of debts owed to men, Fuḍayl," said Hārūn.

"Thanks be to God," cried Fuḍayl, "who has blessed me abundantly, so that I have no complaint to make to His servants."

Then Hārūn placed a purse of a thousand dinars before him.

"This is lawful coin, of my mother's inheritance," he said.

"Commander of the Faithful," said Fuḍayl, "the counsels I have spoken to you have yielded no profit. Even now you have recommenced wrongdoing and resumed injustice."

"What wrongdoing?" demanded Hārūn.

"I call you to salvation, and you cast me into temptation. This is wrongdoing indeed," said Fuḍayl. "I tell you, give back what you possess to its proper owner. You for your part give it to another to whom it should not be given. It is useless for me to speak."

So saying, he rose up from the caliph's presence and flung the gold out of the door.

"Ah, what a man he is!" exclaimed Hārūn, leaving Fuḍayl's house. "Fuḍayl is in truth a king of men. His arrogance is extreme, and the world is very contemptible in his eyes."

Anecdotes of Fuḍayl

One day Fuḍayl was holding in his lap a four-year-old child, and by chance placed his mouth on its cheek as is the wont of fathers.

"Father, do you love me?" asked the child.

"I do," replied Fuḍayl.

"Do you love God?"

"I do."

"How many hearts do you have?" the child asked.

"One," answered Fuḍayl.

"Can you love two with one heart?" demanded the child.

Fuḍayl at once realised that it was not the child speaking, but that in reality it was a Divine instruction. Jealous for God, he began to beat his head and repented. Severing his heart from the child, he gave it to God.

One day Fuḍayl was standing at 'Arafāt. All the pilgrims there were weeping and wailing, humbling themselves and making lowly petition.

"Glory be to God!" cried Fuḍayl. "If so many men were to go to a man at one time and ask him for a silver penny, what do you say? Would that man disappoint so many?"

"No," came the answer.

"Well," said Fuḍayl, "surely it is easier for Almighty God to forgive them all, than for that man to give a silver penny. For He is the most bountiful of the bountiful, so there is good hope that He will pardon all."

Once Fuḍayl's son suffered an obstruction of urine. Fuḍayl came and lifted up his hands.

"O Lord," he prayed, "by my love for Thee deliver him out of this sickness."

He had not yet risen from his knees when the boy was healed.

Fuḍayl would often say in prayer: "Lord God, have mercy! For Thou knowest my repentance; and do not punish me, for Thou hast all power over me." Then he would add, "O God, Thou keepest me hungry, and Thou keepest my children hungry. Thou keepest me naked, and Thou keepest my children naked. Thou givest not to me a lantern by night. All these things Thou doest to Thy friends. By what spiritual station has Fuḍayl earned this felicity from Thee?"

For thirty years no man saw Fuḍayl smile, except on the day when his son died. Then he smiled.

"Master, what time is this for smiling?" he was asked.

"I realised that God was pleased that my son should die," he answered. "I smiled to accord with God's good pleasure."

Fuḍayl had two daughters. When his end approached, he laid a last charge upon his wife.

"When I die, take these girls and go to Mount Abī Qubays. There lift your face to heaven and say, 'Lord God, Fuḍayl laid a charge upon me saying, "Whilst I was alive, I protected these helpless ones as best I could. When Thou madest me a prisoner in the fastness of the grave, I gave them back to Thee."'"

When Fuḍayl was buried, his wife did as he had bidden her. She went out to the mountaintop and conveyed her daughters there. Then she prayed with much weeping and lamentation. At that very moment the Prince of Yemen passed by there with his two sons. Seeing them weeping and making moan, he enquired, "Whence are you come?"

Fuḍayl's wife explained the situation.

"I give these girls to these my sons," the prince announced. "I give each of them as a dowry ten thousand dinars. Are you content with this?"

"I am," their mother replied.

At once the prince furnished litters and carpets and brocades, and conveyed them to Yemen.

6

Ibrāhīm ibn Adham

Abū Isḥāq Ibrāhīm ibn Adham, born in Balkh of pure Arab descent, is described in Sufi legend as a prince who renounced his kingdom (somewhat after the fashion of the Buddha) and wandered westwards to live a life of complete asceticism, earning his bread in Syria by honest manual toil until his death in c. 165 (782). Some accounts state that he was killed on a naval expedition against Byzantium. The story of his conversion is a classic of Muslim hagiography.

The legend of Ibrāhīm ibn Adham

Ibrāhīm ibn Adham's saintly career began in the following manner. He was king of Balkh, and a whole world was under his command; forty gold swords and forty gold maces were carried before and behind him. One night he was asleep on his royal couch. At midnight the roof of the apartment vibrated, as if someone was walking on the roof.

"Who is there?" he shouted.

"A friend," came the reply. "I have lost a camel, and am searching for it on this roof."

"Fool, do you look for the camel on the roof?" cried Ibrāhīm.

"Heedless one," answered the voice, "do you seek for God in silken clothes, asleep on a golden couch?"

These words filled his heart with terror. A fire blazed within him, and he could not sleep any more. When day came he returned to the dais and sat on his throne, thoughtful, bewildered and full of care. The ministers of state stood each in his place; his slaves were drawn up in serried ranks. General audience was proclaimed.

Suddenly a man with aweful mien entered the chamber, so terrible to look upon that none of the royal retinue and servants dared ask him his name; the tongues of all clove to their throats. He advanced solemnly till he stood before the throne.

"What do you want?" demanded Ibrāhīm.

"I have just alighted at this caravanserai," said the man. "This is not a caravanserai. This is my palace. You are mad," shouted Ibrāhīm.

"Who owned this palace before you?" asked the man.

"My father," Ibrāhīm replied.

"And before him?"

"My grandfather."

"And before him?"

"So-and-so."

"And before him?"

"The father of So-and-so."

"Where have they all departed?" asked the man.

"They have gone. They are dead," Ibrāhīm replied.

"Then is this not a caravanserai which one man enters and another leaves?"

With these words the stranger vanished. He was Khiḍr, upon whom be peace. The fire blazed more fiercely still in Ibrāhīm's soul, and the anguish within him augmented momently. Visions by day followed the hearing of voices by night, equally mysterious and incomprehensible.

"Saddle my horse," Ibrāhīm cried at last. "I will go to the hunt. I know not what this thing is that has come upon me today. Lord God, how will this affair end?"

His horse was saddled and he proceeded to the chase. Headlong he galloped across the desert; it was as if he knew not what he was doing. In that state of bewilderment he became separated from his troops. On the way he suddenly heard a voice.

"Awake!"

He pretended not to have heard, and rode on. A second time the voice came, but he heeded it not. A third time he heard the same, and hurled himself farther away. Then the voice sounded a fourth time.

"Awake, before you are stricken awake!"

He now lost all self-control. At that instant a deer started up, and Ibrāhīm prepared to give chase. The deer spoke to him.

"I have been sent to hunt you. You cannot catch me. Was it for this that you were created, or is this what you were commanded?"

"Ah, what is this that has come upon me?" Ibrāhīm cried.

And he turned his face from the deer. He thereupon heard the same words issuing from the pommel of his saddle. Terror and fear possessed him. The revelation became clearer yet, for Almighty God willed to complete the transaction. A third time the selfsame voice proceeded from the collar of his cloak. The revelation was thus consummated, and the heavens were opened unto him.

Sure faith was now established in him. He dismounted; all his garments, and the horse itself, were dripping with his tears. He made true and sincere repentance. Turning aside from the road, he saw a shepherd wearing felt clothes and a hat of felt, driving his sheep before him. Looking closely, he saw that he was a slave of his. He bestowed on him his gold-embroidered cloak and bejewelled cap, together with the sheep, and took from him his clothes and hat of felt. These he donned himself. All the angelic hosts stood gazing on Ibrāhīm.

"What a kingdom has come to the son of Adham," they cried. "He has cast away the filthy garments of the world, and has donned the glorious robes of poverty."

Even so he proceeded on foot to wander over mountains and endless deserts, lamenting over his sins, until he came to Merv. There he saw a man who had fallen from the bridge and was about to perish, swept away by the river. Ibrāhīm shouted from afar.

"O God, preserve him!"

The man remained suspended in the air until helpers arrived and drew him up. They were astonished at Ibrāhīm.

"What man is this?" they cried.

Ibrāhīm departed from that place, and marched on to Nishapur. There he searched for a desolate corner where he might busy himself with obedience to God. In the end he hit upon the famous cave where he dwelt for nine years, three years in each apartment. Who knows what occupied him there through the nights and days? For it needed a mighty man of uncommon substance to be able to be there alone by night.

Every Thursday he would climb above the cavern and collect a bundle of firewood. Next morning he would set out, for Nishapur and there sell the brushwood. Having performed the Friday prayers, he would buy bread with the money he had gained, give half to a beggar and use half himself to break his fast. So he did every week.

One winter's night he was in that apartment. It was extremely cold, and he had to break the ice to wash. All night he shivered, praying through till dawn. By dawn he was in danger of perishing from the cold. By chance the thought of a fire entered his mind. He saw a fur on the ground. Wrapping himself up in the fur, he fell asleep. When he awoke it was broad daylight, and he had become warm. He looked, and saw that the fur was a dragon, its eyes saucers of blood. A mighty terror came upon him.

"Lord God," he cried, "Thou didst send this thing unto me in a shape of gentleness. Now I see it in a dreadful form. I cannot endure it."

Immediately the dragon moved away, twice or thrice rubbed its face in the ground before him, and vanished.

Ibrāhīm ibn Adham goes to Makkah

When the fame of Ibrāhīm ibn Adham's doings spread abroad amongst men, he fled from the cave and set out towards Makkah. In the desert he encountered one of the great men of the Faith, who taught him the Greatest Name of God and then took his departure. Ibrāhīm called upon God by that Name, and immediately he beheld Khiḍr, upon whom be peace.

"Ibrāhīm," said Khiḍr, "that was my brother David who taught you the Greatest Name."

Then many words passed between Khiḍr and Ibrāhīm. Khiḍr was the first who drew Ibrāhīm out, by the leave of God. Ibrāhīm relates as follows concerning the next stage of his pilgrimage.

"On reaching Dhāt al-'Irq I saw seventy men wearing the patchwork frock lying dead there, the blood gushing out of their noses and ears. Circling them, I found one who still had a spark of life in him.

"'Young man,' I cried, 'what has happened here?'

"'Son of Adham,' he answered me, 'keep to the water and the prayer-niche. Go not far away, lest you be banished; and come not too near, lest you be anguished. Let no man be overbold in the presence of Sultan. Have a lively fear of the Friend who slays pilgrims as if they were Greek infidels, and wages war upon pilgrims. We were a Sufi community who had set out into the desert trusting in God, resolved not to utter one word, to think of naught but God, to move and be still only with God in view and to heed none but Him. When we had crossed the desert and were come to the place where pilgrims robe themselves in white, Khiḍr, upon whom be peace, came to us. We greeted him, and he returned our salute, and we were very happy, saying, "Praise be to God, the journey was blessed, the quester has reached his quest, for such a holy person came out to meet us." Forthwith a voice cried within us, "You liars and pretenders, such were your words and covenant! You forgot Me, and busied yourselves with another. Depart! I will not make peace with you until I snatch away your souls in recompense and shed your blood with the sword of jealous wrath." These brave men whom you see lying here are all victims of this retaliation. Beware, Ibrāhīm! You too have the same ambition. Halt, or depart far away!'

"'Why did they spare you, then?' I asked, deeply perplexed by his words.

"'They told me, "They are ripe, you are still raw. Live on a few moments yet, and you too will be ripe. When you are ripe, you too will come in their wake."' So saying, he gave up the ghost."

Ibrāhīm was fourteen years crossing the desert, praying and humbling himself all the way. When he drew near to Makkah, the elders of the Ḥaram hearing of his approach came out to meet him. He thrust himself ahead of the caravan so that no one might recognise him. The servants preceded the elders, and they saw Ibrāhīm going ahead of the caravan; but not having seen him before, they did not recognise him. Coming up to him, they cried, "Ibrāhīm ibn Adham is near at hand. The elders of the Ḥaram have come out to meet him."

"What do you want of that heretic?" Ibrāhīm demanded.

Straightway they set upon him and beat him up.

"The elders of Makkah go out to meet him, and you call him a heretic?" they shouted.

'I say he is a heretic," Ibrāhīm repeated.

When they left him, Ibrāhīm turned to himself.

"Ha!" he cried. "You wanted the elders to come out to meet you. Well, you have collected a few punches. Praise be to God that I have seen you get your wish!"

Ibrāhīm then took up residence in Makkah. A circle of companions formed around him, and he earned his bread by the labour of his hands, working as a carpenter.

Ibrāhīm at Makkah is visited by his Son

When Ibrāhīm ibn Adham quitted Balkh he left behind him a suckling child. The latter, by now grown up, asked his mother one day about his father.

"Your father is lost," she replied.

The son thereupon made proclamation that all who desired to perform the pilgrimage should assemble. Four thousand presented themselves. He gave them all their expenses to cover provisions and camels and led the party Makkawards, hoping that God might grant him sight of his father. Reaching Makkah, they encountered by the door of the Holy Mosque a party of patchwork-frocked Sufis.

"Do you know Ibrāhīm ibn Adham?" the son enquired.

"He is a friend of ours," they told him. "He is entertaining us, and has gone to hunt for food."

The son asked them to direct him, and he went in his track. The party emerging in the lower quarter of Makkah, he saw his father unshod and bareheaded coming along with a load of firewood. Tears sprang to his eyes, but he controlled himself and followed in his father's wake to the market. There his father began to shout.

"Who will buy goodly things for goodly things?"

A baker called to him and took the firewood in exchange for bread. Ibrāhīm brought the bread and laid it before his companions.

"If I say who I am," the son feared, "he will run away."

So he went to take counsel with his mother as to the best way of recovering his father. His mother advised patience.

"Be patient until we make the pilgrimage."

When the boy departed, Ibrāhīm sat down with his associates.

"Today there are women and children on this pilgrimage. Mind your eyes," he charged them.

All accepted his counsel. When the pilgrims entered Makkah and made the circumambulation of the Ka'bah, Ibrāhīm with his companions also circled the Holy House. A handsome boy approached him, and Ibrāhīm looked at him keenly. His friends noticed this and were astonished, but waited until they had finished the circumambulation.

"God have mercy on you!" they then said to Ibrāhīm. "You bade us not to glance at any woman or child, and then you yourself gazed at a handsome lad."

"Did you see?" Ibrāhīm exclaimed.

"We saw," they replied.

"When I left Balkh," Ibrāhīm told them, "I abandoned there a suckling son. I know that the lad is that son."

Next day one of the companions went out before Ibrāhīm to look for the caravan from Balkh. Coming upon it, he observed in the midst of the caravan a tent pitched all of brocade. In the tent a throne was set, and the boy was seated on the throne, reciting the Qur'an and weeping. Ibrāhīm's friend asked if he might enter.

"Where do you come from?" he enquired.

"From Balkh," the boy replied.

"Whose son are you?"

The boy put his hand to his face and began to weep.

"I have never seen my father, "he said, laying aside the Qur'an. "Not until yesterday—I do not know whether it was he or not. I am afraid that if I speak he will run away, as he ran away from us before. My father is Ibrāhīm ibn Adham the King of Balkh."

The man seized him to bring him to Ibrāhīm. His mother rose and went along with him. Ibrāhīm, as they approached him, was seated with his companions before the Yemeni Corner. He espied from afar his friend with the boy and his mother. As soon as the woman saw him she cried aloud and could control herself no longer.

"This is your father."

An indescribable tumult arose. All the bystanders and friends of Ibrāhīm burst into tears. As soon as the boy recovered himself he saluted his father. Ibrāhīm returned his greeting and took him to his breast.

"What religion do you follow?" he asked.

"The religion of Islam," answered his son.

"Praise be to God," cried Ibrāhīm. "Do you know the Qur'an?"

"I do."

"Praise be to God. Have you studied the faith?"

"I have."

Then Ibrāhīm would have departed, but the boy would not let go of him. His mother wailed aloud. Turning his face to heaven, Ibrāhīm cried, "O God, succour me!"

The boy immediately expired in his embrace.

"What happened, Ibrāhīm?" his companions cried out.

"When I took him to my breast," Ibrāhīm explained, "love for him stirred in my heart. A voice spoke to me, 'Ibrāhīm, you claim to love Me, and you love another along with Me. You charge your companions not to look upon any strange woman or child, and you have attached your heart to that woman and child.' When I heard this call, I prayed, 'Lord of Glory, come to my succour! He will so occupy my heart that I shall forget to love Thee. Either take away his life or mine.' His death was the answer to my prayer."

Anecdotes of Ibrāhīm ibn Adham

One day Ibrāhīm ibn Adham was asked, "What befell you, that you quit your kingdom?"

"I was seated on my throne one day," he recalled. "A mirror was held up before me; I looked into that mirror and saw that my lodging was the tomb and therein was no familiar friend. I saw a long journey ahead of me, and I had no provision. I saw a just judge, and I had no defence. I became disgusted of my kingship."

"Why did you flee from Khurasan?" they asked.

"I heard much talk there of the true friend," he replied.

"Why do you not seek a wife?" he was asked.

"Does any woman take a husband for him to keep her hungry and naked?" he countered.

"No," they replied.

"That is why I do not marry," he explained. "Any woman whom I married would remain hungry and naked. If I only could, I would divorce myself. How can I bind another to my saddle?"

Then turning to a beggar who was present, he asked him "Do you have a wife?"

"No," the beggar replied.

"Do you have a child?"

"No."

"Excellent, excellent," Ibrāhīm exclaimed.

"Why do you say that?" asked the beggar.

"The beggar who marries embarks on a ship. When the children come, he is drowned."

One day Ibrāhīm saw a beggar bewailing his lot.

"I guess you bought beggary gratis," he remarked.

"Why, is beggary for sale?" the beggar asked in astonishment.

"Certainly," Ibrāhīm replied. "I bought it with the kingdom of Balkh. I got a bargain."

A man once brought Ibrāhīm a thousand dinars.

"Take," he said.

"I do not accept anything from beggars," Ibrāhīm replied "But I am wealthy," the man retorted.

"Do you want more than you own already?" Ibrāhīm asked.

"Indeed," the man exclaimed.

"Then take it back," said Ibrāhīm. "You are the chief of the beggars. Indeed, this is not beggary. This is plain penury."

Ibrāhīm was told of an ecstatic youth who had extraordinary experiences and disciplined himself severely.

"Bring me to him so that I may see him," he said.

They took him to the youth.

"Be my guest for three days," the youth invited him.

Ibrāhīm stayed there and observed the youth's state attentively. It surpassed even what his friends had said. All night he was sleepless and restless, not reposing or slumbering for a single moment. Ibrāhīm felt a certain jealousy.

"I am so frigid, and he is sleepless and unresting the whole night through. Come, let us investigate his case," he said to himself. "Let us discover if anything from Satan has invaded his state, or whether it is wholly pure and in all respects as it should be. I must examine the foundation of the matter. The foundation and root of the matter is what a man eats."

So he investigated what the youth was eating, and discovered that it came from unhallowed sources.

"God is most great. It is Satanic," Ibrāhīm exclaimed.

"I have been your guest for three days," he said to the youth. "Now you come and be my guest for forty days."

The youth accepted. Now the food Ibrāhīm ate was earned by the labour of his own hands. He took the youth to his home and gave him of his own food. Immediately his ecstasy vanished. All his ardour and passion disappeared. That restlessness and sleeplessness and weeping of his departed.

"What have you done to me?" he cried.

"Yes," Ibrāhīm answered. "Your food was unhallowed. Satan was all the time going and coming in you. As soon as you swallowed lawful food, the manifestations he had been contriving in you became revealed for what they were, the Devil's work."

Sahl ibn Ibrāhīm tells the following story.

I was making a journey with Ibrāhīm ibn Adham, and

on the way I fell sick. He sold all that he possessed and spent it on me. I begged him for something, and he sold his ass and spent the proceeds on me.

"Where is the ass?" I enquired when I recovered.

"I sold it," he replied.

"What shall I sit on?" I demanded.

"Brother," Ibrāhīm answered, "come, sit on my back."

And he lifted me on his back and carried me for three stages.

Every day Ibrāhīm went out to work for hire and laboured till night. All his earnings he expended on behalf of his companions. But by the time he had performed the evening prayer and bought something and had returned to his friends the night was far gone.

One night his companions said, "He is late in coming. Come, let us eat some bread and go to sleep. That will be a hint for him to return earlier in future. He will not keep us waiting so long."

So they did. When Ibrāhīm returned he saw that they were asleep. Supposing that they had not eaten anything and had gone to sleep hungry, he at once lit a fire. He had brought a little flour back with him, so he made dough to give them something to eat when they woke, then they would be able to keep fast next day. His companions awoke to see him with his beard on the floor, blowing on the fire; tears were streaming from his eyes, and he was surrounded by smoke.

"What are you doing?" they asked.

"I saw you were asleep," Ibrāhīm replied. "I said to myself, perhaps you could not find anything and went to sleep hungry. So I am making something for you to eat when you awake."

"See how he thought about us, and how we thought about him," they exclaimed.

"Since you entered on this path, have you ever experienced happiness?" Ibrāhīm was asked.

"Several times," he replied. "Once I was on board ship and the captain did not know me. I was wearing ragged clothes, my hair was untrimmed, and I was in a spiritual ecstasy of which all on board were unaware. They laughed at me and ridiculed me. There was a joker on the ship, and every now and then he would come and grab me by the hair and pluck it out and slap me on the neck. In those moments I felt that I had attained my desire, and was very happy to be so humiliated.

"Suddenly a great wave arose, and all feared that they would perish. 'We must throw one of these fellows overboard,' cried the helmsman. 'Then the ship will be lighter.' They seized me to throw me into the sea. The wave subsided, and the ship resumed an even keel. That moment when they took me by the ear to throw me into the water, I felt that I had attained my desire, and was happy.

"On another occasion I went to a mosque to sleep there. They would not let me be, and I was so weak and exhausted that I could not get up. So they seized me by the foot and dragged me out. Now the mosque had three steps; my head struck against each step in turn, and the blood flowed forth. I felt that I had attained my desire. On each step that they dropped me, the mystery of a whole clime became revealed to me. I said, 'Would that the mosque had more steps, to increase my felicity!'

"On another occasion I was rapt in a state of ecstasy. A joker came and urinated on me. Then too I was happy.

"On yet another occasion I was wrapped in a fur jacket infested by fleas which devoured me unmercifully. Suddenly I remembered the fine clothes which I had deposited in the treasury. My soul cried within me, 'Why, what pain is this?' Then too I felt that I had attained my desire."

"Once," Ibrāhīm related, "I was journeying in the desert putting my trust in God. For some days I found nothing to eat. I remembered a friend of mine, but I said to myself, 'If I go to him, my trust in God will become void.' I entered a mosque with the words on my lips, 'I have put my trust in the Living One who dies not. There is no God but He.' A voice out of heaven cried, 'Glory be to that God who has emptied the face of the earth of those who trust in Him.' I said, 'Why these words?' The voice replied, 'How should that man be truly trusting in God who undertakes a long journey for the sake of a morsel that a profane friend may give him, and then declare "I have put my trust in the

Living One who dies not"? You have given the name of trust in God to a lie!'"

"Once I bought a slave," Ibrāhīm recalled.

"'What is your name?' I asked.

"'What you call me,' he answered.

"'What do you eat?'

"'What you give me.'

"'What do you wear?'

"'What you clothe me withal.'

"'What do you do?'

"'What you command.'

"'What do you desire?' I asked.

"'What has a servant to do with desire?' he replied.

"'Wretch that you are,' I said to myself, 'all your life you have been a servant of God. Well, now learn what it means to be a servant!'

"And I wept so long that I swooned away."

No one had ever seen Ibrāhīm sitting crosslegged.

"Why do you not sit crosslegged?" he was asked.

"I did sit that way one day," he replied. "I heard a voice from the air saying, 'Son of Adham, do servants sit so in the presence of their lords?' I at once sat upright and repented.

"Once I was travelling in the desert trusting in God,"

Ibrāhīm related. "For three days I found nothing to eat. The Devil came to me.

"'Did you abandon your kingdom and so much luxury in order to go on the pilgrimage hungry?' the Devil taunted me. 'You can also make the pilgrimage in style and not suffer so.

"Hearing this speech of the Devil, I lifted my head on high.

"'O God,' I cried, 'dost Thou appoint Thy enemy over Thy friend to torture me? Come to my succour! For I cannot cross this desert without Thy aid.'

"'Ibrāhīm,' a voice came to me, 'cast out what thou hast in thy pocket, that We may bring forth that which is in the Unseen.'

"I put my hand in my pocket. Four silver pennies were there which I had forgotten. As soon as I flung them away the Devil fled from me, and aliment materialised out of the Unseen."

"Once," Ibrāhīm recalled, "I was appointed to look after an orchard. The owner of the orchard came and said to me, 'Bring me some sweet pomegranates.' I brought some, but they were sour.

"'Bring me sweet ones,' the owner repeated. I brought another dishful, but they were also sour.

"'Glory be to God!' the owner cried. 'You have spent so long in an orchard, and you do not know ripe pomegranates?'

"'I look after your orchard, but I do not know what pomegranates taste like because I have never sampled any,' I replied

"'With such self-denial, I suspect you are Ibrāhīm ibn Adham,' the owner said.

"When I heard these words, I departed from that place."

"One night," Ibrāhīm related, 'I saw Jibrīl in a dream come down to earth out of heaven with a scroll in his hand.

"'What do you want?' I asked.

"'I am writing down the names of the friends of God,' Jibrīl replied.

"'Write down my name,' I said.

"'You are not of them,' Jibrīl answered.

"'I am a friend of the friends of God,' I rejoined.

"Jibrīl pondered for a while. Then he said,

"'The command has come. Inscribe Ibrāhīm's name the first of all. For on this Path hope materialises out of despair.'"

Ibrāhīm was travelling in the desert one day when he was accosted by a soldier.

"What are you?" the soldier asked.

"A servant," replied Ibrāhīm.

"Which is the way to habitation?" asked the soldier.

Ibrāhīm pointed to the graveyard.

"You are making fun of me," shouted the soldier, lashing out at Ibrāhīm's head. His head was broken, and the blood gushed forth.

The soldier put a rope round Ibrāhīm's neck and dragged him along. People from the nearby town coming that way stopped at the spectacle.

"Ignoramus, this is Ibrāhīm ibn Adham, the friend of God," they cried.

The soldier fell at Ibrāhīm's feet and implored him to pardon him and acquit him of the wrong he had done him.

"You told me you were a servant," he pleaded.

"Who is there who is not a servant?" Ibrāhīm replied.

"I broke your head, and you prayed for me," said the soldier.

"I prayed that you might be blessed for the way you treated me," was Ibrāhīm's answer. "My reward for the way you treated me was Paradise, and I did not wish that your reward should be Hell."

"Why did you direct me to the cemetery when I asked the way to habitation?" the soldier asked.

"Because every day the graveyard becomes more thronged, and the city more deserted," answered Ibrāhīm.

Once Ibrāhīm passed by a drunkard. His mouth was foul, so he fetched water and washed the drunkard's mouth.

"Do you leave foul the mouth that has mouthed the name of God? That is irreverence!" Ibrāhīm said to himself.

"The ascetic of Khurasan washed your mouth," they told the man when he woke.

"I too now repent," the man declared.

After that Ibrāhīm heard in a dream, "Thou didst wash a mouth for My sake. I have washed thy heart."

I was once on shipboard with Ibrāhīm (relates Raja) when suddenly a wind sprang up and the world grew dark.

"Alas, the ship is sinking!" I cried.

"Fear not that the ship will sink," came a voice from the air. "Ibrāhīm ibn Adham is with you."

Immediately the wind subsided, and the darkened world became bright.

Ibrāhīm wished to embark on a ship, but he had no money.

"Every one must pay a dinar," came the announcement.

Ibrāhīm prayed two *rak'ahs*, and said, "O God, they are demanding money from me and I have none."

Forthwith the whole sea was turned to gold. Ibrāhīm gathered a handful and gave it to them.

One day Ibrāhīm was seated on the bank of the Tigris stitching his threadbare robe. His needle fell into the river.

"You gave up such a mighty kingdom. What did you get in return?" someone asked him.

"Give back my needle," cried Ibrāhīm, pointing to the river.

A thousand fishes put up their heads from the water, each with a golden needle in its mouth.

"I want my own needle," said Ibrāhīm.

A feeble little fish held up Ibrāhīm's needle in its mouth.

"This is the least thing I have gotten by abandoning the kingdom of Balkh," said Ibrāhīm. "The rest you know nothing of."

◆

One day Ibrāhīm came to a well. He let down the bucket, and it came up full of gold. He emptied it and let it down again, and it came up full of pearls. In merry mood he emptied it once more.

"O God," he cried, "Thou art offering me a treasury. I know that Thou art all-powerful, and Thou knowest that I shall not be deluded by this. Give me water, that I may make my ablution."

◆

Once Ibrāhīm was going on the pilgrimage in company.

"Not one of us has a camel or any provisions," said his fellow-pilgrims.

"Rely on God to provide for you," Ibrāhīm told them.

Then he added, "Look at those trees! If it is gold that you desire, they will be turned to gold."

All the acacias had turned to gold by the Power of Almighty God.

One day Ibrāhīm was travelling with a party when they came to a fort. Before the fort was much brushwood.

"We will pass the night here," they said. "There is plenty of brushwood, so we can make a fire."

They kindled a fire and sat in the light of the flames. All ate dry bread, whilst Ibrāhīm stood in prayer.

"If only we had some hallowed meat to roast on this fire," said one.

Ibrāhīm finished his prayer. Then he said, "God is certainly able to give you hallowed meat."

Saying this, he stood once more in prayer. Immediately came the roar of a lion. They watched as a lion approached dragging a wild ass. They took the ass, roasted it and ate it, whilst the lion crouched there watching them.

7

Bishr ibn al-Ḥārith

Abū Naṣr Bishr ibn al-Ḥārīth al-Ḥāfī was born near Merv c. 150 (767) and was converted from a life of dissipation, studied Traditions in Baghdad, then abandoned formal learning for the life of a mendicant, destitute, starving and barefoot. He died in Baghdad in 227 (841). He was admired by Aḥmad ibn Ḥanbal and respected by the caliph al-Ma'mūn.

The conversion of Bishr the Barefoot

Bishr the Barefoot was born in Merv and settled at Baghdad. The beginning of his conversion happened as follows. He had lived a life of dissipation, and one day as he was staggering along the road drunk he found a piece of paper on which was written, "In the Name of God, the Merciful, the Compassionate." He bought some *'iṭr* of roses and perfumed the paper with it, and deposited it reverently in his house. That night a certain holy man had a dream in which he was bidden to tell Bishr:

"Thou hast perfumed my Name, so I have perfumed thee. Thou hast exalted my Name, so I have exalted thee. Thou hast purified my Name, so I have purified thee. By my Majesty, I will surely perfume thy name in this world and the world to come."

"He is a dissolute fellow," thought the saint. "Perhaps I am seeing erroneously."

So he made ablution, prayed and returned to sleep. He saw the selfsame dream a second and a third time. In the morning he arose and went in search of Bishr.

"He is at a wine-party," he was told.

He went to the house where Bishr was.

"Was Bishr here?" he enquired.

"He was," they said. "But he is drunk and incapable."

"Tell him I have a message for him," said the saint.

"A message from whom?" demanded Bishr when he was told.

"A message from God," replied the saint.

"Alas!" cried Bishr, bursting into tears. "Is it a message of chiding or of chastisement? Wait, till I tell my friends. Friends," he addressed his drinking-companions, "I have had a call. I am going. I bid you farewell. You will never see me again at this business."

And from that day onward he lived so saintly, that none heard his name mentioned without heavenly peace invaded his heart. He took to the way of selfdenial, and so overwhelmed was he by the vision of God that he never put shoes on his feet. For that reason he was called Bishr the Barefoot.

"Why do you not wear shoes?" he was asked.

"I was barefooted the day when I made my peace with God," he said, "and ever since I am ashamed to wear shoes. Moreover God Almighty says, 'I have made the earth a carpet for you.' It is not seemly to tread with shoes on the carpet of kings."

Aḥmad ibn Ḥanbal visited Bishr frequently, having a complete faith in him to such a point that his pupils protested.

"Today you are without rival as a scholar of Traditions, the law, theology and every manner of science, yet every moment you go after a dissolute fellow. Is that seemly?"

"Indeed, in all the sciences you have enumerated I have better knowledge than he," Aḥmad ibn Ḥanbal replied. "But he knows God better than I."

So he would pursue Bishr, saying, "Tell me about my Lord."

Anecdotes of Bishr

"Tonight Bishr will be your guest."

This conviction entered Bishr's sister's mind. She swept and watered her house, and waited expectantly for Bishr to arrive. Suddenly Bishr came like one distraught.

"Sister, I am going up to the roof," he announced.

He planted his foot on the stairs and climbed several steps, then remained standing like that till the next day.

When dawn broke, he descended. He went off to pray in the mosque.

"What was the reason you stood all night?" asked his sister when he returned.

"The thought entered my mind," Bishr replied, "that in Baghdad there are so many people whose names are Bishr—one a Jew, one a Christian, one a Magian. My name too is Bishr, and I have attained the great felicity of being a Muslim.

What, I asked myself, did the others do to be excluded, and what did I do to attain such felicity? Bewildered by this thought, I remained rooted to the spot."

Bishr possessed seven bookcases of volumes on Traditions. He buried them all in the ground, and did not transmit them.

"The reason I do not transmit Traditions," he explained, "is that I perceive in myself a lust to do so. If I perceive in my heart a lust to keep silence, then I will transmit."

For a space of forty years Bishr longed for roast meat but had not the money to buy any. For many years his heart yearned for beans, but he ate none. He never drank water from streams dug out by the authorities.

One of the Saints relates, "I was with Bishr once when the weather was extremely cold. I saw him naked and trembling. 'Abū Naṣr' I said, 'in such weather people put on extra clothing. You have taken off your clothes.' 'Yes,'

Bishr replied, 'I remembered the poor. I had no money with which to succour them, so I wanted to share with them physically.'"

Aḥmad ibn Ibrāhīm tells the following story.

"Tell Ma'rūf," Bishr said to me, "that I will call on him after I have said my prayer."

I delivered the message, and we waited together. We performed the midday prayer, and Bishr did not come. We performed the afternoon prayer, and he did not come. We performed the prayer before sleeping.

"Glory be to God," I said to myself, "does a man like Bishr break his word? This is extraordinary."

I kept on the lookout, we being at the door of the mosque. Presently Bishr came along with his prayer rug under his arm. When he reached the Tigris he walked on the water and so came to us. He and Ma'rūf talked till dawn, then he returned walking on the water again. Flinging myself down from the roof, I hurried to him and kissed his hands and feet.

"Pray for me," I implored him.

Bishr prayed. Then he said, "Reveal what you have seen to no man."

So long as he was alive, I told no one.

A crowd was gathered around Bishr, and he was preaching on the theme of satisfaction. One of those present interrupted him.

"Abū Naṣr, you accept nothing from any creature in order to attain prominence. If you are sincere in your self-denial and have truly turned your face from this world, then take offerings from other men so that you may lose your prominence in people's eyes. Give to the poor what you receive, but give in secret; then be unwavering in trusting in God, and obtain your provision from the world unseen."

These words made a powerful impression on Bishr's followers. Bishr answered as follows.

"Attend now! The poor are divided into three classes. One class consists of those who never ask for anything, and if they are given anything they yet decline to accept it. These people are the spiritualists; for when they ask aught from God, God gives them whatever they desire, and if they adjure God their need is at once granted. The second class are those who do not ask, but if they are given anything they accept it. These are the middling folk; they are constant in their trust in God, and they are those who shall sit at the table of Paradise. The third class are those who sit with patience; as far as they can they observe their moment, and repel outward enticements."

"I am satisfied with this statement," the interrupter said. "May God be satisfied with you!"

A throng of people came to Bishr.

"We have come from Syria, and are going on the pilgrimage," they said. "Do you feel inclined to accompany us?"

"On three conditions," Bishr replied. "First, we will take nothing with us; second, we will not ask for anything; third, if we are given anything we will not accept it."

"Not to ask for anything and not to take anything with us—that we are able to concede," they answered. "But if an offering comes along, we cannot not take it."

"You have put your faith not in God," Bishr rebuked them, "but in your pilgrims' provisions."

A man once came to consult Bishr's advice.

"I have two thousand dirhams lawfully acquired. I wish to go on the pilgrimage."

"You want to walk for your own amusement," Bishr replied. "If you are really intent on pleasing God, then go and pay someone's debt, or give the money to an orphan, or someone in poor circumstances. The ease thus given to a Muslim's heart is more acceptable to God than a hundred pilgrimages."

"I put prior the desire to make the pilgrimage," the man said.

"That is because you have obtained these moneys by means that are not good," Bishr commented. "You will never find rest until you have spent them in improper ways."

Bishr related as follows.

Once I saw the Prophet in a dream. He said to me, "Bishr, do you not know why God has chosen you from amongst your contemporaries and has raised you up to high rank?"

"No, Messenger of God," I replied.

"It is because you have followed my Sunnah, and reverenced the righteous, and given good counsel to your brethren, and loved me and the people of my household," the Prophet told me. "For this reason God has advanced you to the station of the pious."

Bishr also told the following story.

One night I saw 'Alī in a dream. I said, "Give me counsel."

"How good a thing," said 'Alī, "is the compassion shown by the rich to the poor for the sake of seeking the reward of the All-merciful. Better still is the disdain shown by the poor towards the rich relying upon the munificence of the Creator of the world."

Bishr lay on his deathbed. A man entered and complained of the tight-fistedness of fate. Bishr gave him his shirt and put on a borrowed shirt, and in that shirt set out into the world beyond.

It is recorded that so long as Bishr was alive, no mule dropped its dung in the streets of Baghdad out of reverence for him, because he walked barefooted. One night a man with a mule observed his beast drop its dung in the road.

"Ah, Bishr the Barefoot is no more," he exclaimed.

Enquiry was made, and so it proved. The man was asked how he knew.

"Because so long as he was alive, on all the streets of Baghdad no mule-dung was to be seen. I observed that the rule had been broken, and so knew that Bishr was no more."

8

Dhū al-Nūn al-Miṣrī

Abū al-Fā'iz Thawbān ibn Ibrāhīm al-Miṣrī, called Dhū al-Nūn, was born at Ikhmīm in Upper Egypt c. 180 (796), studied under various teachers and travelled extensively in Arabia and Syria. In 214 (829) he was arrested on a charge of heresy and sent to Baghdad to prison, but after examination he was released on the caliph's orders to return to Cairo, where he died in 246 (861); his tombstone has been preserved. A legendary figure as alchemist and thaumaturge, he is supposed to have known the secret of the Egyptian hieroglyphs. A number of poems and short treatises are attributed to him, but these are for the most part apocryphal.

Dhū al-Nūn the Egyptian and how he was converted

Dhū al-Nūn the Egyptian told the following story of his conversion.

I was informed that in a certain place an ascetic was living. I set forth to visit him, and found him suspending himself from a tree.

"O body," he was saying, "assist me to obey God, else I will keep you hanging like this until you die of hunger."

A fit of weeping overcame me. The devotee heard me crying.

"Who is this," he called, "who has compassion upon one whose shame is little and whose crimes are many?"

I approached him and gave him greeting.

"What is this state of affairs?" I asked.

"This body of mine gives me no peace to obey God," he replied. "It wants to mingle with other men."

I supposed that he must have shed a Muslim's blood, or committed some other deadly sin.

"Did you not realise," the ascetic said to me, "that once you mingle with other men, everything else follows?"

"What a tremendous ascetic you are!" I cried.

"Would you like to see someone more ascetic than I?" he said

"I would," I said.

"Go into yonder mountain," he said. "There you will see.'

I proceeded thither, and saw a young man squatting in a hermitage; one foot had been amputated and flung out of the cell, and the worms were devouring it. I approached him and saluted him, then I enquired after his circumstances.

"One day," he told me, "I was seated in this hermitage when a woman happened to pass by. My heart inclined towards her and my body demanded of me to go after her. I put one foot out of the cell, then I heard a voice saying, "Are you not ashamed, after serving and obeying God for thirty years, and now you obey Satan and chase a loose woman?" So I cut off the foot that I had set outside the hermitage, and now I sit here waiting for what will transpire and what they will do with me. What business has brought you to such sinners? If you desire to see a man of God, proceed to the top of this mountain."

The mountain was too high for me to reach the top, so I enquired about this man.

"Yes," I was told. "It is a long time now that a man has been serving God in that cell. One day a man came along and disputed with him, saying that daily bread was meant for earning. The devotee vowed that he would eat nothing that involved the acquisition of material possessions. For many days he ate nothing. Then Almighty God sent a cloud of bees to hover around him and give him honey."

The things I had seen and the words I had heard caused a mighty pain to clutch my heart. I realised that whoever puts his trust in God, God cares for him and suffers not his anguish to be in vain. As I went on my way, I saw a blind little bird perched in a tree. It fluttered down from the tree.

"Where will this helpless creature get food and water?" I cried.

The bird dug the earth with its beak and two saucers appeared, one of gold containing grain and the other of silver full of rosewater. The bird ate its fill, then it flew up into the tree and the saucers vanished.

Utterly dumbfounded, Dhū al-Nūn thenceforward put his trust in God completely, and was truly converted. He pushed on several stages, and when night fell he came to a desert. In that desert he sighted a jar of gold and jewels, and on the top of the jar a tablet on which was written the name of God. His companions divided the gold and the jewels between them.

"Give me the tablet on which is written the name of my Friend," Dhū al-Nūn cried.

And he took the tablet. He kissed the tablet all through the day and night, till by the blessing of the tablet he so progressed that one night he dreamed a voice said to him, "All the rest chose the gold and jewels, for they are precious. You chose what was loftier than that, my Name. Therefore I have opened to you the door of knowledge and wisdom."

Dhū al-Nūn then returned to the city. His story continues.

I was walking one day when I reached the margin of a river. By the water I saw a pavilion. I proceeded to make my ablutions, and when I had finished my eye suddenly fell on the roof of the pavilion. On the balcony I saw a very beautiful girl standing. Wanting to prove her, I said, "Maiden, to whom do you belong?"

"Dhū al-Nūn," replied she, "when you appeared from afar I supposed you were a madman. When you came nearer, I supposed you were a scholar. When you came still nearer, I supposed you were a mystic. Now I see you are neither mad, nor a scholar, nor a mystic."

"Why do you say that?" I demanded.

"If you had been a madman," she replied, "you would not have made your ablutions. If you had been a scholar, you would not have gazed at that which is prohibited you. If you had been a mystic, your eye would have fallen upon naught but God."

So saying, she vanished. I then realised that she was not a mortal creature, but had been sent as a warning. A fire invaded my soul, and I flung myself in the direction of the sea.

When I reached the seashore, I saw a company of men embarked in a ship. I also embarked in that ship. After some days had passed, by chance a jewel belonging to a merchant was lost on board. One by one the passengers were taken and searched. Finally they reached the unanimous conclusion that the jewel was on me. They set about belabouring me and treated me with great disrespect, whilst I remained silent. At last I could endure no more.

"O Creator, Thou knowest," I cried.

Thousands of fishes thereupon put their heads out of the water, each with a jewel in its mouth.

Dhū al-Nūn took one of the jewels and gave it to the merchant. All on board when they saw this fell at his feet and begged his pardon. So highly was he considered in the eyes of men. That was why he was called Dhū al-Nūn ("The Man of the Fish").

Dhū al-Nūn is arrested and taken to Baghdad

When Dhū al-Nūn had already attained a high degree, no one recognised his true greatness. The people of Egypt denounced him unanimously as a heretic, and informed the caliph Mutawakkil of his activities. Mutawakkil sent officers to convey him to Baghdad in fetters. When he entered the caliph's court he declared, "This very hour I have learned true Islam from an old woman, and true chivalry from a water-carrier."

"How is that?" he was asked.

"When I reached the caliph's palace," he replied, "and beheld that court in all its magnificence, with the chamberlains and attendants thronging its passages, I wished that some change might take place in my appearance. A woman with a stick in her hand came up and, looking straight at me, addressed me.

"'Do not be afraid of the body before whom they are taking you, for he and you are both servants of one Almighty Lord. Unless God wills it, they can do nothing to His servant.'

"Then on the road I saw a water-carrier. He gave me a draught of pure water. I made a sign to one who was with me to give the man a dinar. He refused to take it.

"'You are a prisoner and in bonds,' he said. 'It would not be true chivalry to take anything from such a prisoner, a stranger in bonds.'"

After that it was ordered that he should be put in prison. Forty days and nights he remained in gaol, and every day the sister of Bishr the Barefoot brought him a loaf, the earnings of her spindle. The day when he came out of prison, the forty loaves remained intact, not one having been eaten. When Bishr's sister heard of this, she became very sad.

"You know that those loaves were lawful food and unsolicited. Why did you not eat them?" she protested.

"Because the plate was not clean," Dhū al-Nūn replied, meaning that it had been handled by the gaoler.

As Dhū al-Nūn came out of the prison he stumbled and cut his forehead. It is related that much blood flowed, but not one drop fell on his face, his hair or his clothes, and all the blood that fell on the ground vanished at once, by the command of Almighty God.

Then they brought him before the caliph, and he was ordered to answer the charges preferred against him. He explained his doctrine in such a manner that Mutawakkil burst into tears, and all his ministers stood in wonder at his eloquence. So the caliph became his disciple, and accorded him high honour.

Dhū al-Nūn and the pious disciple

There was a disciple of Dhū al-Nūn who had forty times observed the forty days' seclusion, forty times he had stood at 'Arafāt, and for forty years he had kept vigil by night. Forty long years he had sat sentinel over the chamber of his heart. One day he came to Dhū al-Nūn.

"I have done all this," he said. "For all that I have suffered, the Friend speaks not one word to me nor favours me with a single glance. He takes no account of me, and reveals nothing to me from the unseen world. All this I say not in order to praise myself. I am simply stating the facts. I have performed all that was in the power of me, poor wretch, to do. I make no complaint against God. I simply state the facts, that I devote my whole heart and soul to His service. But I am telling the story of the sadness of my evil luck, the tale of my misfortune. I do not say this because my heart has grown weary of obedience. Only I fear that if further life remains ahead of me, it will be the same. For a whole lifetime I have knocked in hope, but I have heard no response. Now it is grown hard for me to endure this any longer. Since you are the physician of the afflicted and the sovereign prescriber of the sages, minister now to my wretchedness."

"Go and eat your fill tonight," advised Dhū al-Nūn. "Omit the prayer before sleep, and slumber the whole night through. So it may be that if the Friend will not show Himself kindly, He will at least show Himself reproachful; if He will not look on you with compassion, He will look on you with sternness."

The dervish departed and ate his fill. His heart would not permit him to forgo the prayer before sleep, and so he prayed the prayer and fell asleep. That night he saw the Prophet in a dream.

"Your Friend greets you," the Prophet said. "He says, 'An effeminate wretch and no true man is he who comes to

My court and is quickly sated. The root of the matter is uprightness of life, and no reproaches. God Almighty declares, I have given your heart its desire of forty years, and I grant you to attain all that you hope for, and fulfill all your desire. But convey My greetings to that bandit and pretender Dhū al-Nūn. Say then to him, Pretender and liar, if I do not expose your shame before all the city, then I am not your Lord. See that you no more beguile the hapless lovers of My court and scare them not away from My court.'"

The disciple awoke, and was overcome by weeping. He went and told Dhū al-Nūn what he had seen and heard. When Dhū al-Nūn heard the words, "God sends you greeting and declares you a pretender and a liar", he rolled over and over with joy and wept ecstatically.

Anecdotes of Dhū al-Nūn

Dhū al-Nūn relates as follows.

I was wandering in the mountains when I observed a party of afflicted folk gathered together.

"What befell you?" I asked.

"There is a devotee living in a cell here," they answered. "Once every year he comes out and breathes on these people and they are all healed. Then he returns to his cell, and does not emerge again until the following year."

I waited patiently until he came out. I beheld a man pale of cheek, wasted and with sunken eyes. The awe of him caused me to tremble. He looked on the multitude with compassion. Then he raised his eyes to heaven, and breathed several times over the afflicted ones. All were healed.

As he was about to retire to his cell, I seized his skirt.

"For the love of God," I cried. "You have healed the outward sickness; pray heal the inward sickness."

"Dhū al-Nūn," he said, gazing at me, "take your hand from me. The Friend is watching from the zenith of might and majesty. If He sees you clutching at another than He, He will abandon you to that person, and that person to you, and you will perish each at the other's hand."

So saying, he withdrew into his cell.

One day Dhū al-Nūn's companions came to him and found him weeping.

"Why are you weeping?" they asked.

"Last night when I was prostrating in prayer," he replied, "my eyes closed in sleep. I saw the Lord, and He said to me, 'O Abū al-Fayḍ, I created all creatures and they separated into ten parts. I offered the material world to them; nine of those ten parts turned their faces to the material world. One part remained over. That one part divided also into ten parts. I offered Paradise to them; nine parts turned their faces to Paradise. One part remained over. That one part split likewise into ten parts. I brought Hell before them; all fled and were scattered for fear of Hell. Only one part remained over, those who had not been lured by the material world, nor inclined after Paradise, neither were afraid of Hell. I said to them, "My servants, you looked not upon the material world, you inclined not after Paradise, you were not afraid of Hell. What do you seek?" All raised their heads and cried, "Thou knowest best what we desire."

One day a boy approached Dhū al-Nūn and said, "I have a hundred thousand dinars. I want to spend them in your service. I wish to use that gold on your dervishes."

"Are you of age?" Dhū al-Nūn asked him.

"No," he replied.

"Then you are not entitled to expend," Dhū al-Nūn told him. "Wait with patience until you are of age."

When the boy came of age he returned to Dhū al-Nūn and repented at his hands. Then he gave all that gold to the dervishes, until nothing remained of the hundred thousand dinars.

One day an emergency arose, and nothing remained to the dervishes, for they had spent all the money.

"What a pity there is not another hundred thousand, so that I could spend it on these fine men," said the benefactor.

When Dhū al-Nūn heard him speak these words, he realised that he had not yet penetrated to the inner truth of the mystic life, for worldly things still seemed important to him. He summoned the young man.

"Go to the shop of such-and-such a druggist," he instructed him. "Tell him from me to give you three dirhams' worth of such-and-such a medicine."

The youth went to the druggist's, and presently returned.

"Put the stuff in the mortar and pound it up small," Dhū al-Nūn ordered him. "Then pour on top of it a little oil, until it becomes a paste. Make three pellets of it, and pierce each with a needle. Then bring them to me."

The youth carried out these instructions, and brought the pellets. Dhū al-Nūn rubbed them in his hands and breathed on them, and they turned into three rubies the like of which was never seen.

"Now take these to the market and have them valued," ordered Dhū al-Nūn. "But do not sell them."

The youth took the rubies to the market and displayed them. Each one was priced at a thousand dinars. He returned and told Dhū al-Nūn.

"Now put them in the mortar and pound them, and throw them into water," the latter directed.

The youth did as instructed, and threw the powder into water.

"My child," said Dhū al-Nūn, "these dervishes are not hungry for lack of bread. This is their free choice."

The youth repented, and his soul awoke. The world had no longer any worth in his eyes.

Dhū al-Nūn related as follows.

For thirty years I called men to repent, but only one person came to the court of God in due obedience. The circumstances were these.

One day a prince with his retinue passed by me by the door of the mosque. I spoke these words.

"No one is more foolish than the weakling who tangles with the strong."

"What words are these?" demanded the prince.

"Man is a weakling, yet he tangles with God who is strong," I said.

The young prince grew pale. He arose and departed. Next day he returned.

"What is the way to God?" he asked.

"There is a little way, and there is a greater way," I answered. "Which of the two do you want? If you desire the little way, abandon the world and the lusts of the flesh and give up sinning. If you want the great way, abandon everything but God, and empty your heart of all things."

"By Allah, I will choose only the greater way," said the prince.

The next day he put on the woollen robe, and entered the mystic way. In due course he became a saint.

The following story was told by Abū Ja'far the One-eyed.

I was with Dhū al-Nūn when a group of his followers were present. They were telling stories of inanimate things obeying commands. Now there was a sofa in the room.

"An example," said Dhū al-Nūn, "of inanimate things obeying saints' commands would be if I were to say to that sofa there, 'Waltz around the house' and it started to move."

No sooner had Dhū al-Nūn spoken these words than

the sofa started to circle round the house, then it returned to its place. A youth present burst into tears at the sight, and gave up the ghost. They washed his body on that very sofa, and buried him.

Once a man came up to Dhū al-Nūn and said, "I have a debt, and I have no means of paying it."

Dhū al-Nūn picked up a stone from the ground and gave it to him. The man took the stone to the bazaar. It had turned into an emerald. He sold it for four hundred dirhams and paid his debt.

A certain youth was always speaking against Sufis. One day Dhū al-Nūn took the ring off his finger and handed it to him.

"Take this to market and pawn it for a dinar," he said.

The young man took the ring to market, but they would not take it for more than one dirham. The youth returned with the news.

"Now take it to the jewellers, and see what they value it at," Dhū al-Nūn told him.

The jewellers priced the ring at a thousand dinars.

"You know as much about Sufis," Dhū al-Nūn said to the youth when he returned, "as those stallholders in the market know about this ring."

The youth repented, and disbelieved in the Sufis no more.

Dhū al-Nūn had been longing for *sekbaj* for ten years, but he never gratified that longing. Now it was the eve of festival, and his soul said within him, "How would it be if tomorrow you gave us a mouthful of *sekbaj* as a festival treat?"

"Soul," answered Dhū al-Nūn, "if you want me to do that, then consent with me tonight in chanting the whole Qur'an in the course of two *rak'ahs.*"

His soul consented. The next day Dhū al-Nūn prepared *sekbaj* and set it before his soul. He washed his fingers and stood in prayer.

"What happened?" he was asked.

"Just now," Dhū al-Nūn replied, "my soul said to me, 'At last after ten years I have attained my desire.' 'By God,' I answered, 'you shall not attain that desire.'"

The relater of this story states that Dhū al-Nūn had just spoken these words when a man entered and set a bowl of *sekbaj* before him.

"Master," he said, "I did not come on my own. I was sent. Let me explain. I earn my living as a porter, and I have children. For some time now they have been asking for *sekbaj,* and I have been saving up. Last night I made this *sekbaj* for the festival. Today I saw in a dream the world-adorning beauty of the Messenger of God. 'If you would see me on the morrow of uprising,' said the Prophet, 'take this to Dhū al-Nūn and tell him that Muḥammad, the son of 'Abdullah, the son of 'Abd al-Muṭṭalib, intercedes with him to make truce with his soul for one moment and swallow a few mouthfuls.'"

"I obey," said Dhū al-Nūn, weeping.

As Dhū al-Nūn lay on his deathbed his friends asked him, "What do you desire?"

"My desire," he answered, "is that ere I die, even if it be for only one moment, I may know Him."

He then spoke the following verses.

Fear wasted me,
Yearning consumed me,
Love beguiled me,
God revived me.

One day later he lost consciousness. On the night of his departure from this world, seventy persons saw the Prophet in a dream. All reported that the Prophet said, "The friend of God is coming. I have come out to welcome him."

When he died, there was seen written in green on his brow, "This is the friend of God. He died in the love of God. This is the slain of God by the sword of God."

When they lifted his coffin to carry him to the grave the sun was extremely hot. The birds of the air came and with wings flapping kept his bier shaded from his house to the graveside.

As he was being borne along the road, a *mu'adhdhin* chanted the call to prayer. When he reached the words of attestation, Dhū al-Nūn lifted a finger out of the shroud.

"He is alive!" the shout went up.

They laid down the bier. His finger was pointing, but he was dead. For all that they tried, they could not straighten his finger. When the people of Egypt beheld this, they were all put to shame and repented of the wrongs they had done him. They did things over his dust that cannot be described in words.

9

Abū Yazīd al-Bisṭāmī

Abū Yazīd Ṭayfūr ibn ʻĪsā ibn Surūshān al-Bisṭāmī was born in Bisṭām in north-eastern Persia, the grandson of a Zoroastrian; there he died in 261 (874) or 264 (877), and his mausoleum still stands. The founder of the ecstatic ("drunken") school of Sufism, he is famous for the boldness of his expression of the mystic's complete absorption into the Godhead. In particular his description of a journey into Heaven (in imitation of the Prophet Muḥammad's "ascension"), greatly elaborated by later writers, exercised a powerful influence on the imagination of all who came after him.

Birth and early years

The grandfather of Abū Yazīd al-Bisṭāmī was a Zoroastrian; his father was one of the leading citizens of

Bisṭām. Abū Yazīd's extraordinary career began from the time he was in his mother's womb.

"Every time I put a doubtful morsel in my mouth," his mother would say, "you stirred in my womb and would not keep still until I had put it out of my mouth."

This statement is confirmed by words spoken by Abū Yazīd himself.

"What is best for a man on this path?" he was asked.

"Congenital felicity," he replied.

"And if that is missing?"

"A strong body."

"And if that is lacking?"

"An attentive ear."

"And without that?"

"A knowing heart."

"And without that?"

"A seeing eye."

"And without that?"

"Sudden death."

In due course his mother sent him to school. He learned the Qur'an, and one day his master was explaining the meaning of the verse in the Sūrah of Luqmān, Be thankful to Me, and to thy parents. These words moved the heart of Abū Yazīd.

"Sir," he said, laying down his tablet, "please give me permission to go home and say something to my mother."

The master gave him leave, and Abū Yazīd went home.

"Why, Ṭayfūr," cried his mother, "why have you come home? Did they give you a present, or is it some special occasion?"

"No," Abū Yazīd replied. "I reached the verse where God commands me to serve Him and you. I cannot be manager in two houses at once. This verse stung me to the quick. Either you ask for me from God, so that I may be yours entirely, or apprentice me to God, so that I may dwell wholly with Him."

"My son, I resign you to God, and exempt you from your duty to me," said his mother. "Go and be God's."

"The task I supposed to be the hindmost of all tasks proved to be the foremost," Abū Yazīd later recalled. "That was to please my mother. In pleasing my mother, I attained all that I sought in my many acts of selfdiscipline and service. It fell out as follows. One night my mother asked me for water. I went to fetch her some, but there was none in the jug. I fetched the pitcher, but none was in it either. So I went down to the river and filled the pitcher with water. When I returned to the house, my mother had fallen asleep.

"The night was cold. I kept the jug in my hand. When my mother awoke from sleep she drank some water and blessed me. Then she noticed that the jug was frozen to my hand. 'Why did you not lay the jug aside?' she exclaimed. 'I was afraid that you might wake when I was not present,' I answered. 'Keep the door half-open,' my mother then said.

"I watched till near daybreak to make sure if the door was properly half-open or not, and that I should not have disregarded her command. At the hour of dawn, that which I had sought so many times entered by the door."

After his mother resigned him to God, Abū Yazīd left Bisṭām and for thirty years wandered from land to land, disciplining himself with continuous vigil and hunger. He attended one hundred and thirteen spiritual preceptors and derived benefit from them all. Amongst them was one called Ṣādiq. He was sitting at his feet when the master suddenly said, "Abū Yazīd, fetch me that book from the window."

"The window? Which window?" asked Abū Yazīd.

"Why," said the master, "you have been coming here all this time, and you have not seen the window?"

"No," replied Abū Yazīd. "What have I to do with the; window? When I am before you, I close my eyes to everything else. I have not come to stare about."

"Since that is so," said the teacher, "go back to Bisṭām. Your work is completed."

It was hinted to Abū Yazīd that in a certain place a great teacher was to be found. He came from afar to see him. As he approached, he saw the reputed teacher spit in the direction of Makkah. He at once retraced his steps.

"If he had achieved anything at all in the way," he remarked, "he would never have been guilty of transgressing the Law."'

In this connection it is stated that his house was forty paces from the mosque, and he never spat on the road out of respect for the mosque.

It took Abū Yazīd a full twelve years to reach the Ka'bah. This was because at every oratory he passed he would throw down his prayer rug and perform two *rak'ahs*.

"This is not the portico of an earthly king," he would say, "that one may run thither all at once."

So at last he came to the Ka'bah, but that year he did not got to Madīnah.

"It would not be seemly to make that an appendage of this visitation," he explained. "I will put on pilgrim robes for Madīnah separately."

Next year he returned once more, donning the pilgrim garb separately at the beginning of the desert. In one town he passed through on the way a great throng became his followers, and as he left a crowd went in his wake.

"Who are those men?" he demanded, looking back.

"They wish to keep you company," came the answer.

"Lord God!" Abū Yazīd cried, "I beg of Thee, veil not Thy creatures from Thee through me!"

Then, desiring to expel the love of him from their hearts and to remove the obstacle of himself from their path, having performed the dawn prayer he looked at them and said, "*Verily I am God; there is no god but I; therefore serve Me.*"

"The man has become mad!" they cried. And they left him and departed.

Abū Yazīd went on his way. He found on the road a skull on which was written, *Deaf, dumb, blind—they do not understand.*

Picking up the skull with a cry, he kissed it.

"This seems to be the head," he murmured, "of a Sufi annihilated in God—he has no ear to hear the eternal voice, no eye to behold the eternal beauty, no tongue to praise

God's greatness, no reason to understand so much as a mote of the true knowledge of God. This verse is about him."

Once Abū Yazīd was going along the road with a camel on which he had slung his provisions and saddle.

"Poor little camel, what a heavy load it is carrying," someone cried. "It is really cruel."

Abū Yazīd, having heard him say these words over and over, at last replied.

"Young man, it is not the little camel that lifts the load."

The man looked to see if the load was actually on the camel's back. He observed that it was a full span above its back, and that the camel did not feel any weight at all.

"Glory be to God, a wondrous deed!" the man exclaimed.

"If I conceal from you the true facts about myself, you thrust out the tongue of reproach," said Abū Yazīd. "If I disclose them to you, you cannot bear the facts. What is one to do with you?"

After Abū Yazīd had visited Madīnah, the order came to him to return to care for his mother. He accordingly set out for Bisṭām, accompanied by a throng. The news ran through the city, and the people of Bisṭām came out to welcome him a good way from the town. Abū Yazīd was likely to be so preoccupied with their attentions that he would be detained from God. As they approached him, he drew a loaf out of his sleeve. Now it was Ramaḍān; yet he stood and ate the loaf. As soon as the people of Bisṭām saw this, they turned away from him.

"Did you not see?" Abū Yazīd addressed his companions "I obeyed an ordinance of the sacred Law, and all the people rejected me."

He waited patiently until nightfall. At midnight he entered Bisṭām and, coming to his mother's house, he stood a while listening. He heard sounds of his mother performing his ablutions and praying.

"Lord God, care well for our exile. Incline the hearts of the shaykhs towards him, and vouchsafe him to do all things well.'

Abū Yazīd wept when he heard these words. Then he knocked on the door.

"Who is there?" cried his mother.

"Your exile," he replied.

Weeping, his mother opened the door. Her sight was dimmed.

"Ṭayfūr," she addressed her son, "do you know what has dimmed my sight? It is because I have wept so much being parted from you, and my back is bent double from the load of grief I have endured."

Ascension of Abū Yazīd

Abū Yazīd related as follows.

I gazed upon God with the eye of certainty after that He had advanced me to the degree of independence from all creatures and illumined me with His light, revealing to me the wonders of His secrets and manifesting to me the grandeur of His He-ness.

Then from God I gazed upon myself, and considered well the secrets and attributes of my self. My light was darkness beside the light of God; my grandeur shrank to very meanness beside God's grandeur; my glory beside God's glory became but vainglory. There all was purity, here all was foulness.

When I looked again, I saw my being by God's light. I realised that my glory was of His grandeur and glory. Whatsoever I did, I was able to do through His omnipotence. Whatever the eye of my physical body perceived, it perceived through Him. I gazed with the eye of justice and reality; all my worship proceeded from God, not from me, and I had supposed that it was I who worshipped Him.

I said, "Lord God, what is this?"

He said, "All that I am, and none other than I."

Then He stitched up my eye, not to be the means of seeing and so that I might not see, and He instructed the gaze of my eye in the root of the matter, the He-ness of Himself. He annihilated me from my own being, and made me to be everlasting through His own everlastingness, and He glorified me. He disclosed to me His own Selfhood, unjostled by my own existence. So God, the one Truth, increased in me reality. Through God I gazed on God, and I beheld God in reality.

There I dwelt a while, and found repose. I stopped up the ear of striving; I withdrew the tongue of yearning into the throat of disappointment. I abandoned acquired knowledge, and removed the interference of the soul that bids to evil. I remained still for a space, without any instrument, and with the hand of God's grace I swept superfluities from the pathway of root principles.

God had compassion on me. He granted me eternal knowledge, and put into my throat a tongue of His goodness. He created for me an eye out of His light, and I saw all creatures through God. With the tongue of His goodness I communed with God, and from the knowledge of God I acquired knowledge, and by His light I gazed on Him.

He said, "O thou all without all with all, without instrument with instrument!"

I said, "Lord God, let me not be deluded by this. Let me not become self-satisfied with my own being, not to yearn for Thee. Better it is that Thou shouldst be mine without me, than that I should be my own without Thee. Better it is that I should speak to Thee through Thee, than that I should speak to myself without Thee."

He said, "Now give ear to the Law, and transgress not My commands and forbiddings, that thy strivings may earn Our thanks."

I said, "Insomuch as I profess the faith and my heart firmly believes, if Thou givest thanks, it is better that Thou shouldst thank Thyself rather than Thy slave; and if Thou blamest, Thou art pure of all fault."

He said, "From whom didst thou learn?"

I said, "He who asks this question knows better than he who is asked; for He is both the Desired and the Desirer, the Answered and the Answerer."

When He had perceived the purity of my inmost soul, then my soul heard a shout of God's satisfaction; He sealed me with His good pleasure. He illumined me, and delivered me out of the darkness of the carnal soul and the foulnesses of the fleshly nature. I knew that through Him I lived; and of His bounty I spread the carpet of gladness in my heart.

He said, "Ask whatsoever thou wilt."

I said, "I wish for Thee, for Thou art more excellent than bounty, greater than generosity, and through Thee I have found content in Thee. Since Thou art mine, I have rolled up the scroll of bounty and generosity. Keep me not from Thee, and proffer not before me that which is inferior to Thee."

For a while He did not answer me. Then, laying the crown of munificence on my head, He spoke.

"Truth thou speakest, and reality thou seekest, in that thou hast seen the truth and heard the truth."

I said, "If I have seen, through Thee I have seen, and if I have heard, through Thee I have heard. First Thou heardest, then I heard."

And I uttered many praises to Him. Consequently He gave me wings of majesty, so that I flew in the arenas of His glory and beheld the wonders of His handiwork. Perceiving my weakness and recognising my need, He strengthened me with His own strength and arrayed me with His own adornment.

He laid the crown of munificence on my head, and opened unto me the door of the palace of Unity. When He perceived that my attributes were annihilated in His attributes, He bestowed on me a name of His own presence and addressed me with His own Selfhood. Singleness became manifest; duality vanished.

He said, "Our pleasure is that which is thy pleasure, and thy pleasure is that which is Our pleasure. Thy speech admits no defilement, and none takes thee to task on account of thy I-ness."

Then He made me to taste the stab of jealousy, and revived me anew. I came forth pure from the furnace of testing. Then He spoke.

"Whose is the Kingdom?"

I said, "Thine."

He said, "Whose is the Command?"

I said, "Thine."

He said, "Whose is the Choice?"

I said, "Thine."

Since these words were the very same as He had heard at the beginning of the transaction, He desired to demonstrate to me that, had not His mercy preceded, creation would never have found repose, and that but for Love, Omnipotence would have wreaked destruction on all things. He gazed on me with the eye of Overwhelming through the medium of Allcompelling, and once more no trace of me was visible.

In my intoxication I flung myself into every valley. I melted my body in every crucible in the fire of jealousy. I galloped the steed of questing in the broad expanse of the wilderness; no better game I saw than utter indigence, nothing I discovered better than total incapacity. No lamp I saw brighter than silence, no speech I heard better than speechlessness. I became a dweller in the palace of silence; I clothed myself in the stomacher of fortitude, till matters reached their crux. He saw my outward and inward parts void of the flaw of fleshly nature. He opened a fissure of relief in my darkened breast, and gave me a tongue of divestiture and unity.

So now I have a tongue of everlasting grace, a heart of light divine, an eye of godly handiwork. By his succour I speak, with His power I grasp. Since through Him I live, I shall never die.

Since I have reached this stage, my token is eternal; my expression everlasting; my tongue is the tongue of unity, my spirit is the spirit of divestiture. Not of myself I speak, that I should be mere narrator, neither through myself do I speak, that I should be mere remembrancer. He moves my tongue according as He wills, and in all this I am but an interpreter. In reality the speaker is He, not I.

Now, having magnified me, He spoke again.

"The creatures desire to see thee."

I said, "I desire not to see them. If Thou likest to bring me forth before the creatures, I will not oppose Thee. Array me in Thy Unity, that when Thy creatures see me and gaze upon Thy handiwork, they will have seen the Artificer, and I shall not be there at all."

This desire He granted me; and He laid the crown of munificence on my head, and caused me to surpass the station of my fleshly nature.

Then He said, "Come before My creatures."

I took one step out of the Presence. At the second step I fell headlong. I heard a cry.

"Bring back My beloved, for he cannot be without Me, neither knows he any path save to Me."

Abū Yazīd also related the following.

When I reached Unity—and that was the first moment that I gazed upon Unity—for many years I ran in that valley on the feet of understanding; till I became a bird whose body was of Oneness, whose wings were of Everlastingness. I kept flying in the firmament of Unconditionedness. When I had vanished from the things created, I spoke.

"I have reached the Creator."

Then I lifted up my head from the valley of Lordship. I quaffed a cup, the thirst for which I never slaked in all eternity. Then for thirty thousand years I flew in the expanse of His Unity, and for thirty thousand years more I flew in Divinity, and for thirty thousand years more I flew in Singularity. When ninety thousand years had come to an end, I saw Abū Yazīd, and all that I saw, all was I.

Then I traversed four thousand wildernesses, and reached the end. When I gazed, I saw myself at the beginning of the degree of the prophets. Then for such a while I went on in that infinity, that I said,

"No one has ever reached higher than this. Loftier than this no station can be."

When I looked well, I saw that my head was at the sole of the foot of a prophet. Then I realised that the end of the state of the saints is but the beginning of the states of the prophets; to the end of the prophets there is no term.

Then my spirit transcended the whole Dominion, and Heaven and Hell were displayed to it; but it heeded naught Whatever came before it, that it could not suffer. To the soul of no prophet it reached, without it gave greeting. When it reached the soul of God's Chosen One, upon him be peace, there it beheld a hundred thousand seas of fire without end, and a thousand veils of light. Had I so much as dipped my foot in the first of those seas, I would have been consumed and given myself over to destruction. Therefore I became so bewildered with awe and confusion, that naught remained of me. However I desired to be able to see but the tent-peg of the pavilion of Muḥammad, God's Messenger, I had not the boldness. Though I had attained to God, I had not the boldness to attain to Muḥammad.

Then Abū Yazīd said, "O God, whatsoever thing I have seen, all has been I. There is no way for me to Thee, so long as this 'I' remains; there is no transcending my selfhood for me What must I do?"

The command came, "To be delivered out of thy thouness, follow after Our beloved, the Arab Muḥammad. Anoint thine eye with the dust of his foot, and continue following after him.

Abū Yazīd and Yaḥyā ibn Mu'ādh

Yaḥyā ibn Mu'ādh wrote a letter to Abū Yazīd saying, "What do you say of a man who has quaffed a cup of wine, and become intoxicated from eternity to eternity"?

Abū Yazīd replied, "That I know not. What I do know is this, that here is a man who in a single night and a day drains all the oceans of eternity to eternity and then asks for more."

Yaḥyā ibn Mu'ādh wrote again, "I have a secret to tell you, but our rendezvous is in Paradise. There under the shadow of Ṭūbā I will tell it you." And he sent along with the letter a loaf saying, "The shaykh must avail himself of this, for I kneaded it with water from the well of Zamzam."

In his reply Abū Yazīd referred to Yaḥyā's secret saying, "As for the rendezvous you mention, with His remembrance, I enjoy even now possession of Paradise and the shade of the tree Ṭūbā. So far as the loaf is concerned, however, that I cannot avail myself of. You stated with what water you kneaded it, but you did not mention what seed you sowed."

So Yaḥyā ibn Mu'ādh conceived a great yearning to visit Abū Yazīd. He arrived at the hour of the prayer before sleeping.

"I could not disturb the shaykh then," Yaḥyā recalled. "At the same time I could not contain myself till morning. So I proceeded to the place in the desert where they told me he was to be found. I saw the shaykh perform the prayer before sleeping, then till the next day he stood on the tips of his toes. I stood rooted in amazement, and heard him all night engaged in prayer. When dawn came, he uttered the words, 'I take refuge with Thee from asking of Thee this station.'"

Yaḥyā then recovering himself greeted Abū Yazīd, and enquired of him what had befallen him in the night.

"More than twenty stations were enumerated to me," Abū Yazīd told him. "I desire not one of these, for they are all stations of veiling."

"Master, why did you not ask God for gnosis, seeing that He is the King of kings and has said, 'Ask whatsoever you will?'" demanded Yaḥyā.

"Be silent!" Abū Yazīd cried. "I am jealous of myself to know Him, for I desire none but He to know Him. Where His knowledge is, what business have I to intervene? That indeed is His will, Yaḥyā, only He, and no other, shall know Him."

"By the majesty of God," Yaḥyā implored, "grant me some portion of the gift you were vouchsafed last night."

"If you were given the election of Adam, the holiness of Jibrīl, the friendship of Ibrāhīm, the yearning of Mūsā, the purity of 'Īsā, and the love of Muḥammad," Abū Yazīd replied, "still you would not be satisfied. You would seek for more, transcending all things. Keep your vision fixed on high, and descend not; for whatever you descend into, by that you will be veiled."

Abū Yazīd and his disciple

There was a certain ascetic who was one of the great saints

of Bisṭām. He had his own followers and admirers, and at the same time he was never absent from the circle of Abū Yazīd. He listened to all his discourses, and sat with his companions.

One day he remarked to Abū Yazīd, "Master, today is thirty years that I have been keeping constant fast. By night too I pray, so that I never sleep at all. Yet I discover no trace in myself of this knowledge of which you speak. For all that I believe in this knowledge, and I love this preaching."

"If for three hundred years," said Abū Yazīd, "you fast by day and pray by night, you will never realise one atom of this discourse."

"Why?" asked the disciple.

"Because you are veiled by your own self," Abū Yazīd replied.

"What is the remedy for this?" the man asked.

"You will never accept it," answered Abū Yazīd.

"I will so," said the man. "Tell me, so that I may do as you prescribe."

"Very well," said Abū Yazīd. "This very hour go and shave your beard and hair. Take off these clothes you are wearing, and tie a loincloth of goat's wool about your waist. Hang a bag of nuts round your neck, then go to the marketplace. Collect all the children you can, and tell them, 'I will give a nut to everyone who slaps me.' Go round all the city in the same way; especially go everywhere people know you. That is your cure."

"Glory be to God! There is no god but God," cried the disciple on hearing these words.

"If an infidel uttered that formula, he would become a believer," remarked Abū Yazīd. "By uttering the same formula you have become a polytheist."

"How so?" demanded the disciple.

"Because you counted yourself too grand to be able to do as I have said," replied Abū Yazīd. "So you have become a polytheist. You used this formula to express your own importance, not to glorify God."

"This I cannot do," the man protested. "Give me other directions."

"The remedy is what I have said," Abū Yazīd declared.

"I cannot do it," the man repeated.

"Did I not say that you would not do it, that you would never obey me?" said Abū Yazīd.

Anecdotes of Yazīd

"For twelve years," said Abū Yazīd, "I was the blacksmith of my soul. I thrust my soul into the furnace of discipline and made it red hot in the flames of arduous endeavour, then I placed it upon the anvil of reproach and hammered it with the hammer of self-blame, till I had fashioned out of my soul a mirror. For five years I was my own mirror, and I polished that mirror with every manner of godly service and obedience. After that I gazed upon my own reflection for a year, and I saw about my waist an infidel girdle of delusion and coquetry and self-regard, because I relied upon my own acts of obedience and approved of my own conduct. For five years further I laboured till that girdle was snapped and I was a Muslim anew. I looked upon all creatures, and saw that they were dead. I said four Allahu akbars over them, and returning from their obsequies without the jostling of God's creatures by God's succour I attained to God."

Whenever Abū Yazīd arrived at the door of a mosque, he would stand a while and weep.

"Why do you do so?" he was asked.

"I feel myself to be as a menstruating woman who is ashamed to enter the mosque and defile the mosque," he replied.

On one occasion Abū Yazīd set out on the journey to Ḥijāz, but no sooner had he gone forth when he returned.

"You have never failed in your purpose before," it was remarked. "Why did you do so now?"

"I had just turned my face to the road," he replied, "when I saw a black man standing with a drawn sword. 'If you return, well and good. If not, I will strike your head from your body. You have left God in Bisṭām,' he added, 'and set out for the Holy House.'"

"A man encountered me on the road," Abū Yazīd recalled.

"'Where are you going?' he demanded.

"'On the pilgrimage,' I replied.

"'How much have you got?'

"'Two hundred dirhams.'

"'Come, give them to me,' the man demanded. 'I am a man with a family. Circle round me seven times. That is your pilgrimage.'

"I did so, and returned home."

Pir 'Umar reports that when Abū Yazīd wished to go into seclusion, in order to worship or to meditate, he would enter his apartment and secure closely every aperture.

"I am afraid," he would say, "that some voice or some noise may disturb me."

That of course was a pretext.

'Īsā al-Bisṭāmī reports, "I associated with the shaykh for thirteen years, and I never heard the shaykh utter a single word. Such was his habit; he would put his head on his knees. Occasionally he would raise his head, utter a sigh, and then return to his meditation."

Al-Sahlajī comments on the foregoing, that that was how Abū Yazīd behaved when he was in that state of "contraction"; otherwise, on days when he was in the state of "expansion" everyone benefited greatly from his discourse.

"On one occasion," al-Sahlajī continues, "as he was in seclusion he uttered the words, 'Glory be to me! How great is my dignity!' When he was himself again, his disciples told him that such words had proceeded from his tongue.

'God is your antagonist, and Abū Yazīd is your antagonist,' he replied. If I speak such words again, cut me in pieces.'

"And he gave each of his disciples a knife, saying, 'If such words come to me again, slay me with these knives.'

"It so transpired that he spoke the same words a second time. His disciples made to kill him. The whole apartment was filled with Abū Yazīd. His companions pulled bricks out of the walls and each struck at him with his knife. The knives were as effective as if they were being struck at water; no blow had the slightest effect. After a while that form shrank, and Abū Yazīd appeared as small as a sparrow, sitting in the prayer niche. His companions entered and told him what had passed. 'This is Abū Yazīd whom you see now,' he remarked. 'That was not Abū Yazīd.'"

Once Abū Yazīd took a red apple into his hand and looked at it.

"This is a beautiful apple," he said.

A voice spoke within him.

"Abū Yazīd, art thou not ashamed to apply My name to a fruit?"

For forty days his heart was oblivious to the name of God.

"I have taken an oath," the shaykh declared, "that I will never eat the fruit of Bisṭām so long as I live."

"One day I was seated," Abū Yazīd recalled, "when the thought entered my mind, 'I am the shaykh of the time, the saint of the age.' As soon as this thought occurred to me, I knew that I had been guilty of a great error. I rose up and proceeded on the road to Khurasan. I halted in a hospice and swore that I would not leave it until God sent me someone who should reveal me again to myself.

"Three days and three nights I remained there. On the fourth day I saw a one-eyed man approaching on a camel. Observing him closely, I saw in him the marks of divine awareness. I signalled to the camel to halt, and immediately it lowered its two forelegs to the ground. The man gazed upon me.

"'You bring me all this way,' he said, 'to open an eye that was closed, to unlatch a door that was locked, and to drown the people of Bisṭām along with Abū Yazīd?'

"I swooned away. 'Whence do you come?' I asked. 'Since the moment you swore that oath, I have come three thousand leagues.' Then my visitor added, 'Beware, Abū Yazīd! Keep watch over your heart.'

"With that he turned his face from me and departed."

Dhū al-Nūn sent Abū Yazīd a prayer rug. Abū Yazīd returned it to him.

"What use is a prayer rug to me?" he demanded. "Send me a cushion to lean my back against!" (He implied that he had passed beyond the stage of prayer and had reached the goal.)

Dhū al-Nūn then sent him a good pillow. Abū Yazīd returned that too, for by that time he had melted away and nothing was left of him but skin and bones.

"He who has for a cushion," he said, "the goodness and loving kindness of God, that man has no need of the pillow of one of God's creatures."

"I once passed a night in the desert," Abū Yazīd recalled. "I wrapped my head in my habit and fell asleep. Suddenly a state came upon me (he meant nocturnal emission) that required me to wash. Now the night was extremely cold, and when I awoke my soul was sluggish about washing in cold water. 'Wait till the sun comes up, then attend to this business,' my soul said.

"Observing my soul's sluggishness and indifference to the requirements of religion, I arose and broke the ice with that selfsame frock and washed myself, then remained with the frock around me until I dropped and fainted. When I came to the frock had suddenly dried."

Abū Yazīd often wandered about amongst the tombs. One night he was returning from the cemetery when a young nobleman approached playing a lute. "God save us," Abū Yazīd exclaimed. The youth lifted the lute and dashed it against Abū Yazīd's head, breaking both his head and the lute. The youth was drunk, and did not realise whom he was striking.

Abū Yazīd returned to his convent and waited till morning. Then he summoned one of his companions.

"What do people give for a lute?" he asked him.

The companion informed him. He wrapped the sum in a cloth, added a piece of sweetmeat, and sent these to the youth.

"Tell the young gentleman," he said, "that Abū Yazīd asks his pardon. Say to him, 'Last night you struck me with that lute and it broke. Accept this money in compensation, and buy another. The sweetmeat is to remove from your heart the sorrow over the lute's being broken.'"

When the young nobleman realised what he had done, he came to Abū Yazīd and apologised. He repented, and many young men repented along with him.

One day Abū Yazīd was walking with a party of disciples. The road narrowed, and just then a dog approached from the opposite direction. Abū Yazīd retired, giving the dog right of way.

The chance thought of disapproval occurred to one of the disciples. "Almighty God honoured man above all other creatures. Abū Yazīd is the 'king of the gnostics' yet with all this dignity, and such a following of disciples, he makes way for a dog. How can that be?"

"Young man," Abū Yazīd replied, "this dog mutely appealed to me, 'What shortcoming was I guilty of in the dawn of time, and what exceptional merit did you acquire, that I was clad in the skin of a dog whereas you were robed in honour as king of the gnostics?' This was the thought that came into my head, so I made way for the dog."

One day Abū Yazīd was proceeding along the way when presently a dog ran alongside of him. Abū Yazīd drew in his skirt.

"If I am dry," said the dog, "no damage has been done. If I am wet, seven waters and earths will make peace between us. But if you draw your skirt to yourself like a Pharisee, you will not become clean, not though you bathe in seven oceans."

"You are unclean outwardly," commented Abū Yazīd. "I am inwardly unclean. Come, let us work together, that through our united efforts we may both become clean."

"You are not fit to travel with me and be my partner," the dog replied. "For I am rejected of all men, whereas you are accepted of men. Whoever encounters me throws a stone at me; whoever encounters you greets you as King of the Gnostics. I never store up a single bone for the morrow; you have a whole barrel of wheat for the morrow."

"I am not fit to travel along with a dog," said Abū Yazīd. "How then shall I travel along with the Eternal and Everlasting One? Glory be to that God, who educates the best of creatures by means of the least of creatures!"

Abū Yazīd continued, "A sadness invaded me, and I despaired of being an obedient servant of God. I said to myself, 'I will go to the market and buy a girdle [worn by some non- Muslims] to tie round my middle, that my reputation may vanish from among men.' So I went searching for a girdle. I saw a shop with a girdle hanging. 'They will give me this for only one dirham,' I told myself. Then I said, 'How much will you give this for?' 'A thousand dinars,' said the shopkeeper. I cast my head down. Then I heard a voice from heaven saying, 'Did you not realise that they will not give for less than a thousand dinars a girdle for binding round the waist of such a man as you?' My heart rejoiced, for I then knew that God cares for His servant."

One night Abū Yazīd dreamed that the angels of the first heaven descended.

"Rise up," they said to him, "let us commemorate God."

"I have not the tongue to commemorate Him," he replied.

The angels of the second heaven descended and said the same words, and his answer was the same. So it continued till the angels of the seventh heaven descended; to them he gave the same reply.

"Well, when will you have the tongue to commemorate God?" they asked.

"When the inhabitants of Hell are fixed in Hell, and the inhabitants of Paradise take their place in Paradise, and the resurrection is past, then," said he, "Abū Yazīd will go around the throne of God and will cry Allah, Allah!"

In Abū Yazīd's neighbourhood there lived a Zoroastrian. He had a child, and this child used to weep because they had no lamp. Abū Yazīd with his own hand brought a lamp to their house. The child was hushed at once.

"Since Abū Yazīd's light has entered," they said, "it would be a pity for us to continue in our own darkness."

They became Muslims forthwith.

One night Abū Yazīd could find no joy in worship.

"Look and see if there is anything of value in the house," he said.

His disciples looked, and discovered half a bunch of grapes.

"Fetch them and give them away," Abū Yazīd commanded. "My house is not a fruiterer's shop."

And he rediscovered his composure.

One day a man reported to Abū Yazīd, "In Tabarestan a certain man had passed away. I saw you there with Khiḍr, peace be upon him; he had laid his hand on your neck, and your hand rested on his back. When the mourners returned from the funeral, I saw you soar into the air."

"Yes," said Abū Yazīd. "What you say is perfectly true."

A man who did not believe in Abū Yazīd came to him one day to put him to the test.

"Reveal to me the answer to such-and-such a problem," he said.

Abū Yazīd perceived the unbelief within him.

"In a certain mountain there is a cave," he told him. "In that cave lives one of my friends. Ask him to reveal the answer to you."

The man hastily proceeded to the cave. There he saw a huge and terrible dragon. As soon as his eyes fell upon it he fainted away, and fouled his clothes. When he recovered he flung himself out of that place, leaving his shoes behind. So he returned to Abū Yazīd. Falling at his feet, he repented.

"Glory be to God!" Abū Yazīd exclaimed. "You cannot look after your shoes out of fear for a creature. Being in awe of God, how can you look after the 'revelation' which you came seeking in your disbelief?"

One day a man entered and questioned Abū Yazīd on the topic of shame. Abū Yazīd answered him, and the man turned to water. Another entered just then and perceived a pool of pale water.

"Master, what is this?" he asked.

"A man entered and questioned me about shame," Abū Yazīd replied. "I answered him. He could not endure what I said, and so turned into water out of shame."

Ḥātim the Deaf said to his disciples, "Whosoever of you on the day of resurrection does not intercede for the inhabitants of Hell, he is not one of my disciples."

This statement was reported to Abū Yazīd.

"I say," declared Abū Yazīd, "that he is my disciple who stands on the brink of Hell and takes by the hand every one being conveyed to Hell and dispatches him to Heaven, and then enters Hell in his place."

Once the army of Islam flagged in the war against Byzantium, and was near to being defeated. Suddenly they heard a shout, "Abū Yazīd, give help!" At once a he came from the direction of Khurasan, so that fear fell upon the army of the infidels and the army of Islam won the day.

Abū Yazīd was asked, "How did you attain to this degree and achieve this station?"

"One night when I was a child," he answered, "I came out from Bisṭām. The moon was shining, and the world was at rest. I beheld a Presence, besides which eighteen thousand worlds seemed but a mote. A deep emotion possessed me and I was overmastered by a mighty ecstasy. 'Lord God,' I cried, 'so mighty a palace, and so empty! Works so tremendous, and such loneliness!' A voice from heaven replied, 'The palace is not empty because none comes to it; it is empty because We do not desire all and sundry to enter it. Not every unwashed of face is worthy to inhabit this palace.'

"I made the resolve to pray for all creatures. Then the thought came to me, 'The station of intercession belongs to Muḥammad, upon him be peace.' So I observed my manners I heard a voice address me, 'Because of this one observance of good manners I have exalted your name, so that until the resurrection men shall call you King of the Gnostics.'"

"The first time I entered the Holy House," stated Abū Yazīd, "I saw the Holy House. The second time I entered it, I saw the Lord of the House. The third time I saw neither the House nor the Lord of the House."

By this Abū Yazīd meant, "I became lost in God, so that I knew nothing. Had I seen at all, I would have seen God." Proof of this interpretation is given by the following anecdote.

A man came to the door of Abū Yazīd and called out.

"Whom are you seeking?" asked Abū Yazīd.

"Abū Yazīd," replied the man.

"Poor wretch!" said Abū Yazīd. "I have been seeking Abū Yazīd for thirty years, and cannot find any trace or token of him."

This remark was reported to Dhū al-Nūn. He commented, "God have mercy on my brother Abū Yazīd! He is lost with the company of those that are lost in God."

So complete was Abū Yazīd's absorption in God, that every day when he was called by a disciple who had been his inseparable companion for twenty years, he would say, "My son, what is your name?"

"Master," the disciple said one day, "you are mocking me. For twenty years now I have been serving you, and every day you ask me my name." "My son," replied Abū Yazīd, "I do not deride you. But His name has entered my heart, and has expelled all other names. As soon as I learn a new name, I promptly forget it."

"Almighty God," said Abū Yazīd, "admitted me to His presence in two thousand stations, and in every station He offered me a kingdom, but I declined it. God said to me, 'Abū Yazīd, what do you desire?' I replied, 'I desire not to desire.'"

"You walk on the water!" they said.

"So does a piece of wood," Abū Yazīd replied.

"You fly in the air!"

"So does a bird."

"You travel to the Ka'bah in a single night!"

"Any conjurer travels from India to Demavand in a single night."

"Then what is the proper task of true men?" they asked.

"The true man attaches his heart to none but God," he replied.

"I triply divorced the world," said Abū Yazīd, "and alone proceeded to the Alone. I stood before the Presence and cried, 'Lord God, I desire none but Thee. If I possess Thee, I possess all.'

"When God recognised my sincerity, the first grace that He accorded me was that he removed the chaff of the self from before me."

"What is the Throne?" Abū Yazīd was asked.

"It is I," he replied.

"What is the Footstool?"

"I."

"What is the Tablet and the Pen?"

"I."

"God has servants the like of Ibrāhīm and Mūsā and 'Īsā."

"All are I."

"God has servants the like of Jibrīl and Mīkāl and Isrāfīl."

"All are I."

The man was silent.

"Whoever has become effaced in God," said Abū Yazīd, "and has attained the Reality of all that is, all is God."

It is related that Abū Yazīd seventy times attained propinquity to the presence of the Almighty. Each time he returned, he bound a girdle about him and then broke it.

When his life drew towards its close, he entered the prayer niche and bound a girdle about him. He put on upside down his fur jacket and his cap. Then he said, "O God, I do not vaunt of the discipline of a whole lifetime. I do not parade my all night prayers. I do not speak of my fasting all my life. I do not enumerate the times I have recited the Qur'an. I do not tell of my spiritual occasions and litanies and proximities. Thou knowest that I do not look back on anything, and that this of which I give account by my tongue is not said in boasting, or because I rely thereon. I give account of all this, because I am ashamed of all that I have done. Thou hast invested me with the grace of seeing myself so. All that is nothing; count it as naught. I am an old Torkoman of seventy years whose hair has grown white in pagandom. Now I come from the desert crying Tangri Tangri. Only now I learn to say Allah Allah. Only now I break my girdle. Only now I set foot in the circle of Islam. Only now I make my tongue move with the attestation of the Faith. All that Thou doest is without cause; Thou acceptest not on account of obedience, and Thou rejectest not on account of disobedience. All that I have done I reckon as but dust. Whatsoever Thou hast seen of me not pleasing to Thy presence, do Thou draw the line of pardon through it. And wash the dust of disobedience from me; for I have myself washed away the dust of the presumption that I have obeyed Thee."

10

‘Abdullah ibn al-Mubārak

Abū ‘Abd al-Raḥmān ‘Abdullah ibn al-Mubārak al-Ḥanẓalī al-Marwazī, born in 118 (736) of a Turkish father and a Persian mother, was a noted authority on Traditions and a famous ascetic. He studied under many teachers in Merv and elsewhere, and became erudite in many branches of learning, including grammar and literature. A wealthy merchant who distributed much in alms to the poor, he died at Hit on the Euphrates in 181 (797). He composed many works on Traditions, and one of these, on the theme of asceticism, has survived.

The conversion of ‘Abdullah ibn al-Mubārak

The circumstances of ‘Abdullah ibn al-Mubārak’s conversion were as follows. He became infatuated with a girl, so much so that he could not rest. One night during the winter he stood beneath the wall of his beloved’s apartment until morning, waiting to catch a glimpse of her. All night it snowed. When the call to prayer sounded, he supposed that it was for the prayer before sleeping. Seeing the daybreak, he realised that he had been absorbed all night in his longing for his beloved.

"Shame on you, son of Mubārak!" he cried. "On such a blessed night you stood on your feet till morning because of your private passion, yet if the imam is over long in reciting a Sūrah during prayer you are quite frantic."

Anguish gripped his heart forthwith, and he repented and devoted himself busily to worship. So complete was his devotion, that one day his mother, entering the garden, saw him sleeping under a rosebush whilst a snake with a narcissus in its mouth was driving flies away from him.

After that he set forth from Merv and stayed for a time in Baghdad, associating with the Sufi masters there. Then he proceeded to Makkah where he resided for a space, after which he returned to Merv. The people of Merv welcomed him back warmly, and set up classes and study-groups. At that time half of the people were followers of Traditions and half devoted themselves to jurisprudence. So today 'Abdullah is known as "the Approved of the Two Sects" because he was in accord with each, and both claimed him as their own. 'Abdullah founded two colleges in Merv, one for traditionists and the other for jurisprudents. He then left for Ḥijāz, and took up residence in Makkah again.

In alternate years he would perform the pilgrimage, and go out to the wars, and a third year he would engage in commerce. The profits of his trading he divided among his followers. He used to give dates to the poor, and count the date-stones; whoever ate more dates, he would offer a dirham for every stone.

So scrupulous was he in his piety, that on one occasion he had alighted at an inn. Now he had a valuable horse; he proceeded to prayer. Meanwhile his horse wandered into a field of wheat. He abandoned his horse there and proceeded on foot, saying, "He has devoured the crop of the authorities." On another occasion he made the journey all the way from Merv to Damascus to return a pen which he had borrowed and forgotten to give back.

One day as he was passing through a certain place they informed a blind man living there that 'Abdullah was coming. "Ask of him all that you require."

"Stop, 'Abdullah," the blind man called. 'Abdullah halted.

"Pray to God to restore my sight," the man begged.

'Abdullah lowered his head and prayed. At once the man saw again.

'Abdullah ibn al-Mubārak and 'Alī ibn al-Mūwaffaq

'Abdullah was living at Makkah. One year, having completed the rites of the pilgrimage, he fell asleep. In a dream he saw two angels descend from heaven.

"How many have come this year?" one asked the other.

"Six hundred thousand," the other replied.

"How many have had their pilgrimage accepted?"

"Not one."

"When I heard this," 'Abdullah reports, "I was filled with trembling. 'What?' I cried. 'All these people have come from afar out of the distant ends of the earth and with great pain and weariness *from every deep ravine,* traversing wide deserts, and all their labour is in vain?' 'There is a cobbler in Damascus called 'Alī ibn al-Muwaffaq,' said the angel. 'He has not come on the pilgrimage, but his pilgrimage is accepted and all his sins have been forgiven.'

"When I heard this," 'Abdullah continued, "I awoke saying, 'I must go to Damascus and visit that person.' So I went to Damascus and looked for where he lived. I shouted, and someone came out. 'What is your name?' I asked. "Alī ibn al-Muwaffaq,' he replied. 'I wish to speak with you,' I said. 'Say on,' he replied. 'What work do you do?' 'I cobble.' I then told him of my dream. 'What is your name?' he enquired when I had done. 'Abdullah ibn al-Mubārak,' I replied. He uttered a cry and fell in a faint. When he recovered I said to him, 'Tell me your story.'

"The man told me, 'For thirty years now I have longed to make the pilgrimage. I had saved up three hundred and fifty dirhams from my cobbling. This year I had resolved to go to Makkah. One day the good lady within becoming pregnant, she smelt the smell of food coming from next door. "Go and fetch me a bit of that food," she begged me. I went and knocked on the neighbour's door and explained the situation. My neighbour burst into tears. "My children have eaten nothing for three days together," she said. "Today I saw a donkey lying dead, so I hacked off a piece and cooked it. It would not be lawful food for you." My heart burned within me when I heard her tale. I took out the three hundred and fifty dirhams and gave them to her. "Spend these on the children," I said. "This is my pilgrimage."'

"The angel spoke truly in my dream," 'Abdullah declared, "and the Heavenly King was true in His judgement."

'Abdullah ibn al-Mubārak and his slave

'Abdullah had a slave. A man told him, "That slave of yours plunders the dead and gives you the proceeds."

This information distressed 'Abdullah. One night he followed on his slave's heels. He went to a cemetery and opened a grave. In the grave was a prayer-niche, where the slave stood at prayer. 'Abdullah, who had watched all this from a distance, crept nearer. He saw that the slave was clothed in sackcloth and had put a collar round his neck. Rubbing his face in the earth, he was wailing. Observing this, 'Abdullah crept away weeping and sat apart in a corner.

The slave remained in that place until dawn. Then he came up and covered over the grave, and proceeded to the mosque and said his morning prayers.

"My God," he cried, "day has returned. My temporal lord will ask me for money. Thou art the riches of the bankrupt. Give Thou to me from whence Thou knowest."

Immediately a light shone out of the sky, and a silver dirham dropped into the slave's hand. 'Abdullah could not bear to watch any more. He rose up and took the head of the slave into his bosom and kissed him.

"A thousand lives be the ransom of such a slave!" he exclaimed. "You were the master, not I."

"O God," cried the slave, perceiving what had happened, "now that my veil has been stripped away and my secret is revealed, no more repose remains for me in this world. I implore Thee by Thy might and glory, suffer me not to be a cause of stumbling. Take away my soul."

His head was still lying in 'Abdullah's bosom when he expired. 'Abdullah laid him out and wrapped him in a winding-sheet, then he buried him in that same sackcloth in the selfsame grave.

That night 'Abdullah saw the Master of the World in a dream, and the Friend of God Ibrāhīm with him, each come down riding a heavenly horse.

"'Abdullah," they said, "why did you bury our friend in sackcloth?"

11

Sufyān al-Thawrī

Abū 'Abdullah Sufyān ibn Sa'īd al-Thawrī was born in 97 (715) at Kūfah and studied first under his father, and later with many learned men, attaining high proficiency in Traditions and theology. In 158 (775) he collided with the authorities and was compelled to go into hiding in Makkah; he died in 161 (778) at Basra. He founded a school of jurisprudence which survived for about two centuries; living a strictly ascetic life, he was claimed by the Sufis as a saint.

Sufyān al-Thawrī and the Caliphs

The scrupulousness of Sufyān al-Thawrī manifested itself even before he was born. One day his mother was on the roof of her house and put in her mouth a few pickles from her neighbour's roof. Sufyān gave such a violent kick against his mother's womb that she thought she had lost him.

It is reported that the caliph of those days was praying before Sufyān, and whilst at prayer he twirled his moustache.

"This is not a proper kind of prayer," Sufyān called out. "Tomorrow on the resurrection plain this prayer will be flung into your face like a dirty rag."

"Speak a little more gently," said the caliph.

"If I should hold my hand back from such a responsibility," Sufyān answered, "my urine would turn to blood."

The caliph was angered by these remarks, and ordered him to be put on the gallows.

"Then no one else will be so bold before me," he said.

On the day when the gallows were erected, Sufyān was lying with his head in the bosom of a great saint and his feet in the lap of Sufyān ibn 'Uyaynah, fast asleep. The two saints, learning that the gallows were being prepared, said to one another, "Let us not tell him." At this point Sufyān awoke

"What is happening?" he asked.

They told him, exhibiting much distress.

"I am not so greatly attached to life," Sufyān commented. "But one must discharge one's duty so long as one is in this world."

His eyes filling with tears, he prayed, "Lord God, seize them with a mighty seizing!"

The caliph at that moment was seated on his throne surrounded by the pillars of state. A thunderbolt struck the palace, and the caliph with his ministers was swallowed by the earth.

"What a well-received and quickly answered prayer!" exclaimed those two noble saints.

Another caliph sat on the throne who believed in Sufyān. It so happened that Sufyān fell ill. Now the caliph had a Christian physician, a great master and extremely clever. He sent him to Sufyān to treat him. When he examined his urine, he remarked,

"This is a man whose liver has turned to blood out of the fear of God. It is flowing little by little out of his bladder. The religion which such a man holds," he added, "cannot be false."

And he immediately turned Muslim.

"I thought I was sending the physician to the bed of a sick man," the caliph commented. "In reality I sent the sick man to treat the physician."

Anecdotes of Sufyān al-Thawrī

One day Sufyān with a friend was passing the door of a notable. The friend gazed at the portico. Sufyān rebuked him.

"If you and your like did not gaze so at their palaces, they would not commit such extravagance," he said. "By gazing you become partners in the sin of this extravagance."

A neighbour of Sufyān's died, and Sufyān went out to pray at his funeral. After that he heard people saying, "He was a good man."

"If I had known that other men approved of him," said Sufyān, "I would never have taken part in his funeral. Unless a man is a hypocrite, the others do not approve of him!"

One day Sufyān put on his clothes all awry. When this was pointed out to him, he was on the point of adjusting them, but then abstained.

"I put on this shirt for God's sake," he said. "I do not wish to change it for the sake of men."

A youth missed the pilgrimage, and he sighed.

"I have performed forty pilgrimages," Sufyān told him. "I bestow them all on you. Will you bestow this sigh on me?"

"I do," said the youth.

That night Sufyān dreamed that a voice said to him, "You have made such a profit on the transaction that, if it were divided up amongst all the pilgrims at 'Arafāt, they would be rich indeed."

One day Sufyān was eating a piece of bread when a dog happened along. He gave the bread to the dog, bit by bit.

"Why did you not eat it with your wife and child?" he was asked.

"If I give bread to the dog,?' he replied, "he keeps watch over me all through the night so that I can pray. If I give it to my wife and child, they hold me back from my devotions."

Once Sufyān was travelling to Makkah in a litter. A companion was with him, and Sufyān wept all the way.

"Do you weep out of fear for your sins?" asked his friend. Sufyān stretched out his hand and plucked some stubble.

"My sins are many," he replied. "Yet though my sins are many, they mean no more to me than this handful of stubble. What makes me afraid is whether the faith I am offering is really faith or no."

An illustration of the compassion Sufyān showed to all God's creatures is provided by the following story. One day he saw in the market a bird in a cage, fluttering and making a pitiful sound. He bought it and set it free. Every night the bird would come to Sufyān's home and watch all night while Sufyān prayed, perching on him from time to time.

When Sufyān died and was being borne to the grave, that bird insisted on joining the procession and wailed pitifully along with the rest of the mourners. When Sufyān was committed to the dust, the bird dashed itself to the ground. A voice issued from the tomb, "Almighty God has forgiven Sufyān for the compassion he showed to His creatures." The bird died too, and joined Sufyān.

12

Shaqīq al-Balkhī

Abū 'Alī Shaqīq ibn Ibrāhīm al-Azdī al-Balkhī, a man of wide learning, began his career as a merchant but later turned to the ascetic way. He made the pilgrimage to Makkah, and was martyred fighting in the holy wars in 194 (810).

The career of Shaqīq al-Balkhī

Shaqīq al-Balkhī was a master of many sciences, and wrote many books. He taught Ḥātim the Deaf, whilst he learned the Way from Ibrāhīm ibn Adham. He claimed to have studied under 1,700 teachers, and to have acquired several camels' loads of books. The circumstances of his conversion were as follows.

Shaqīq went to Turkestan on a trading expedition. On the way he paused to look at a temple, where he saw an idolater worshipping an idol and making humble obeisance.

"You have a Creator who is living and omnipotent and omniscient," he told the man. "Worship Him. Have some shame; do not worship an idol from which neither good nor evil comes."

'If it is as you say," the idolater replied, "is He not able to provide you with your daily bread in your own city? Must you then come all this way here?"

These words awakened Shaqīq to the truth, and he turned back towards Balkh. A Zoroastrian happened to travel along with him.

"What are you engaged upon?" asked the Zoroastrian.

"Trading," Shaqīq replied.

"If you are going in search of sustenance that has not been preordained for you, you can travel till the resurrection and you will not attain it," said the other. "And if you are going after sustenance that has been foreordained for you, do not trouble to go; it will come to you of itself."

These words awakened Shaqīq still further, and his love for worldly things grew chill.

Finally Shaqīq returned to Balkh, where his friends gave him a warm welcome; for he was famous for his generosity. Now the Prince of Balkh at that time was 'Alī ibn 'Īsā ibn Hāmān, and he kept hunting-dogs. It so happened that one of his dogs was missing.

"It is with Shaqīq's neighbour," they told him.

The man was arrested and accused of stealing the dog. They beat him about, and he turned to Shaqīq for protection. Shaqīq went to the Prince.

"Give me three days, and I will bring your dog back to you. Set my friend free," he begged.

The Prince set Shaqīq's neighbour free. Three days later by chance a man found and captured the dog.

"I must take this dog to Shaqīq," he thought. "He is a generous man, and will give me something."

So he brought the dog to Shaqīq. Shaqīq brought it to the Prince, and thus he was quit of his pledge. Thereupon he resolved to turn his back on the world entirely.

Later there was a great famine in Balkh, so that men were devouring one another. In the market Shaqīq saw a young slave laughing happily.

"Slave, what occasion for merriment is this?" Shaqīq demanded. "Do you not see how the people are suffering from hunger?"

"Why should I be worried?" the slave answered. "My master owns a whole village and has plenty of grain. He will never let me go hungry."

Shaqīq lost all self-control on hearing this reply.

"O God," he cried, "this slave is so happy in having a master who owns a stack of corn. Thou art the King of Kings, and hast undertaken to give us our daily bread. Why then should we be anxious?"

He thereupon abandoned all worldly occupation and made sincere repentance. He set forth on the path to God, in whom he put perfect trust. He used to say, "I am the pupil of a slave."

Ḥātim the Deaf relates the following anecdote.

I went with Shaqīq to the holy war. One day the

fighting was very fierce; the ranks were drawn up so closely that nothing could be seen but the tips of lances, and arrows were raining from the sky.

"Ḥātim," Shaqīq called to me, "how are you enjoying yourself? May be you are thinking it is last night, when you were sleeping in your bedclothes with your wife!"

"Not at all," I replied.

"In God's name why not?" Shaqīq cried. "That is how I feel. I feel as you did last night in your bed-clothes."

Then night came on, and Shaqīq laid down and, wrapping himself in his gown, fell fast asleep. So completely did he rely upon God that in the midst of so many enemies he slept soundly.

One day Shaqīq was lecturing when news ran through the city that the infidels were at the gates. Shaqīq ran out and routed the unbelievers, then he returned. A disciple placed a handful of flowers near the Master's prayer rug. He picked them up and smelt them.

An ignorant fellow saw this and shouted,

"An army at the gates, and the imam of the Muslims holds flowers to his nose!"

"The hypocrite sees the smelling of flowers all right, but he does not see the routing of the infidels," Shaqīq commented.

Shaqīq al-Balkhī before Hārūn al-Rashīd

When Shaqīq set out on the Makkah pilgrimage and reached Baghdad, Hārūn al-Rashīd summoned him.

"Are you Shaqīq the Ascetic?" Hārūn demanded when he came into his presence.

"I am Shaqīq," he replied, "but not the Ascetic."

"Counsel me," Hārūn commanded.

"Then attend," Shaqīq proceeded. "Almighty God has set you in the place of Abū Bakr the Trusty, and requires trustiness from you as from him. He has set you in the place of 'Umar the Discriminator, and requires from you as from him discrimination between truth and falsehood. He has set you in the place of 'Uthmān of the Two Lights, and requires from you as from him modesty and nobility. He has set you in the place of 'Alī the Well-approved, and requires from you as from him knowledge and justice."

"Say more," Hārūn cried.

"God has a lodging-place called Hell," Shaqīq said. "He has appointed you its doorkeeper, and has equipped you with three things—wealth, sword and whip. 'With these three things,' He commands, 'keep the people away from Hell. If any man comes to you in need, do not grudge him money. If any man opposes God's commandment, school him with this whip. If any man slays another, lawfully exact retaliation on him with this sword.' If you do not these things, you will be the leader of those that enter Hell."

"Say more," Hārūn repeated.

"You are the fountain, and your agents are the rivulets," said Shaqīq. "If the fountain is bright, it is not impaired by the darkness of the rivulets. But if the fountain is dark, what hope is there that the rivulets will be bright?"

"Say more," Hārūn said again.

"Suppose you are thirsting in the desert, so that you are about to perish," Shaqīq went on. "If in that moment you come upon a draught of water, how much will you be willing to give for it?"

"As much as the man demands," said Hārūn. "And if he will not sell save for half your kingdom?"

"I would give that," Hārūn replied.

"And suppose you drink the water and then it will not come out of you, so that you are in danger of perishing," Shaqīq pursued. "Then someone tells you, 'I will cure you, but I demand half your kingdom.' What would you do?"

"I would give it," answered Hārūn.

"Then why do you vaunt yourself of a kingdom," said Shaqīq, "the value of which is one draught of water which you drink, and then it comes out of you?"

Hārūn wept, and sent Shaqīq away with all honour.

13

Dāwūd al-Ṭā'ī

Abū Sulaymān Dāwūd ibn Nuṣayr al-Ṭā'ī of Kūfā was a man of notable erudition, a pupil of Abū Ḥanīfah; he was converted to the ascetic life by Ḥabīb al-Rā'ī and threw all his books into the Euphrates. He died between 160 (777) and 165 (782).

The poverty of Dāwūd al-Ṭā'ī

From the beginning Dāwūd al-Ṭā'ī was overwhelmed by an inner grief and always avoided the society of his fellow creatures. The cause of his conversion was that he heard a mourning-woman recite these verses.

On which of your cheeks has decay begun,
And which of your eyes has started to run?

Great sorrow invaded his heart, and all composure deserted him. In this state he went to lessons with his teacher Abū Ḥanīfah.

"What has transpired with you?" Abū Ḥanīfah asked.

Dāwūd related to him the foregoing incident.

"The world has lost its attractions for me," he added. "Something has happened inside of me which I cannot understand, nor can I discover an explanation of it in any book or legal pronouncement."

"Turn away from other men," Abū Ḥanīfah prescribed.

So Dāwūd turned his face from other men and shut himself up in his house. After a long interval, Abū Ḥanīfah went to see him.

"This is not the solution, for you to hide in your house and utter not a word. The proper course is for you to sit at the feet of the imams and listen to them propounding novel ideas. You should attend to what they have to say patiently, uttering not a word. Then you will know those problems better than they."

Recognising the good sense of what Abū Ḥanīfah said, Dāwūd resumed his studies. For a year he sat at the feet of the imams, never opening his mouth and accepting their pronouncements with patience, being content simply to listen and not to reply.

"This one year's patience," he remarked at the end of that' time, "is equivalent to thirty years' strenuous work."

He then encountered Ḥabīb al-Rā'ī, who initiated him into the mystic path. He set forth upon it manfully. He flung his books into the river, went into retirement and cut off all expectation of other men.

Now he had received twenty dinars as an inheritance. These he consumed in twenty years. Certain of the shaykhs reproved him for this.

"The path stands for giving to others, not keeping to oneself."

"I hold on to this amount to secure my peace of mind," he explained. "I can make do with this until I die."

He spared himself no austerity, to such an extent that he would dip bread in water and then sip the water, saying, "Between this and eating the bread I can recite fifty verses of the Qur'an. Why should I waste my life?"

Abū Bakr ibn 'Ayyāsh reports, "I went to Dāwūd's chamber and saw him holding a piece of dry bread and weeping. 'What has happened, Dāwūd?' I asked. 'I want to eat this piece of bread,' he replied, 'and I do not know whether it is hallowed or unhallowed."'

Another reports, "I called on him, and saw a pitcher of water placed in the sun. I asked, 'Why do you not place it in the shade?' 'When I put it there, it was in the shade,' he replied. 'Now I am too ashamed before God to indulge myself.'"

Anecdotes of Dāwūd

It is said that Dāwūd owned a great palace with many apartments. He would occupy one apartment until it fell into ruins; then he would move to another apartment.

"Why do you not repair the apartment?" he was asked.

'I have made a covenant with God not to repair this world," he replied.

Gradually the whole palace collapsed, nothing remaining except the portico. On the night on which Dāwūd died, the portico also fell in.

"The roof of the apartment is broken," remarked another visitor. "It is about to fall."

'I have not looked at this roof for twenty years," answered Dāwūd.

"Why do you not marry?" Dāwūd was asked.

"I do not wish to deceive a believing woman," he replied.

"How is that?"

"If I propose to a woman," Dāwūd explained, "that will mean that I have undertaken to manage her affairs. Since I cannot attend both to my religious duties and the world, that means that I will have deceived her."

"Well, at least comb your beard," they said.

"That implies being at leisure to do it," he answered.

One moonlit night Dāwūd went up on his roof and gazed at the sky. He fell to meditating on the splendor of God's kingdom, and wept until he was beside himself. He fell off on to the roof of his neighbour. The latter, thinking that a thief was on his roof, rushed up with a sword. Seeing Dāwūd there, he took him by the hand.

"Who threw you down here?" he asked.

"I do not know," Dāwūd replied. "I was beside myself. I have no idea at all."

Once Dāwūd was seen running to prayers.

"What is the hurry?" he was asked.

"This army at the gates of the city," he replied. "They are waiting for me."

"Which army?" they exclaimed.

"The men of the tombs," he replied.

Hārūn al-Rashīd asked Abū Yūsuf to take him to visit Dāwūd. Abū Yūsuf went to Dāwūd's house, but was refused admission. He begged Dāwūd's mother to intercede.

"Admit him," his mother pleaded.

"What business have I with worldlings and evildoers?" Dāwūd replied, refusing to comply.

"I implore you, by the right of my milk, admit him," his mother said.

"O God," said Dāwūd, "Thou hast said, 'Observe the right of thy mother, for My good pleasure is in her good pleasure.' Otherwise, what business have I with them?

He then granted audience. They entered and seated themselves. Dāwūd began to preach, and Hārūn wept copiously. When he withdrew, he put down a gold moidore.

"This is hallowed," he said.

"Remove it," Dāwūd said. "I have no need of it. I sold a house which was mine by hallowed inheritance, and live on the proceeds. I have asked God that when that money is spent He shall take my soul, so that I may not be in need of any man. I am hopeful that God has answered my prayer."

Hārūn and Abū Yūsuf then returned to the palace. Abū Yūsuf went to see the keeper of the purse.

"How much is left of Dāwūd's money?" he asked.

"Two dirhams," the keeper replied. "He has been spending a silver penny daily."

Abū Yūsuf calculated. Another day, standing with his back to the prayer-niche, he announced, "Today Dāwūd has died." Enquiry was made, and it was found to be so.

"How did you know?" they asked.

"I calculated from his expenditure that today nothing remained to him," Abū Yūsuf explained. "I knew that his prayer would be answered."

14

Al-Muḥāsibī

The account given by 'Aṭṭār of al-Muḥāsibī, one of the greatest figures in the history of Islamic mysticism, is surprisingly jejune. Born in Basra in 165 (781), Abū 'Abdullah al-Ḥārīth ibn Asad al-Baṣrī al-Muḥāsibī early in his life moved to Baghdad where he studied Traditions and theology and was closely involved with the leading personalities and prominent events of his times. He died in 243 (857). The influence of his teachings and writings upon later mystical theorists, including in particular Abū Ḥāmid al-Ghazālī, was profound and far-reaching. Many of his books and pamphlets have been preserved, the most important being the *Kitāb al-Ri'āyah* (edited by Dr. Margaret Smith, London, 1940).

The austerity of Ḥārīth al-Muḥāsibī

Ḥārīth al-Muḥāsibī inherited thirty thousand dinars from

his father.

"Take it to the Treasury. Let the authorities have it," he ordered.

"Why?" they asked.

"The Prophet said," he explained, "and it is a true Tradition that the Qadarites are the Magians of this community. My father was a Qadarite. The Prophet also said that a Muslim cannot inherit from a Magian. My father was a Magian, as you see, and I am a Muslim."

God's providence in preserving him was such that, when he stretched out his hand towards food whose lawfulness was doubtful, a nerve in the back of his finger became taut so that the finger did not obey the command to move. Thus he knew that the morsel in question was not proper.

"Ḥārīth came to me one day and was visibly hungry," reported Junayd. "'Uncle, I will bring some food,' I said. 'That would be welcome,' he answered. So I went to the larder and looked for some food. I found some remains of a wedding-feast which had been brought to us for supper. I brought this and offered it to him. His finger would not obey him. He put morsel in his mouth, but despite all his efforts it would not go down. He turned it about in his mouth, then at last he got and put it out in the porch and took his departure.

"Later I questioned him about what had happened. Ḥārīth said, 'I was certainly hungry, and I wanted to please you. But God has given me a special sign, that any food that is doubtful will not go down my throat and my finger refuses to touch it. For all that I tried, it would not go down. Where did that. food come from?' 'From the house of a kinsman of mine,' he replied.

"Then I said, 'Today will you come to my house?' 'I will,' he replied. So we entered, and fetched a piece of dry bread, and we ate. Ḥārīth remarked, 'This is the kind of thing to offer dervishes.'"

15

Aḥmad ibn Ḥarb

Aḥmad ibn Ḥarb al-Nīsabūrī was a noted ascetic of Nishapur, a reliable traditionist and a fighter in the holy wars. He visited Baghdad in the time of Aḥmad ibn Ḥanbal and taught there; he died in 234 (849) at the age of 85.

Aḥmad ibn Ḥarb and the Zoroastrian

Aḥmad ibn Ḥarb had for neighbour a Zoroastrian named Bahram. Now this neighbour had sent a partner out on a trading mission, and on the way thieves had carried off all his goods.

"Rise up," Aḥmad called to his disciples when he heard the news. "Such a thing has happened to our neighbour. Let us go and condole with him. Even though he is a Zoroastrian, yet he is a neighbour."

When they reached the door of his house Bahram was kindling his Zoroastrian fire. He ran forward and kissed his sleeve. Bahram, thinking that perhaps they were hungry, though bread was scarce made to lay the table.

"Do not trouble yourself," Aḥmad said. "We have come to sympathise. I heard that your goods had been stolen."

"Yes, that is so," said Bahram. "But I have three reasons to be grateful to God. First, because they stole from me and not from someone else. Second, that they took only a half. Third, that even if my worldly goods are gone, I still have my religion; and the world comes and goes."

These words pleased Aḥmad.

"Write this down," he told his disciples. "The odour of Islam issues from these words." Then he added, turning to Bahram, "Why do you worship this fire?"

"So that it may not burn me," Bahram replied. "Secondly, as today I have given it so much fuel, tomorrow it will not be untrue to me but will convey me to God."

"You have made a great mistake," commented Aḥmad. "Fire is weak and ignorant and faithless. All the calculations you have based on it are false. If a child pours a little water on it, it will go out. A thing so weak as that–how can it convey you to One so mighty? A thing that has not the strength to repel from itself a little earth–how can it convey you to God? Moreover, to prove it is ignorant: if you sprinkle musk and filth upon it, it will burn them both and not know that one is better than the other–that is why it makes no distinction between filth and frankincense. Again, it is now seventy years that you have been worshipping it, and I have never worshipped it; come, let us both put a hand in the fire, and you will see that it burns both our hands. It will not be true to you."

These words struck the Zoroastrian to the heart.

"I will ask you four questions," he said. "If you answer them all, I will accept your Faith. Say: why did God create men? And having created them, why did He provide for them? Why does He cause them to die? And having caused them to die, why does He raise them up again?"

"He created them that they might be His servants," Aḥmad replied. "He provided for them that they might know Him to be the All-provider. He causes them to die that they may know His overwhelming Power. He makes them to live again that they may know Him to be Omnipotent and Omniscient."

As soon as Aḥmad had finished, Bahram recited the attestation.

"I bear witness that there is no god but God, and I bear witness that Muḥammad is the Apostle of God."

Thereupon Aḥmad cried aloud and fainted. Presently he recovered consciousness.

"Why did you faint?" his disciples asked.

"The moment that he raised his finger in attestation," Aḥmad replied, "a voice called to me in my inmost heart. 'Aḥmad,' the voice said, 'Bahram was a Zoroastrian for seventy years, but at last he believed. You have spent seventy years in the Faith; now at the end what will you have to offer?'"

Aḥmad ibn Ḥarb and Aḥmad the Merchant

There lived in Nishapur two men, one named Aḥmad ibn Ḥarb and the other called Aḥmad the Merchant.

Aḥmad ibn Ḥarb was a man so wrapped up in the recollection of God, that when the barber wished to trim his moustache he kept moving his lips.

"Keep still just while I trim these hairs," said the barber.

"You busy yourself with your own affairs," answered Aḥmad ibn Ḥarb.

And each time the barber trimmed, some part of his lips was nicked.

On one occasion he received a letter and for a long while intended to answer it but did not find a spare moment. Then one day the *mu'adhdhin* was chanting the call to prayer. Just while he was saying "It is time" Aḥmad called to a companion.

"Answer my friend's letter. Tell him not to write to me any more, because I have not the leisure to reply. Write, 'Be busy with God. Farewell!"

As for Aḥmad the Merchant, he was so wrapped up in love of worldly things that one day he asked his maidservant for food. The maidservant prepared a dish and brought it to him, but he went on with his calculations until night fell, and he dropped off to sleep. When he woke next morning he called to the maid.

"You did not make that food."

"I did make it. But you were so taken up with your calculations."

She cooked a dish a second time and laid it before her master, but again he did not find the leisure to eat it. A third time the girl prepared food for him, and still he found no opportunity. The maid came and found him asleep, so she rubbed some of the food on his lips. Aḥmad the Merchant awoke.

"Bring the basin," he called, thinking that he had eaten.

Aḥmad ibn Ḥarb and his son

Aḥmad ibn Ḥarb had a little son whom he was training to trust in God.

"Whenever you want food or anything," he told him, "go to this window and say, 'Lord God, I need bread.'"

Each time the child went to that place, the parents had so arranged to place in the window what the child desired.

One day they were out of the house when the child was overcome by the pangs of hunger. As usual he came under the window and prayed.

"Lord God, I need bread."

Immediately food was sent down to him by the window. The household returned to find him sitting down and eating.

"Where did you get this from?" they asked.

"From the one who gives me every day," he replied. So they realised that he was well established in this way.

16

Ḥātim al-Aṣamm

Abū 'Abd al-Raḥmān Ḥātim ibn 'Unwān al-Aṣamm ("the Deaf"), a native of Balkh, was a pupil of Shaqīq al-Balkhī. He visited Baghdad, and died at Washjard near Tirmidh in 237 (852).

Anecdotes of Ḥātim the Deaf

Ḥātim the Deaf's charity was so great that when a woman came to him one day to ask him a question and at that moment she broke wind, he said to her, "Speak louder. I am hard of hearing." This he said in order that the woman should not be put to shame. She raised her voice, and he answered her problem. So long as that old woman was alive, for close on fifteen years Ḥātim made out that he was deaf, so that no one should tell the old woman that he was not so. After her death he gave his answers readily. Until then, he would say to everyone who spoke to him, "Speak louder." That was why he was called Ḥātim the Deaf.

One day Ḥātim was preaching in Balkh.

"O God," he prayed, "whoever in this congregation today is the greatest and boldest sinner and has the blackest record, do Thou forgive him."

Now there was present in that congregation a man who robbed the dead. He had opened many tombs and stolen the winding-sheets. That night he went about his usual business of robbing the dead. He had actually removed the earth from a grave when he heard a voice proceeding out of the tomb.

"Are you not ashamed? This morning you were pardoned at Ḥātim's gathering, and tonight you are at your old business again?"

The grave-robber jumped out of the tomb, and ran to Ḥātim. He told him what had happened, and repented.

Sa'd ibn Muḥammad al-Rāzī reports the following.

For many years I was a disciple of Ḥātim, and in all that time I only once saw him angry. He had gone to the market, and there he saw a man who had seized hold of one of his apprentices and was shouting.

"Many times he has taken my goods and eaten them, and does not pay me the price of them."

"Good sir, be charitable," Ḥātim interposed.

"I know nothing of charity. I want my money," the man retorted.

All Ḥātim's pleading was without effect. Growing angry, he took his cloak from his shoulders and flung it to the ground there in the midst of the bazaar. It was filled with gold, all true coin.

"Come, take what is owing to you, and no more, or your hand will be withered," he said to the tradesman.

The man set about picking up the gold until he had taken his due. He could not contain himself, and stretched out the hand again to pick up more. His hand immediately became withered.

One day a man came to Ḥātim and said, "I possess much wealth, and I wish to give some of this wealth to you and your companions. Will you accept?"

"I am afraid," Ḥātim answered, "that when you die I shall have to say, 'Heavenly Provider, my earthly provider is dead.'"

Ḥātim recalled, "When I went out to the wars a Turk seized me and flung me to the ground to kill me. My heart was not concerned or afraid. I just waited to see what he would do. He was feeling for his sword, when suddenly an arrow pierced him and he fell from me. 'Did you kill me, or did I kill you?' I exclaimed."

When Ḥātim came to Baghdad the caliph was told, "The ascetic of Khurasan has arrived." The caliph promptly sent for him.

"O caliph the ascetic," Ḥātim addressed the caliph as he entered.

"I am not an ascetic," replied the caliph. "The whole world is under my command. You are the ascetic."

"No, you are the ascetic," Ḥātim retorted. "God says, *Say, the enjoyment of this world is little. You* are contented with a little. You are the ascetic, not I. I will not submit to this world or the next; how then am I an ascetic?"

17

Sahl ibn ʻAbdullah al-Tustarī

Abū Muḥammad Sahl ibn ʻAbdullah al-Tustarī was born at Tostar (Ahwaz) c. 200 (815), studied with Sufyān al-Thawrī, and met Dhū al-Nūn al-Miṣrī. A quiet life was interrupted in 261 (874) when he was compelled to seek refuge in Basra, where he died in 282 (896). A short commentary on the Qur'an is attributed to him, and he made important contributions to the development of Sufi theory, being influential through his pupil Ibn Salīm who founded the Sālimiyah school.

Early years

Sahl ibn ʻAbdullah al-Tustarī gives the following account of himself.

I remember when God said, "Am I not your Lord?" and I said, "Yes indeed." I also remember myself in my mother's womb.

I was three years old when I began to pray all night. My uncle Muḥammad ibn Sawwār wept to see me pray.

"Sahl, go to sleep. You make me anxious," he said.

I kept watch on my uncle secretly and openly. Then matters reached the point that one day I said to him, "Uncle, I have a hard state to contend with. I seem to see my head prostrate before the Throne."

"Keep this state secret, my boy, and tell no one," he advised. Then he added, "Recollect when you are in your bedclothes rolling from side to side. As your tongue moves, say, 'God is with me, God is watching over me, God is witnessing me.'"

I used this formula, and informed my uncle so.

"Say the words seven times each night," he counselled me.

I informed him that I had done so.

"Say them fifteen times."

I did as my uncle directed, and a sweetness invaded my heart therefrom. A year passed. Then my uncle said, "Keep my instructions and continue that practice until you go to the grave. The fruits thereof will be yours in this world and the next."

Years passed, and I used the same formula until the sweetness of it penetrated my most secret heart.

"Sahl," said my uncle, "when God is with any man and God sees him, how can he disobey God? God watch over you, that you may not disobey."

After that I went into seclusion. Then they sent me to school.

"I am afraid that my concentration may be scattered," I said. "Make it a condition with the teacher that I remain with him for an hour and learn some lessons, then I am to return to my true occupation."

On these terms I went to school and learned the Qur'an, being then seven years old. From that time I fasted continuously, my only food being barley bread. At twelve a problem occurred to me which no one was able to solve. I asked them to send me to Basra to propound that problem. I came to Basra and questioned the learned men of that city, but no one could answer me. From there I proceeded to Abbadan, to a man called Ḥabīb ibn Ḥamzah. He answered my question. I remained with him for some time, and derived much benefit from his instruction.

Then I came to Tostar. By that time my diet had been reduced to the point that they would buy barley for me for a dirham, grind it and bake it into bread. Every night about dawn I would break my fast with an ounce of that bread, without relish or salt. In that way the dirham lasted me a year.

After that I resolved to break my fast once every three days, then once every five days, then once every seven days, and so on until I reached once every twenty days. (According to one report, Sahl claimed to have reached once every seventy days.) Sometimes I would eat just one almond every forty days.

I made trial for many years of satiety and hunger. In the beginning my weakness resulted from hunger and my strength came from satiety. After a time my strength derived from hunger and my weakness from satiety. Then I prayed, "O God, close Sahl's eyes to both, that he may see satiety in hunger, and hunger in satiety, both proceed from Thee."

One day Sahl said, "Repentance is a duty incumbent upon a man every moment, whether he be of the elect or the common folk, whether he be obedient to God or disobedient."

There was a certain man in Tostar who laid claim to be learned and an ascetic. He protested against this statement of Sahl's.

"He says that the disobedient must repent of his disobedience, and the obedient of his obedience."

And he turned the people against Sahl, making him out to be a heretic and an infidel. All, commons and nobles alike, took up his charge. Sahl refrained from disputing with them to correct their misunderstanding. Fired by the pure flame of religion, he wrote down on paper a list of all his possessions, farms, houses, furniture, carpets, vessels, gold and silver. Then he gathered the people and scattered the pages over their heads. He gave to every man all that was inscribed on the page that he picked up, as a token of gratitude for their relieving him of his worldly goods. Having given everything away, he set out for Ḥijāz.

"My soul," he addressed himself, "now I am bankrupt. Make no further demand on me, for you will not get anything."

His soul agreed not to ask him for anything, until he reached Kūfah.

"So far," his soul then said, "I have not asked you for anything. Now I desire a piece of bread and a fish. Give me that much to eat, and I will not trouble you again all the way to Makkah."

Entering Kūfah, Sahl observed an ass-mill with a camel tied to it.

"How much do you give to hire this camel for a day?" he asked.

"Two dirhams," they told him.

"Release the camel and tie me in its place, and give me one dirham for up to the evening prayer," Sahl demanded.

They released the camel and tied Sahl to the ass-mill. At nightfall they gave him a dirham. He bought bread and a fish and laid it before him.

"Soul," he addressed himself, "every time you want this, resolve with yourself that tomorrow till sunset you will do mule's work to get what you want."

Then Sahl proceeded to the Ka'bah, where he met many Sufi masters. From there he returned to Tostar, to find Dhū al-Nūn awaiting him.

Anecdotes of Sahl

'Amr Layth fell sick, so that all the physicians were powerless to treat him.

"Is there anyone who can pray for a cure?" it was asked.

"Sahl is such a man whose prayers are answered," came the reply.

His help was therefore invoked. Having in mind God's command to "obey those in authority" he responded to the appeal.

"Prayer," he stated when he was seated before 'Amr, "is effective only in the case of one who is penitent. In your prison there are men wrongfully detained."

'Amr released them all, and repented.

"Lord God," prayed Sahl, "like as Thou hast shown to him the abasement due to his disobedience, so now display to him the glory gained by my obedience. Like as Thou hast clothed his inward parts with the garment of repentance, so now clothe his outward parts with the garment of health."

As soon as Sahl had uttered this prayer, 'Amr Layth recovered his health completely. He offered Sahl much money, but this he declined, and left his presence.

"If you had accepted something," objected one of his disciples, "so that we might have applied it to discharging the debt we have incurred, would that not have been better?"

"Do you need gold? Then look!" replied Sahl.

The disciple looked and behold, the whole plain and desert were filled with gold and rubies.

"Why," said Sahl, "should one who enjoys such favour with God accept anything from one of God's creatures?"

Whenever Sahl partook in a mystic audition he went into ecstasy and would continue rapt for five days, eating no food. If it was winter, the sweat would pour from him and drench his shirt.

When he was in that state, and the *'ulamā'* questioned him, he would say, "Do not question me, for in this mystic moment you will get no benefit from me and my words."

Sahl used to walk on the water without his feet being so much as moistened.

"People say," someone observed, "that you walk on water."

"Ask the *mu'adhdhin* of this mosque," Sahl replied. "He is a truthful man."

"I asked him," the man said. "The *mu'adhdhin* told me, 'I never saw that. But in these days he entered a pool to wash. He fell into the pool, and if I had not been on the spot he would have died there.'"

When Abū 'Alī al-Daqqāq heard this story, he commented, "He had many miraculous powers, but he wished to keep them hidden."

One day Sahl was seated in the mosque when a pigeon dropped to the ground, exhausted by the heat.

"Shāh al-Kirmānī has died," remarked Sahl.

When they looked into the matter, it proved to be exactly as Sahl said.

Many lions and other wild beasts used to visit Sahl, and he would feed and tend them. Even today Sahl's house in Tostar is called "the house of the wild beasts."

After his long vigils and painful austerities Sahl lost his physical control, suffering from blennorrhoea, so much so that he had to go to the privy several times an hour. To ease matters, he always kept a jar handy because he could not govern himself. When the time for prayer came round, however, the flow ceased. He would then perform his ablutions and pray, and resume as before. Whenever he mounted the pulpit, his blennorrhoea ceased completely, and all his pain would vanish. As soon as he came down from the pulpit, his ailment would show itself again. In all this, he never failed to observe even a little of the sacred Law.

On the day when Sahl's demise approached, his four hundred disciples were in attendance at his sickbed.

"Who will sit in your place, and who will preach from your pulpit?" they asked.

Now there was a certain Zoroastrian named Shadh-Del.

"Shadh-Del will sit in my place," answered Sahl, opening his eyes.

"The shaykh has lost his reason," muttered the disciples.

Having four hundred disciples, all men of learning and religion, he appoints a Zoroastrian to his place!"

"Cease your clamour!" cried Sahl. "Go and bring Shadh-Del to me."

The disciples fetched the Zoroastrian.

"When three days have elapsed after my death," Sahl said when his eyes fell on him, "after the afternoon prayers go into my pulpit and sit in my place, and preach to the people."

With these words Sahl died. Three days later, after the afternoon prayers, as many again assembled. Shadh-Del entered and mounted the pulpit, while the people stared.

"Whatever is this? A Zoroastrian, with the Magian hat on his head and a girdle tied about his waist!"

"Your leader," said Shadh-Del, "has made me his messenger to you. He said to me, 'Shadh-Del, has the time not come for you to cut the Magian girdle?' Behold, now I cut it."

And he took a knife and cut the girdle.

"He also said," he went on, "'Has the time not come for you to put off the Magian hat from your head?' Behold I have put it off."

Then Shadh-Del said, "I bear witness that there is no god but God, and I bear witness that Muḥammad is the Messenger of God." He went on, "The shaykh said, say, 'He who was your shaykh and your master counselled you well, and it is a rule of discipleship to accept the master's counsel. Behold, Shadh-Del has cut the outward girdle. If you wish to see me at the resurrection, I solemnly adjure you, every one of you, cut your inward girdles.'"

Great commotion arose in the congregation when Shadh-Del finished, and there followed amazing spiritual manifestations.

On the day when Sahl was borne to the grave, many people thronged the streets. Now there was a Jew of seventy years in Tostar; when he heard the noise and clamour, he ran out to see what was happening. As the procession reached him, he cried out,

"Men, do you see what I see? Angels are descending from heaven and stroking his bier with their wings!"

And immediately he uttered the attestation and became a Muslim.

One day Sahl was seated with his companions when a certain man passed by.

"This man holds a secret," Sahl said.

By the time they looked, the man had gone.

After Sahl's death, one of his disciples was sitting by his grave when the same man passed by.

"Sir," the disciple addressed him, "the shaykh who lies in this tomb once said that you hold a secret. By that God who has vouchsafed this secret to you, make me a demonstration."

The man pointed to Sahl's grave.

"Sahl, speak!" he said.

A voice spoke loudly within the tomb.

"There is no god but God alone, Who has no partner."

"They say," said the man, "that whosoever believes that there is no god but God, there is no darkness for him in the grave. Is that true or no?"

Sahl cried from the grave, "It is true!"

18

Ma'rūf al-Karkhī

Abū Maḥfūẓ Ma'rūf ibn Fayrūz al-Karkhī is said to have been born of Christian parents; the story of his conversion to Islam by the Shiite imam 'Alī ibn Mūsā al-Riḍā is generally discredited. A prominent mystic of the Baghdad school, he died in 200 (815).

How Ma'rūf al-Karkhī chose Islam

Ma'rūf al-Karkhī's mother and father were both Christians. When they sent him to school, his master said to him, "Say, God is the third of three."

"No," answered Ma'rūf. "On the contrary, He is God, the One."

The teacher beat him, but to no avail. One day the schoolmaster beat him severely, and Ma'rūf ran away and could not be found.

"If only he would come back," his mother and father said. "Whichever religion he wished to follow, we would agree with him."

Ma'rūf came to 'Alī ibn Mūsā al-Riḍā and accepted Islam at his hands. Some time passed. Then one day he made his way home and knocked at the door of his father's house.

"Who is there?" they asked.

"Ma'rūf," he replied.

"What faith have you adopted?"

"The religion of Muḥammad, the Messenger of God."

His mother and father immediately became Muslims.

After that Ma'rūf fell in with Dāwūd al-Ṭā'ī and underwent a severe discipline. He proved himself so devout and practised such austerities that the fame of his steadfastness was noised abroad.

Muḥammad ibn Manṣūr al-Ṭūsī relates that he encountered Ma'rūf in Baghdad.

"I observed a scar on his face. I said to him, 'I was with you yesterday and did not notice this mark then. What is it?' 'Do not ask about things that do not concern you,' he replied. 'Ask only about matters that are profitable to you.' 'By the right of Him we worship,' I pleaded, 'tell me.'

"Then he said, 'Last night I was praying, and I wished that I might go to Makkah and circumambulate the Ka'bah. I approached the well of Zamzam to take a drink of water. My foot slipped, and my face struck the well. That was how I got this scar.'"

Once Ma'rūf went down to the Tigris to make his ablutions, leaving his Qur'an and prayer rug in the mosque. An old woman stole in and took them, and went off with them. Ma'rūf ran after her. When he caught up with her he addressed her, lowering his head so that his eyes might not fall on her.

"Have you a son who can chant the Qur'an?"

"No," she replied.

"Then give me back the Qur'an. You can have the prayer rug."

The woman was amazed at his clemency, and set down both the Qur'an and the prayer rug.

"No, take the prayer rug," repeated Ma'rūf. "It is lawfully yours."

The woman hastened away in shame and confusion.

Anecdotes of Ma'rūf

One day Ma'rūf was walking along with a group of his followers when a gang of youths came that way. They behaved outrageously all the way to the Tigris.

"Master," Ma'rūf's companions entreated him, "pray to Almighty God to drown them all, that the world may be rid of their foul presence."

"Lift up your hands," Ma'rūf bade them. Then he prayed.

"O God, as Thou hast given them a happy life in this world, even so grant them a happy life in the world to come."

"Master, we know not the secret of this prayer," said his companions in astonishment.

"He with whom I am speaking knows the secret," Ma'rūf replied. "Wait a moment. Even now this secret will be revealed."

When the youths beheld the shaykh, they broke their lutes and poured away the wine they were drinking. Trembling overcame them, and they fell before the shaykh and repented.

"You see," Ma'rūf remarked to his companions. "Your desire has been fulfilled completely, without drowning and without anyone suffering."

Sarī al-Saqaṭī relates the following story.

One festival day I saw Ma'rūf picking date stones.

"What are you doing?" I asked him.

"I saw this child weeping," he told me. "I said, 'Why are you crying?' He told me, 'I am an orphan. I have no father and no mother. The other children have new clothes, and I have none. They have nuts, and I have none.' So I am gathering these stones to sell them and buy him nuts, then he may run along and play."

"Let me attend to this and spare you the care," I said.

Sarī went on, "I took the child and clothed him, and bought him nuts, and made him happy. Immediately I saw a great light shine in my heart, and I was transformed."

Ma'rūf had an uncle who was governor of the city. One day he was passing some wasteland when he observed Ma'rūf sitting there eating bread. Before him there was a dog, and Ma'rūf was putting one morsel in his own mouth and then one in the dog's.

"Are you not ashamed to eat bread with a dog?" cried his uncle.

"It is out of shame that I am giving bread to the poor," replied Ma'rūf.

Then he raised his head and called to a bird in the air. The bird flew down and perched on his hand, covering his head and eyes with his wings.

"Whosoever is ashamed before God," said Ma'rūf, "every thing is ashamed before him."

At once his uncle was filled with confusion.

One day Ma'rūf broke his ritual purity. Immediately he made ablution in sand.

"Why look," they said to him. "Here is the Tigris. Why are you making ablution in the sand?"

"It can be," he replied, "that I may be no more by the time I reach it."

A crowd of Shiites were jostling one day at the door of Riḍā, and they broke Ma'rūf al-Karkhī's ribs, so that he fell seriously ill.

Sarī al-Saqaṭī said to him, "Give me your last testament."

"When I die," said Ma'rūf, "take my shirt and give it in alms. I desire to go out of this world naked, even as I came naked from my mother's womb."

When he died, so great was the fame of his humanity and humility that men of all religions, Jews, Christians and Muslims alike, claimed him as one of them.

His servant reported that Ma'rūf had said, "Whoever is able to lift my bier from the ground, I am of that people."

The Christians were unable. The Jews were likewise unable to lift it. Then the Muslims came and lifted it. They prayed over him, and in that very place they committed him to the ground.

Sarī reported the following.

After Ma'rūf died I saw him in a dream. He was standing beneath the Throne with his eyes wide open, like one stupefied and distraught. A cry came from God to the angels.

"Who is this?"

"Lord God, Thou knowest best," the angels answered.

"It is Ma'rūf," came the Command. "He has become dazzled and stupefied by reason of Our love. Only by seeing Us will he come to his senses. Only by meeting Us will he rediscover himself."

19

Sarī al-Saqaṭī

Abū al-Ḥasan Sarī ibn al-Mughallis al-Saqaṭī, said to be a pupil of Maʻrūf al-Karkhī, uncle of al-Junayd, was a prominent figure in the Baghdad circle of Sufis and attracted the opposition of Aḥmad ibn Ḥanbal. A dealer in secondhand goods, he died in 253 (867) at the age of 98.

The career of Sarī al-Saqaṭī

Sarī al-Saqaṭī was the first man to preach in Baghdad on the mystic truths and the Sūḥ "unity". Most of the Sufi shaykhs of Iraq were his disciples. He was the uncle of Junayd and the pupil of Maʻrūf al-Karkhī; he had also seen Ḥabīb al-Rāʻī.

To begin with he lived in Baghdad, where he had a shop. Hanging a curtain over the door of his shop, he would go in and pray, performing several *rak'ahs* daily in this fashion.

One day a man came from Mount Lokam to visit him. Lifting aside the curtain, he greeted him.

"Shaykh So-and-so from Mount Lokam greets you," he said.

"He dwells in the mountains," commented Sarī. "So his efforts amount to nothing. A man ought to be able to live in the midst of the market and be so preoccupied with God, that not for a single instant is he absent from God."

It is said that in his transactions he never looked for a greater profit than five per cent. Once he bought almonds for sixty dinars. Almonds then became scarce. A broker called on him.

"Sell then," said Sarī.

"For how much?" the broker asked.

"Sixty-six dinars."

"But the price of almonds today is ninety dinars," the broker objected.

"It is my rule not to take more than five per cent," Sarī replied. "I will not break my rule."

"I also do not think it right to sell your goods for less," said the broker.

So the broker did not sell, and Sarī made no concession.

To start with Sarī used to sell odds and ends. One day the bazaars of Baghdad caught fire.

"The bazaars are on fire," they told him.

"Then I have also become free," he remarked.

Afterwards an inspection was made and it was found that Sarī's shop had not been burned. When he saw that, he gave all that he possessed to the poor and took up the Sufi way.

"What was the beginning of your spiritual career?" he was asked.

"One day," he said, "Ḥabīb al-Rā'ī passed by my shop. I gave him something to give to the poor. 'God be good to you,' he replied. The day he intoned that prayer the world lost its attraction for me.

"The following day Ma'rūf al-Karkhī came along bringing an orphan child. 'Clothe this child,' he begged me. I clothed the child. 'May God make the world hateful to your heart, and give you rest from this work,' he cried. I gave up worldly things completely, thanks to the blessing of Ma'rūf's prayer."

Sarī and the courtier

One day Sarī was preaching. Now one of the caliph's boon companions called Aḥmad al-Yazīd the Scribe came along in all his finery, surrounded by a crowd of servants and slaves.

"Wait while I listen to this fellow's sermon," he said. "We have been to a good few places where we should not have gone. I have had my fill of them."

He entered and sat down in Sarī's audience.

"In all eighteen thousand worlds," Sarī was saying, "there is nothing weaker than man. Yet of all the species that God has created, none is so disobedient to God's command as man. If he is good, he is so good that the very angels envy his estate; if he is bad, he is so bad that the Devil himself is ashamed to associate with him. What a marvellous thing is man, so weak, yet he disobeys God who is so mighty!"

These words were as an arrow sped from Sarī's bow into Aḥmad's soul. He wept so bitterly that he fainted. Then weeping he arose and returned to his home. That night he ate nothing and uttered not a word.

The next day he came on foot to Sarī's assembly, anxious and pale of cheek. When the meeting ended, he went home. On the third day he came again, alone and on foot. At the close of the assembly he came up to Sarī.

"Master," he said, "your words have taken hold of me and made the world loathsome to my heart. I want to give up the world and retire from the society of men. Expound to me the way of the Travellers."

"Which path do you want?" Sarī asked him. "That of the Way, or that of the Law? That of the multitude, or that of the elect?"

"Expound both," the courtier requested.

"The way of the multitude is this," said Sarī, "that you observe prayer five times daily behind the imam, and that you give alms–if it be in money, half a dinar out of every twenty. The way of the elect is this, that you thrust the world behind you altogether and do not concern yourself with any of its trappings; if you are offered it, you will not accept it. These are the two ways."

The courtier went out and set his face towards the

wilderness. Some days later an old woman with matted hair and scratches on her cheeks came to Sarī.

"Imam of the Muslims, I had a son, young and fresh of countenance," she said. "One day he came to your assembly laughing and strutting, and returned weeping and wailing. Now it is some days since he has vanished, and I do not know where he is. My heart is burning because he is parted from me. Please do something for me."

Her desperate pleading moved Sarī to compassion.

"Do not grieve," he told her. "Only good will ensue. When he comes back, I will inform you. He has abandoned the world and turned his back on the worldlings. He has become a true penitent."

After a space, one night Aḥmad reappeared.

"Go, tell the old lady," Sarī bade his servant. Then he looked upon Aḥmad. His cheeks were pale, he was wasted, the tall cypress of his stature was bent double.

"Kindly master," he cried, "forasmuch as you have guided me to peace and delivered me out of darkness, now may God give you peace and bestow upon you joy in both worlds."

They were thus conversing when Aḥmad's mother and his wife entered, bringing his little son. When his mother's eyes fell upon Aḥmad and she saw him in a state she had never seen before, she cast herself upon his breast. His wife too stood on one side of him wailing, whilst his son wept on the other. A hubbub went up from them all, and Sarī too burst into tears. The child flung himself at his father's feet. But despite all their efforts to persuade him to return home, it was all to no effect.

"Imam of the Muslims," Aḥmad protested, "why did you tell them? They will be my undoing."

"Your mother entreated me over and over, so at last I consented to tell her," Sarī replied.

Aḥmad prepared to return to the desert.

"While still alive, you have made me a widow and your child an orphan," cried his wife. "When he asks for you, what am I to do? There is no other way. You must take the boy with you."

"I will do that," Aḥmad answered.

He stripped him of his fine clothes and flung a strip of goat's wool over him. He put a wallet in his hand.

"Now be on your way," he said.

"I cannot stand this," cried his wife when she saw the child in that state. She snatched the boy to her.

"I give you charge of myself too," said Aḥmad. "If you so desire, set me free."

Then Aḥmad returned to the wilderness. Some years went by. Then one night, at the time of the prayer of sleeping, a man came to Sarī's hospice.

"Aḥmad sent me," he said, entering. "He says, 'My affairs have come to a critical pass. Help me.'"

Sarī went out. He found Aḥmad lying on the ground in a sepulchre, on the point of expiring. His tongue was still moving. Sarī listened. Aḥmad was saying, "For the like of this let the workers work." Sarī raised his head from the dust, wiped it, and laid it on his breast. Aḥmad opened his eyes and saw the shaykh.

"Master, you have come in time," he cried. "My affairs have come to a critical pass."

Then he ceased to breathe. Weeping, Sarī set out for the city to arrange his affairs. He saw a multitude coming forth from the city.

"Where are you going?" he asked.

"Do you not know?" they replied. "Last night a voice was heard from Heaven proclaiming, 'Whoever desires to pray over an elect friend of God, say, Go to the cemetery of Shūnīziyah.'"

Anecdotes of Sarī

Junayd reported the following.

One day when I visited Sarī I found him in tears.

"What happened?" I asked.

"The thought occurred to me," he replied, "that tonight I would hang out a jar for the water to cool. In a dream I saw a *ḥūrī* who told me, when I asked her who she belonged to, 'I belong to the man who does not hang out a jar for the water to get cool.' The *ḥūrī* then dashed my jar to the ground. See there!"

I saw the broken shards. For a long time the pieces still lay there.

The following was also reported by Junayd.

One night I had been sleeping peacefully, and when I awoke my secret soul insisted that I should go to the mosque of Shūnīziyah. I went there, and saw by the mosque a person of terrible mien. I was afraid.

"Junayd, are you afraid of me?" he asked.

"Yes," I replied.

"If you knew God as He should be known," he said, "you would fear none but Him."

"Who are you?" I demanded.

"Iblīs," he answered.

"I wanted to see you," I told him.

"The moment you thought of me, you forgot God without being aware of it," he said. "What was your object in wanting to see me?"

"I wanted to ask whether you had any power over the poor," I told him.

"No," he answered.

"Why is that?" I asked.

"When I want to trap them with worldly things, they flee to the next world," he said. "And when I want to trap them with the next world, they flee to the Lord, and there I cannot follow them."

"If you cannot master them, then do you see them?" I enquired.

"I see them," he answered. "When they are at concert and in ecstasy, I see the source of their lamentation."

With that he vanished. I entered the mosque, to find Sarī there with his head on his knees.

"He lies, that enemy of God," he said, raising his head. "They are too precious for Him to show them to Iblīs."

Sarī had a sister. She asked for permission to sweep his apartment, but he refused her.

"My life is not worthy of this," he told her.

One day she entered and saw an old woman sweeping out his room.

"Brother, you did not give me permission to wait upon you. Now you have brought one not of your kindred."

"Sister, let not your heart be troubled," Sarī replied. "This is the lower world. She fell in love with me, and was denied me. So now she asked permission of Almighty God to be a part of my life. She has been given the task of sweeping my chamber."

20

Aḥmad ibn Khiḍrūyah

Abū Ḥāmid Aḥmad ibn Khiḍrūyah al-Balkhī, a prominent citizen of Balkh married to the pious daughter of the governor of that city, associated with Ḥātim al-Aṣamm and Abū Yazīd al-Bisṭāmī. He visited Nishapur, and died in 240 (864) at the age of 95.

Aḥmad ibn Khiḍrūyah and his wife

Aḥmad ibn Khiḍrūyah had a thousand disciples, every one of whom walked on the water and flew in the air. Aḥmad dressed himself in soldier's uniform. Fāṭimah, his wife, was a portent in the Sufi way. She was a daughter of the Prince of Balkh. Having repented, she sent a messenger to Aḥmad.

"Ask my hand from my father."

Aḥmad did not respond. So she sent a second envoy.

"Aḥmad, I thought you were manlier than this. Be a guide, not a highwayman!"

Aḥmad then sent an emissary to ask her father for her hand. Her father, seeking God's blessing thereby, gave her to Aḥmad. Fāṭimah bade farewell to worldly concerns and found repose dwelling in solitude with Aḥmad.

So matters continued, until one day Aḥmad resolved to visit Abū Yazīd. Fāṭimah accompanied him, and when they entered Abū Yazīd's presence she lifted her veil from her face and engaged Abū Yazīd in conversation. Aḥmad was dismayed by this, jealousy overmastering his heart.

"Fāṭimah, what boldness was this you showed with Abū Yazīd?" he cried.

"You are intimate with my natural self. Abū Yazīd is intimate with my spiritual way. You rouse my passion, but he brings me to God," Fāṭimah replied. "The proof of this is that he can dispense with my company, whereas you need me."

Abū Yazīd was bold with Fāṭimah, until one day his eyes fell upon her hands and he noticed that they were stained with henna.

"Fāṭimah, why have you put on henna?" he asked.

"Abū Yazīd, until now you have never looked at my hands and noticed the henna," Fāṭimah replied. "Hitherto I have been at ease with you. Now that your eyes have fallen on my hands, it is unlawful for me to keep your company."

"I have petitioned God," said Abū Yazīd, "to make women in my eyes no more noticeable than a wall, and so

He has made them in my sight."

After that Aḥmad and Fāṭimah proceeded to Nishapur, where they were warmly received. When Yaḥyā ibn Mu'ādh al-Rāzī passed through Nishapur on his way to Balkh, Aḥmad wished to arrange a party for him. He consulted Fāṭimah.

"What do we need for a party for Yaḥyā?" he asked her.

"So many oxen and sheep," she told him. "Accessories too—so many candles and so much *'iṭir* of roses. Besides all this, we need several asses."

"Why, what is the reason for killing asses?" asked Aḥmad.

"When a nobleman comes to dine," explained Fāṭimah, "the dogs of the quarter must get a share of the feast."

Such was the spirit of true chivalry that imbued Fāṭimah that Abū Yazīd declared, "If any man desires to see a true man hidden in women's clothes, let him look at Fāṭimah."

Aḥmad ibn Khiḍrūyah wrestles with his soul

Aḥmad ibn Khiḍrūyah related the following.

For a long time I had repressed my carnal soul. Then one day a party set out for the wars, and a great desire to accompany them arose within me. My soul reminded me of a number of Traditions concerning the rewards in Heaven for fighting in the cause of God. I was amazed.

"My soul is not always so eager to obey," I said. "Perhaps this is because I always keep my soul fasting. My soul cannot endure hunger any longer, and wishes to break its fast." So I said, "I do not break the fast on a journey."

"I quite agree," replied my soul.

"Perhaps my soul says that because I command it to pray by night. It wishes to go on this journey so as to sleep at night and find rest." So I said, "I will keep you awake till dawn."

"I quite agree," said my soul.

I was still more amazed. Then I reflected that perhaps my soul said that because it wanted to mix with people, being weary of solitude and hoping to find solace in company. So I said, "Wherever I carry you, I will put you down in a place apart and will not sit with other men."

"I quite agree," my soul repeated.

Reduced to impotence, I had resorted to humble petition to God, praying that He might disclose to me the cunning machinations of my soul, or make my soul confess. Then my soul spoke.

"Every day you slay me a hundred times by opposing my desires, and other men are not aware. There at least in the wars I shall be killed once and for all and get deliverance, and the report will be noised through all the world, 'Bravo, Aḥmad ibn Khiḍrūyah! They killed him, and he achieved the martyr's crown.'"

"Glory be to Him," I cried, "who created a soul to be a hypocrite while alive, and a hypocrite still after death. It will never be a true Muslim, either in this world or the next. I thought that you were seeking to obey God. I did not realise that you were tying the girdle."

Thereafter I redoubled my struggle against my soul.

Anecdotes of Aḥmad ibn Khiḍrūyah

A thief broke into Aḥmad ibn Khiḍrūyah's house. He searched everywhere but could not find anything. He was about to leave disappointed when Aḥmad called out to him.

"Young fellow, take the bucket and draw water from the well and purify yourself, then attend to your prayers. When something comes I will give it to you, so that you shall not leave my house empty-handed."

The youth did as Aḥmad bade him. When daylight returned, a gentleman brought a hundred dinars and gave them to the shaykh.

"Take this as a reward for your night of prayer," he said to the thief.

The thief suddenly trembled all over. He burst into tears.

"I had mistaken the road," he cried. "I worked for God just one night, and He has favoured me so."

Repenting, he returned to God. He refused to take the gold, and became one of Aḥmad's disciples.

On one occasion Aḥmad came to a Sufi hospice wearing ragged clothes. In Sufi fashion he devoted himself wholly to spiritual tasks. The brethren of that hospice inwardly doubted his sincerity.

"He does not belong to this hospice," they whispered to their shaykh.

Then one day Aḥmad went to the well and his bucket fell in. The other Sufis upbraided him. Aḥmad came to the Superior.

"Recite the Fātiḥah, that the bucket may come up from the well," he begged.

"What kind of demand is this?" said the astounded shaykh.

"If you will not recite it," said Aḥmad, "then give me permission to do so."

The shaykh gave him leave, and Aḥmad recited the Fātiḥah. The bucket immediately rose to the surface. When the Superior saw this, he put his cap off his head.

"Young man, who are you, that my threshing-floor is but chaff in comparison with your grain?" he asked.

"Tell your companions," answered Aḥmad, "to look on travellers with less disrespect."

Once a man came to Aḥmad ibn Khiḍrūyah and said, "I am sick and poor. Teach me a way whereby I may be delivered out of this trial."

"Write the name of each trade there is on a piece of paper," replied Aḥmad. "Put the papers in a pouch, and bring them to me."

The man wrote down all the trades and brought the papers to Aḥmad. Aḥmad thrust his hand in the pouch and drew out one paper. The name "thief" was written on it.

"You must become a thief," he told the man.

The man was astounded. For all that he rose up and betook himself to a gang of highway robbers.

"I have a fancy for this job," he told them. "How do I do it?"

"There is one rule governing this work," they told him. "Whatever we order you to do, you must do it."

"I will do exactly as you order," he assured the thieves.

He was with them for a number of days. Then one day a caravan arrived. The thieves waylaid the caravan, and brought to their new colleague one of the travellers who was a man of great wealth.

"Cut his throat," they told him.

The man hesitated.

"This prince of the thieves has killed so many people. It is better," he said to himself, "that I should slay him rather than this merchant."

"If you have come to do a job, you must do as we order," said the head of the gang. "Otherwise, go and find other work."

"If I must carry out orders," said the man, "I will carry out God's orders, not this thief's."

Drawing his sword, he let the merchant go and struck off the head of the prince of the thieves. Seeing this, the other bandits fled. The goods remained intact, and the merchant escaped with his life. He gave the man much gold and silver, so that he became independent.

Once a dervish was received by Aḥmad in hospitality. Aḥmad lit seventy candles.

"This is not pleasing to me," said the dervish. "Making a fuss bears no relation to Sufism."

"Go then," said Aḥmad, "and extinguish every candle I have not lit for the sake of God."

All that night the dervish was pouring water and earth, but could not extinguish even one of the candles.

"Why so surprised?" Aḥmad addressed the dervish next morning. "Come with me, and you will see things really to wonder at."

They went off and came to the door of a church. When the Christian deacons saw Aḥmad and his companions, the archdeacon invited them to enter. He laid a table and bade Aḥmad to eat.

"Friends do not eat with foes," Aḥmad observed.

"Offer us Islam," said the archdeacon.

So Aḥmad offered them Islam, and seventy of his retinue accepted conversion. That night Aḥmad had a dream in which God spoke to him.

"Aḥmad, you lit seventy candles for Me. I have lit for you seventy hearts with the light of the Faith."

21

Yaḥyā ibn Mu'ādh

Abū Zakariyyā' Yaḥyā ibn Mu'ādh al-Rāzī, a disciple of Ibn Karram, left his native town of Rayy and lived for a time in Balkh, afterwards proceeding to Nishapur where he died in 258 (871). A certain number of poems are attributed to him.

Yaḥyā ibn Mu'ādh al-Rāzī and his debt

Yaḥyā ibn Mu'ādh had incurred a debt of a hundred thousand dirhams. He had borrowed all this money and expended it on gifts to holy warriors, pilgrims, poor men, scholars and Sufis. His creditors were pressing him for repayment, and his heart was much preoccupied thereby.

One night he dreamed that the Prophet spoke to him.

"Yaḥyā, be not over-anxious, for I am pained on account of your anxiety. Arise, go to Khurasan. There a woman has set aside three hundred thousand dirhams to meet the hundred thousand you have borrowed."

"Messenger of God," cried Yaḥyā, "which is that city, and who is that person?"'

"Go from city to city and preach," said the Prophet. "Your words bring healing to men's hearts. Just as I have come to you in a dream, so now I will visit that person in a dream."

So Yaḥyā came to Nishapur. They set up a pulpit for him before the cupola.

"Men of Nishapur," he cried, "I have come here at the direction of the Prophet, on him be peace. The Prophet declared, 'One will discharge the debt you owe.' I have a debt of a hundred thousand silver dirhams. Know that always my words possessed a beauty, but now this debt has come as a veil over that beauty."

"I will give fifty thousand dirhams," one man volunteered.

"I will give forty thousand," offered another.

Yaḥyā declined to accept their gifts.

"The Master, peace be upon him, indicated one person," he said.

He then began to preach. On the first day seven corpses were removed from the gathering. Then, seeing that his debt was not discharged in Nishapur, Yaḥyā set out for Balkh. There he was detained for a while to preach. He extolled riches over poverty. They gave him a hundred thousand dirhams. But his words did not please a certain shaykh living in those parts, seeing that he had preferred riches.

"May God not bless him!" he exclaimed.

When Yaḥyā left Balkh he was set on by highwaymen and robbed of all the money.

"That is the result of that shaykh's prayer," they said.

So he proceeded to Herat, some say by way of Merv. There he related his dream. The daughter of the Prince of Herat was in the audience. She sent him a message.

"Imam, cease worrying about the debt. The night the Prophet spoke to you in a dream, he also spoke to me. I said, 'Messenger of God, I will go to him.' 'No,' the Prophet replied, 'he will come to you.' I have therefore been waiting for you. When my father gave me in marriage, the things others receive in copper and brass he made for me of silver and gold. The silver things are worth three hundred thousand dirhams. I bestow them on you. But I have one requirement, that you preach here for four days more."

Yaḥyā held forth for four days longer. On the first day ten corpses were taken up, on the second twenty-five, on the third forty, and on the fourth seventy. Then on the fifth day Yaḥyā left Herat with seven camels' loads of silver. When he reached Balham, being accompanied by his son, transporting all that wealth, his son demurred.

"When he enters the town, he must not give it all immediately to the creditors and the poor and leave me with nothing of it."

At dawn Yaḥyā was communing with God, his head bowed to the ground. Suddenly a rock fell on his head.

"Give the money to the creditors," he cried. Then he expired.

The men of the Way lifted him on their shoulders and bore him to Nishapur, where they laid him in the grave.

Yaḥyā ibn Mu'ādh al-Rāzī and his brother

Yaḥyā ibn Mu'ādh had a brother who went to Makkah and took up residence near the Ka'bah. From there he wrote a letter to Yaḥyā.

"Three things I desired. Two have been realised. Now one remains. Pray to God that He may graciously grant that one desire as well. I desired that I might pass my last years in the noblest place on earth. Now I have come to the Sacred Territory, which is the noblest of all places. My second desire was to have a servant to wait on me and make ready my ablution water. God has given me a seemly servant-girl. My third desire is to see you before I die. Pray to God that he may vouchsafe this desire."

Yaḥyā replied to his brother as follows.

"As for your saying that you desired the best place on earth, be yourself the best of men, then live in whatever place you wish. A place is noble by reason of its inhabitants, not vice versa.

"Then as for your saying that you desired a servant and have now got one, if you were really a true and chivalrous man, you would never have made God's servant your own servant, detaining her from serving God and diverting her to serve yourself. You should yourself be a servant. You desire to be a master, but mastership is an attribute of God. Servanthood is an attribute of man. God's servant must be a servant. When God's servant desires a station proper to God, he makes himself a Pharaoh.

"Finally, as to your saying that you desire to see me, if you were truly aware of God, you would never remember me. So associate with God, that no memory of your brother ever comes into your mind. There one must be ready to sacrifice one's son; how much more a brother! If you have found Him, what am I to you? And if you have not found Him, what profit will you gain from me?"

22

Shāh ibn Shujā‘

Abū al-Fawāris Shāh ibn Shujā‘ al-Kirmānī, said to be of a princely family and author of works on Sufism which have not survived, died sometime after 270 (884).

Shāh ibn Shujā‘ al-Kirmānī and his children

Shāh ibn Shujā‘ al-Kirmānī had one son. On his breast he had written in green the word Allah. In due course the boy, overcome by the wayward impulses of youth, amused himself by strolling with lute in hand. He had a fine voice, and as he sauntered he would play the lute and sing tearful tunes.

One night, being drunk, he went out on to the streets playing his lute and singing songs. When he came to a certain quarter, a bride newly come there rose up from her husband's side and came to look at him. The husband thereupon awoke and, missing his wife, also stared at the spectacle.

"Boy," he called to him, "has not the time come to repent?"

These words struck the youth to the heart.

"It has come. It has come," he cried.

Rending his robe and breaking his lute, he betook himself to his room and for forty days ate nothing. Then he emerged and took his way.

"What I was vouchsafed only after forty years, he has been granted after forty days," remarked Shāh ibn Shujā'.

Shāh ibn Shūjā' also had a daughter. The kings of Kirmān asked for her hand in marriage. He requested three days' grace, and during those three days he went from mosque to mosque, till at last he caught sight of a dervish praying earnestly. Shāh ibn Shūjā' waited patiently until he had finished his prayers, then he addressed him.

"Dervish, do you have any family?"

"No," the dervish replied.

"Do you want a wife who can recite the Qur'an?"

"Who is there who will give such a wife to me?" said the dervish. "All I possess is three dirhams."

"I will give you my daughter," said Shāh ibn Shūjā'. "Of these three dirhams you possess, spend one on bread and one on 'aṭṭar of roses, then tie the marriage-knot."

They agreed accordingly. That same night Shāh ibn Shūjā' despatched his daughter to his house. Entering the dervish's house, the girl saw some dry bread beside a jug of water.

"What is this bread?" she demanded.

"It remained over from yesterday. I kept it for tonight," the dervish told her.

Thereupon the girl made to leave the house.

"I knew," the dervish observed, "that the daughter of Shāh ibn Shujā' would never be able to live with me and put up with my poverty."

"Sir, it is not on account of your lack of means that I am leaving you," the girl replied. "I am leaving because of your lack of faith and trust, in that you set aside bread from yesterday, not relying on God's provision for the morrow. At the same time I am surprised at my father. For twenty years he has kept me at home, always saying 'I will give you to a godfearing man.' Now he has given me to a fellow who does not rely on God for his daily bread."

"Is there any atonement for this sin?" the dervish asked.

"Yes," said the girl. "The atonement is, that only one of the two remains in this house—myself, or the dry bread."

23

Yūsuf ibn al-Ḥusayn

Abū Ya'qūb Yūsuf ibn al-Ḥusayn al-Rāzī travelled extensively from his native Rayy, visiting Arabia and Egypt where he met and studied under Dhū al-Nūn al-Miṣrī. He returned to preach in Rayy, dying there in 304 (916).

The conversion of Yūsuf ibn al-Ḥusayn al-Rāzī

The spiritual career of Yūsuf ibn al-Ḥusayn al-Rāzī began in the following circumstances. He was travelling in Arabia with a company of his fellows when he arrived in the territory of a certain tribe. When the daughter of the Prince of the Arabs caught sight of him, she fell madly in love with him, for he was possessed of great beauty. Waiting her opportunity, the girl suddenly flung herself before him. Trembling, he left her and departed to a more distant tribe.

That night he was sleeping with his head on his knees, when he dreamed he was in a place the like of which he had never seen. One was seated on a throne there in kingly wise, surrounded by a company clad in green robes. Wishful to know who they might be, Yūsuf edged his way towards them. They made way for him, treating him with much respect.

"Who are you?" he enquired.

"We are angels," they replied, "and he who is seated on the throne there is Yūsuf, upon whom be peace. He has come to pay a visit to Yūsuf ibn al-Ḥusayn."

Let Yūsuf tell the rest of the story in his own words. Overcome with weeping, I cried, "Who am I, that God's prophet should come to visit me?"

Thereupon Yūsuf, upon him be peace, descended from his throne, took me in his embrace, and seated me on the throne.

"Prophet of God," I cried, "who am I that you should be so gracious to me?"

"In the hour," Yūsuf answered, "when that lovely girl flung herself before you, and you committed yourself to God and sought His protection, God displayed you to me and the angels. God said, 'See, Yūsuf! You are that Yūsuf who inclined after Zulaykhah only to repel her. He is that Yūsuf who did not incline after the daughter of the King of the Arabs, and fled.' God Himself sent me with these angels to visit you. He sends you the good tidings that you are of God's elect."

Then Yūsuf added, "In every age there is a portent. The

portent in this age is Dhū al-Nūn al-Miṣrī. He has been vouchsafed the Greatest Name of God. Go unto him."

When Yūsuf awoke (the narrative continues) he was filled with a great ache. A powerful yearning overmastered him, and he turned his face towards Egypt, desirous to know the Great Name of God. Arriving at the mosque of Dhū al-Nūn, he spoke the greeting and sat down. Dhū al-Nūn returned his greeting. For a whole year Yūsuf sat in a remote corner of the mosque, not daring to question Dhū al-Nūn.

After a year Dhū al-Nūn asked, "Whence is this young man come?"

"From Rayy," he replied.

For another year Dhū al-Nūn said nothing, and Yūsuf continued to occupy the same corner.

At the end of the second year Dhū al-Nūn asked, "On what errand has this young man come?"

"To visit you," he replied.

For another year Dhū al-Nūn was silent. Then he asked, "Does he require anything?"

"I have come that you may teach me the Greatest Name," Yūsuf replied.

For a further year Dhū al-Nūn held his peace. Then he handed Yūsuf a wooden vessel covered over.

"Cross the River Nile," he told him. "In a certain place there is an elder. Give this bowl to him, and remember whatever he tells you."

Yūsuf took the bowl and set forth. When he had gone a part of the way, a temptation assailed him.

"What is this moving about in this bowl?"

He uncovered the bowl. A mouse jumped out and ran away. Yūsuf was filled with bewilderment.

"Where am I to go? Shall I go to this elder, or return to Dhū al-Nūn?"

Finally he proceeded to the elder, carrying the empty bowl. When the elder beheld him, he smiled.

"You asked him for God's Great Name?" he asked.

"Yes!" Yūsuf replied.

"Dhū al-Nūn saw your impatience, and gave you a mouse," the elder said. "Glory be to God! You cannot look after a mouse. How then will you keep the Greatest Name?"

Put to shame, Yūsuf returned to the mosque of Dhū al-Nūn.

"Yesterday I asked leave of God seven times to teach you the Greatest Name," Dhū al-Nūn told him. "God did not give permission, meaning that the time is not yet. Then God commanded me, 'Make trial of him with a mouse.' When I made trial of you, this is what happened. Now return to your own city, till the proper time comes."

"Before I leave, give me a testament," Yūsuf begged.

"I will give you three testaments," said Dhū al-Nūn, "one great, one middling, and one small. The great testament is this, that you forget all that you have read, and wash away all that you have written, so that the veil may be lifted."

"This I cannot do," said Yūsuf.

"The middling testament is this, that you forget me and tell my name to no man," said Dhū al-Nūn. "To say that my monitor declared this or my shaykh ordered that is all self-praise."

"This too I cannot do," said Yūsuf.

"The small testament is this," said Dhū al-Nūn, "that you counsel men and call them to God."

"This I can do, God willing," said Yūsuf.

"On condition, however," Dhū al-Nūn added, "that in counselling men you do not have men in sight."

"So I will do," Yūsuf promised.

Then he proceeded to Rayy. Now he came from the nobility of Rayy, and the citizens came out to welcome him. When he began his preaching, he expounded the mystic realities. The people, accustomed to exoteric doctrine, rose up in anger against him, for in that time only formal learning was current. Yūsuf fell into disrepute, to such an extent that no one came to his lectures.

One day he turned up to preach as usual, but seeing no one in the hall he was about to return home. At that moment an old woman called to him.

"Did you not promise Dhū al-Nūn that in counselling men you would not have them in sight, and would speak only for God's sake?"

Astonished at her words, Yūsuf began to preach. Thereafter he continued so for fifty years, whether anyone was present or no.

Yūsuf ibn al-Ḥusayn and Ibrāhīm al-Khawwāṣ

Ibrāhīm al-Khawwāṣ became a disciple of Yūsuf ibn al-Ḥusayn. Through the blessing of his companionship he attained to such remarkable spiritual advancement that he would travel through the desert without provision and mount. It is to him that we owe the following story.

One night (Ibrāhīm said) I heard a voice which said to me, "Go and say to Yūsuf ibn al-Ḥusayn, 'You are of the rejected'." So grievous were these words for me to hear, that if a mountain had been flung on my head that would have been easier to bear than that I should repeat what I had heard to him.

Next night I heard in even more menacing tones, "Say to him, 'You are of the rejected'." Rising up, I washed and begged God's forgiveness, and sat in meditation till the third night, when the same voice came to me. "Say to him, 'You are of the rejected'. If you do not deliver this message, you will receive such a blow that you will not rise again."

So full of sorrow I rose up and went to the mosque, where I saw Yūsuf seated in the prayer-niche.

"Do you remember any verse?" he asked me when he saw me.

"I do," I replied. I recollected a verse in Arabic which I recited to him. Delighted, he rose up and remained on his feet for a long while, tears as if flecked with blood streaming from his eyes. Then he turned to me.

"Since first light till now," he said, "they have been reciting the Qur'an before me, and not one drop came to my eyes. Now through that single verse you spoke such a state has manifested–a veritable torrent has flowed from my eyes. Men are right when they say I am a heretic. The voice of the Divine Presence speaks truly, that I am of the rejected. A man who is so affected by a verse of poetry, while the Qur'an makes no impression whatever upon him—he is surely rejected."

I was bewildered by what I saw and heard. My belief in him was shaken. Afraid, I rose up and set my face towards the desert. By chance I fell in with Khiḍr, who addressed me.

"Yūsuf ibn al-Ḥusayn has received a blow from God. But his place is in the topmost heights of Heaven. A man must stride so far and manfully upon the path of God, that even if the hand of rejection is struck against his forehead, yet his place is in the topmost heights of Heaven. If he falls on this path from kingship, yet he will not fall from the rank of minister."

Yūsuf ibn al-Ḥusayn and the handmaiden

A certain merchant in Nishapur bought a Turkish handmaiden for a thousand dinars. He had a creditor living in another town, and wanted to go in haste and recover his money from him. In Nishapur there was no one in whom he trusted sufficiently to commit the girl to his keeping. So he called on Abū 'Uthmān al-Ḥīrī and explained his predicament to him. At first Abū 'Uthmān refused, but the merchant implored him earnestly.

"Admit her into your harem. I will return as soon as possible."

So finally he consented, and the merchant departed. Involuntarily Abū 'Uthmān's glance fell upon the girl and he fell uncontrollably in love with her. Not knowing what to do, he rose up and went to consult his teacher Abū Ḥafṣ al-Ḥaddād.

"You must go to Rayy, to consult Yūsuf ibn al-Ḥusayn," Abū Ḥafṣ told him.

Abū 'Uthmān set out at once towards Iraq. When he reached Rayy he enquired where Yūsuf ibn al-Ḥusayn was living.

"What have you to do with that damned heretic?" they asked him. "You look a religious man yourself. His society will be bad for you."

They said many such things to him, so that Abū 'Uthmān regretted having come there and returned to Nishapur.

"Did you see Yūsuf ibn al-Ḥusayn?" Abū Ḥafṣ asked him.

"No," he replied.

"Why not?"

"I heard that he was such and such a man," Abū 'Uthmān related what the people of Rayy had told him. "So I did not go to him, but returned."

"Go back and see him," Abū Ḥafṣ urged.

Abū 'Uthmān returned to Rayy and again asked for Yūsuf's house. The people of Rayy told him a hundred times as much as before.

"But I have important business with him," he explained.

So at last they indicated the way to him. When he reached Yūsuf's house, he saw an old man seated there. A beardless and handsome boy was before him, laying before him a bowl and a goblet. Light streamed from his face. Abū 'Uthmān entered and spoke the greeting and sat down. Shaykh Yūsuf began to speak, and uttered such lofty words that Abū 'Uthmān was amazed.

"For God's sake, master," he cried, "with such words and such contemplating, what is this state that is on you? Wine, and a beardless boy?"

"This beardless boy is my son, and very few people know that he is my son," Yūsuf replied. "I am teaching him the Qur'an. A bowl happened to be thrown into this dustbin. I picked it out and washed it and filled it with water, so that anyone who wished for water might drink, for I had no pitcher."

"For God's sake," Abū 'Uthmān repeated, "why do you act so that men say of you what they say?"

"I do it for this reason," Yūsuf answered, "so that no one may send a Turkish handmaiden to my house as a confidant."

When Abū 'Uthmān heard these words he fell down at the shaykh's feet. He realised that the man had attained a high degree.

24

Abū Ḥafṣ al-Ḥaddād

Abū Ḥafṣ ‘Amr ibn Salamah al-Ḥaddād, a blacksmith of Nishapur, visited Baghdad and met Junayd who admired his devotion; he also encountered al-Shiblī and other mystics of the Baghdad school. Returning to Nishapur, he resumed his trade and died there in 265 (879).

How Abū Ḥafṣ al-Ḥaddād was converted

As a young man Abū Ḥafṣ al-Ḥaddād fell in love with a serving wench so desperately that he could not compose himself.

“There is a Jewish magician living in the suburbs of Nishapur,” his friends told him. “He will prescribe for you.”

Abū Ḥafṣ went and described his situation to the Jew.

"You must not pray for forty days, or obey God in any way, or do any good deed," the Jew advised him. "You should not mention God's name on your tongue, or form any good intentions whatsoever. Then I may devise something by magic to procure you your goal."

Abū Ḥafṣ conducted himself accordingly for forty days. Then the Jew composed the talisman, but without success.

"Without doubt some good has come into being through you," the Jew said. "Otherwise I am certain that this object would have been achieved."

"I have done nothing," Abū Ḥafṣ assured him. "The only thing I can think of is that as I came here I kicked a stone out of the way so that no one might trip over it."

"Do not vex the God," said the Jew, "whose command you gainsay for forty days, and who of His generosity suffered not to go to waste even this little trouble you took."

These words kindled a fire within Abū Ḥafṣ's heart. So strong was it, that he was converted at the hands of the Jew.

He continued to practise his trade as a blacksmith, concealing the miracle that had happened to him. Every day he earned one dinar. At night he gave his earnings to the poor, and dropped money into widows' letter-boxes surreptitiously. Then at the time of the prayer of sleep he would go begging, and break his fast on that. Sometimes he would gather the remains of leeks or the like which people had washed in the public basin and make his meal of them.

So he continued for a time. Then one day a blind man passed through the market reciting this verse: "I take refuge with God from the accursed Satan. In the Name of God, the Merciful, the Compassionate. Yet there would appear to them from God that they never reckoned with." This verse occupied his heart, and something came upon him so that he lost consciousness. In place of the tongs he put his hand in the furnace and pulled out the red-hot iron. He laid it on the anvil, and the apprentices set to hammering it. They then noticed he was turning the iron with his hand.

"Master, what ever is this?" they cried.

"Strike!" he shouted at the apprentices.

"Master, where shall we strike?" they asked. "The iron is clean."

Thereupon Abū Ḥafṣ came to his senses. He saw the red-hot iron in his hand and heard the cry, "It is clean. Where shall we strike?" Flinging the iron from his hand, he abandoned his shop for any to pillage.

"I desired so long deliberately to give up this work, and failed, until this event came upon me and forcibly wrested me from myself. Though I kept trying to abandon this work, all was to no purpose until the work abandoned me."

And he applied himself to severe self-discipline, and took up the life of solitude and meditation.

Abū Ḥafṣ al-Ḥaddād and Junayd

Abū Ḥafṣ resolved to make the pilgrimage. Now he was an illiterate and did not understand Arabic. When he came to Baghdad, the Sufi disciples whispered together.

"It is a great disgrace that the Shaykh of Shaykhs of Khurasan should require an interpreter to understand their language."

Junayd sent his disciples out to welcome him. Abū Ḥafṣ knew what "our companions" were thinking, and at once he began to speak in Arabic so that the people of Baghdad were amazed at the purity of his speech. A number of the great scholars gathered before him and questioned him on self-sacrificing love.

"You are able to express yourselves. You say," Abū Ḥafṣ replied.

"As I see it," said Junayd, "true self-sacrifice means that you should not regard yourself as self-sacrificing, and that you should not attribute to yourself whatever you may have done."

"Excellent," commented Abū Ḥafṣ. "But as I see it, self sacrifice means acting with justice towards others, and not seeking justice for oneself."

"Act on that, our companions," said Junayd.

"To act rightly requires more than words," retorted Abū Ḥafṣ.

"Rise up, our companions," Junayd commanded when he heard this reply. "Abū Ḥafṣ exceeds in self-sacrifice Adam and all his seed."

Abū Ḥafṣ kept his companions in great awe and discipline. No disciple dared to be seated before him or to cast his glance on him. They always stood before him, and would not sit without his command. He himself sat in their midst like a sultan.

"You have taught your companions the manners due to a sultan," Junayd observed.

"You can only see the superscription," Abū Ḥafṣ replied. "But from the address it is possible to indicate what is in the letter."

Then Abū Ḥafṣ said, "Order them to make broth and *ḥalwā*."

Junayd directed one of his disciples to make them. When he brought the dishes, Abū Ḥafṣ proceeded.

"Call a porter and put them on his head. Let him carry them until he is tired out. Then, whatever house he has reached, let him call out, and whoever comes to the door, let him give them to him."

The porter obeyed these instructions. He went on until he felt tired and could go no farther. Setting the dishes down by the door of a house, he called out. The owner of the house, an elder, replied.

"If you have brought broth and *ḥalwā*, I will open the door."

"I have," replied the porter.

"Bring them in," said the elder, opening the door.

"I was amazed," the porter related. "I asked the old man, 'What is going on? How did you know that I had brought broth and *ḥalwā*?' The old man answered, 'Last night when I was at my prayers, the thought came into my mind that my children had been begging me for them for a long time. I know that my prayer has not been in vain.'"

There was a disciple who waited on Abū Ḥafṣ with great politeness. Junayd gazed at him many times, for his conduct delighted him.

"How many years has he been in your service?" he asked Abū Ḥafṣ.

"Ten years," Abū Ḥafṣ replied.

"He is perfect in his manners and wonderfully dignified. An admirable young man," Junayd observed.

"Yes," Abū Ḥafṣ said. "Seventeen thousand dinars he has expended on our cause, and borrowed another seventeen thousand and spent them as well. And yet he dares not address one question to us."

Abū Ḥafṣ then set out into the desert. He gave the following account of what happened to him there.

In the desert (he said) I saw Abū Turāb. I had not eaten for sixteen days. I approached a pool to drink, and fell to meditating.

"What has halted you here?" asked Abū Turāb.

"I was waiting to see as between knowledge and certainty, which would prevail, that I might adopt the victor," I replied. "If the victory went to knowledge, I would drink; if certainty prevailed, I would continue on my way."

"You are certainly advancing," said Abū Turāb.

When Abū Ḥafṣ arrived in Makkah he saw a throng of

poor and destitute pilgrims there. He desired to bestow something on them, and became extremely agitated. He was so overcome by his feelings that he picked up a stone and cried,

"By Thy majesty, if Thou dost not give me something I will break all the lamps in the mosque."

He then proceeded to circle the Ka'bah. Immediately a man came up to him and gave him a purse of gold, which he spent on the poor.

Having completed the pilgrimage, he returned to Baghdad. There Junayd's companions went out to welcome him.

"What present have you brought us from your journey?" asked Junayd.

"Perhaps one of 'our companions' is unable to live as he should," replied Abū Ḥafṣ. "This that I have to say can be my offering. If you observe in a brother a lack of good manners, discover in yourself an excuse for him and excuse him to yourself accordingly. If the dust of misunderstanding does not rise as a result of that excuse, and you are in the right, discover some better excuse and excuse him to yourself again. If still the dust does not rise, go on inventing another excuse, even to forty times. If still the dust does not rise, and you are in the right, and those forty excuses do not measure up to the fault he has committed, then sit down and say to yourself, 'What a stubborn and unenlightened soul you are! What an opinionated and unmannerly and boorish fellow you are! Your brother offers forty excuses for his offence, and you do not accept them and continue in the same course! I have washed my hands of you. You know what you want; do as you please.'"

Junayd marvelled at these words. "Who can have such strength?" he asked himself.

Abū Ḥafṣ and Shiblī

Shiblī gave hospitality to Abū Ḥafṣ for four months. Every day he produced a different kind of dish and several sorts of sweetmeat.

When Abū Ḥafṣ came to bid him farewell, he said, "Shiblī, when you come to Nishapur I will teach you true entertainment and generosity."

"Why, what have I done, Abū Ḥafṣ?" asked Shiblī.

"You took too great pains. Extravagance is not the same as generosity," said Abū Ḥafṣ. "One should treat a guest exactly as oneself. That way, his coming will not be a burden to you, and his departure will not be an occasion of gladness. When you go to extravagant lengths, his coming is burdensome to you and his departure a relief. No man who feels like that towards a guest is truly generous."

When Shiblī came to Nishapur he stayed with Abū Ḥafṣ. Forty persons were in the party, and at night Abū Ḥafṣ lit forty-one lamps.

"Did you not say one should not act extravagantly?" remarked Shiblī.

"Then get up and put them out," answered Abū Ḥafṣ.

Shiblī got up, but for all his efforts he could not extinguish more than one lamp.

"Shaykh, how is this?" he asked.

"You were forty persons, emissaries of God. For the guest is an emissary of God. Naturally I lit a lamp in the name of each one, for the sake of God, and one for myself. Those forty which I lit for God you were unable to put out, but the one lit for myself you extinguished. All that you did in Baghdad you did for my sake; I did what I did for God's sake. So the former was extravagance, the latter not."

25

Abū al-Qāsim al-Junayd

Abū al-Qāsim al-Junayd ibn Muḥammad al-Khazzāz al-Nihāwandī, son of a glass-merchant and nephew of Sarī al-Saqaṭī, close associate of al-Muḥāsibī, was the greatest exponent of the 'sober' school of Sufism and elaborated a theosophical doctrine which determined the whole course of orthodox mysticism in Islam. He expounded his theories in his teachings, and in a series of letters written to various contemporaries which have survived. The head of a large and influential school, he died in Baghdad in 298 (910).

Early years

From childhood Junayd was given to spiritual sorrow, and was an earnest seeker after God, well disciplined, thoughtful and quick of understanding and of a penetrating intuition.

One day he returned home from school to find his father in tears.

"What happened?" he enquired.

"I took something by way of alms to your uncle Sarī," his father told him. "He would not accept it. I am weeping because I have given my whole life to save these five dirhams, and then this offering is not meet for one of the friends of God to receive."

"Give me the money, and I will give it to him. That way he may take it," said Junayd.

His father gave him the dirhams, and Junayd went off. Coming to his uncle's house, he knocked at the door.

"Who is that?" came a voice.

"Junayd," answered the boy. "Open the door and take this due offering of alms."

"I will not take it," cried Sarī.

"I beg you to take it, by the God who has dealt so graciously with you and so justly with my father," cried Junayd.

"Junayd, how did God deal graciously with me and justly with him?" demanded Sarī.

"God was gracious to you," Junayd replied, "in vouchsafing you poverty. To my father God was just in occupying him with worldly affairs. You are at liberty to accept or reject as you please. He, whether he likes it or not, must convey the due alms on his possessions to the one deserving of it."

This answer pleased Sarī.

"Child, before I accept these alms, I have accepted you."

So saying, Sarī opened the door and took the alms. He assigned to Junayd a special place in his heart.

Junayd was only seven years old when Sarī took him on the pilgrimage. In the Mosque of the Sanctuary the question of thankfulness was being discussed by four hundred shaykhs. Each shaykh expounded his own view.

"You also say something," Sarī prompted Junayd.

"Thankfulness," said Junayd, "means that you should not disobey God by means of the favour which He has bestowed on you, nor make of His favour a source of disobedience."

"Well said, O consolation of true believers," cried the four hundred. They were unanimous that a better definition could not be devised.

"Boy," said Sarī, "it will soon come to pass that your special gift from God will be your tongue."

Junayd wept when he heard his uncle say this.

"Where did you acquire this?" Sarī demanded.

"From sitting with you," Junayd replied.

Junayd then returned to Baghdad, and took up selling glasses. Every day he would go to the shop and draw down the blind and perform four hundred *rak'ahs*. After a time he abandoned the shop and withdrew to a room in the porch of Sarī's house, where he busied himself with the guardianship of his heart. He unrolled the prayer rug of meticulous watchfulness, that no thought of anything but God should pass through his mind.

Junayd put to the proof

For forty years Junayd persevered in his mystic course. For thirty years he would perform the prayer before sleeping, then stand on his feet repeating "Allah" until dawn, saying the dawn prayer with the ablution he had made the previous night.

"After forty years had gone by," he said, "the conceit arose in me that I had attained my goal. Immediately a voice out of Heaven spoke to me. 'Junayd,' the voice cried, 'the time has come for Me to show you the loop of your Magian girdle.' When I heard these words I exclaimed, 'O God, what sin has Junayd committed?' 'Do you look for a more grievous sin than this,' the voice replied, 'that you exist?'"

Junayd sighed and lowered his head.

"He who is not worthy of union," he murmured, "all his good works are but sins."

He continued to sit in his room, crying "Allah, Allah" all night. The long tongues of slander were shot out against him, and his conduct was reported to the caliph.

"He cannot be inhibited without any proof," said the caliph.

"Many people are being seduced by his words," they stated.

Now the caliph possessed a handmaiden of unrivalled beauty. He had purchased her for three thousand dinars, and loved her dearly. The caliph commanded that she should be arrayed in fine raiment and precious jewels.

"Go to such a place," she was instructed. "Stand before Junayd and unveil your face, and display your jewels and raiment to him. Say to him, 'I am possessed of much wealth, and my heart has grown weary of worldly affairs. I have come so that you may propose to me, that in your society I may devote myself to the service of God. My heart finds repose in no one but you.' Display yourself to him. Unveil, and strive your utmost to persuade him."

She was despatched to Junayd with a servant. The handmaiden came before Junayd and carried out her instructions to the letter and more. Involuntarily Junayd's glance fell upon her. He remained silent and made no answer. She repeated her story. Junayd hung his head; then he raised his head.

"Ah," he exclaimed, and breathed on the girl. The girl immediately fell to the ground and expired.

The servant who had accompanied returned to the caliph and reported what had transpired. Fire fell upon the caliph's soul, and he repented of what he had done.

"He who acts towards others as he should not, sees what he ought not to see," he observed. Rising up, he proceeded to call on Junayd.

"Such a man one cannot summon to attend on oneself," he commented. "O master, how did your heart allow it," asked the caliph, "to consume so fair a form?"

"Prince of the Believers," Junayd replied, "your compassion for the faithful was so great, that you desired to cast to the winds my forty years of discipline, of keeping vigil and self mortification. Yet who am I in all this? Do not, that you may not be done to!"

After that Junayd's affairs prospered. His fame reached to all parts of the world. However much he was persecuted, his repute increased a thousandfold. He began to preach. As he explained once, "I did not preach to the public until thirty of the great saints indicated to me that it was proper for me to call men to God."

"For thirty years I sat watching over my heart," he said. "Then for ten years my heart watched over me. Now it is twenty years that I know nothing of my heart and my heart knows nothing of me."

"For thirty years," he said again, "God has spoken with Junayd by the tongue of Junayd, Junayd not being there at all, and men were not aware."

Junayd preaches

When Junayd's tongue was loosened to utter great words, Sarī al-Saqaṭī urged him that it was his duty to preach in public. Junayd was hesitant, not desiring to do so.

"While the master is there, it is not seemly for the disciple to preach," he demurred.

Then one night Junayd saw the Prophet in a dream.

"Preach," the Prophet said.

Next morning he arose to go and report to Sarī, but he found Sarī standing at the door.

"Hitherto," Sarī told him, "you were inhibited, waiting for others to tell you to preach. Now you must speak, because your words have been made the means of a whole world's salvation. You would not speak when the disciples asked you to. You did not speak when the shaykhs of

Baghdad interceded with you. You did not speak at my urging. Now that the Prophet has commanded you, you must speak."

"God forgive me," Junayd replied. "How did you know that I saw the Prophet in a dream?"

"I saw God in a dream," Sarī explained. "God said, 'I have sent the Messenger to tell Junayd to preach from the pulpit.'"

"I will preach then," consented Junayd. "Only on one condition, that it be to no more than forty persons."

One day Junayd was preaching, and forty persons were present. Of these eighteen expired, and twenty-two fell to the ground unconscious. They were lifted up and carried to their homes.

Another day Junayd was preaching in the cathedral. In the congregation there was a Christian lad, but no one knew that he was a Christian. He approached Junayd and said, "According to the Prophet's saying, 'Beware of the insight of the believer, for he sees by the light of God.'"

"The pronouncement is," replied Junayd, "that you should become a Muslim and cut your Christian girdle, for this is the time of Muslimdom."

The boy immediately became a Muslim.

After Junayd had preached a number of times, the people cried out against him. He gave up preaching, and retired to his room. For all that he was urged to resume, he would not do so.

"I am content," he replied. 'I cannot contrive my own destruction."

Some time later he mounted the pulpit and began to preach without any prompting.

"What was the inner wisdom in this?" he was asked.

"I came upon a Tradition," he replied, "according to which the Prophet said, 'In the last days the spokesman of the people will be he that is the worst of them. He will preach to them.' I know that I am the worst of the people. I am preaching because of what the Prophet said, so that I may not oppose his words."

Anecdotes of Junayd

Once Junayd's eye pained him, and he sent for the doctor.

"If your eye is throbbing, do not let any water get to it," the doctor advised.

When he had gone, Junayd performed his ablutions and prayed, and then went to sleep. When he awoke, his eye was well again. He heard a voice saying, "Junayd forsook his eye to gain Our good pleasure. If with the same intention he had begged of Us all the inhabitants of Hell, his petition would have been granted."

The physician called and saw that his eye was healed.

"What did you do?" he asked.

"I performed the ablutions for prayer," Junayd answered.

Thereupon the physician, who was a Christian, declared his conversion.

"This is the Creator's cure, not the creature's," he commented. 'It was my eye that was sick, not yours. You were the physician, not I."

"Once," said Junayd, "I desired to see Iblīs. I was standing at the mosque door, when I espied an old man approaching from afar. As I looked at him, a horror rose within me.

"Who are you?" I demanded.

"Your desire," he replied.

"Accursed one," I cried, "what thing held you back from prostrating to Adam?"

"How do you imagine, Junayd," Iblīs replied, "that I would prostrate to any but Him?"

Junayd described his sense of bewilderment, hearing the Devil say these words.

"A voice addressed me in my secret heart," he recalled. "The voice said, 'Say, You are a liar. If you had been a true servant, you would have obeyed His command. You would never have disregarded it and flirted with denial.'"

When Iblīs heard this speech, he uttered a loud cry. "By Allah, Junayd, you have destroyed me!" And he vanished.

"In these days brothers in the faith have become few and far to find," a man said in Junayd's presence.

"If you are looking for someone to bear your burden, such men are indeed few and far to find," Junayd countered. "But if you are seeking to carry somebody's load, such brothers are to be found in plenty with me."

Whenever Junayd spoke on the Divine Unity, every time he began with a different expression which no one could understand. One day Shiblī was in Junayd's audience and uttered the word Allah.

If God is absent, to mention the absent One is a sign of absence, and absence is a thing proscribed," Junayd said. "If God is present, to mention His name while contemplating Him present is a mark of irreverence."

A man brought five hundred dinars and offered them to Junayd.

"Do you possess anything besides this?" Junayd asked him.

"Yes, a lot," the man replied.

"Do you need more?"

"Yes, I do."

"Then take it away," Junayd said. "You have a better right to it. I possess nothing, and I need nothing."

A man rose up where Junayd was preaching and began to beg.

"This man is perfectly healthy," thought Junayd. "He can earn his living. Why does he beg, and impose on himself this humiliation?"

That night Junayd dreamed that a covered dish was set before him.

"Eat," he was bidden.

When he lifted the lid, he saw the man who had begged lying dead on the dish.

"I do not eat the flesh of men," he protested.

"Then why did you do so in mosque yesterday?" he was asked.

Junayd realised that he had been guilty of slander in his heart, and that he was being taken to task for an evil thought.

"I woke in terror," Junayd recollected. "I purified myself and said two *rak'ahs,* then I went out to search for the beggar. I saw him on the bank of the Tigris, picking out of the water scraps of vegetables people had washed there and eating them. Raising his head, he saw me approaching and addressed me. 'Junayd,' he said, 'have you repented of the thoughts you had concerning me?' 'I have,' I replied. 'Then go. *It is He Who accepts repentance from His servants.* This time keep a watch over your thoughts.'"

"I learned sincere belief from a barber," Junayd recalled, and he told the following story.

Once when I was in Makkah, a barber was trimming a gentleman's hair. I said to him, "For the sake of God, can you shave my hair?"

"I can," he said. His eyes filling with tears, he left the gentleman still unfinished.

"Get up," he said. "When God's name is spoken, everything else must wait."

He seated me and kissed my head, and shaved off my hair. Then he gave me a screw of paper with a few small coins in it.

"Spend this on your needs," he said.

I thereupon resolved that the first present that came my way I would give him in charity. Not long afterwards a bag of gold arrived from Basra. I took it to the barber.

"What is this?" he asked.

"I made up my mind," I explained, "that the first present that came my way I must give to you. This has just arrived."

"Man," he exclaimed, "have you no shame before God? You said to me, 'For the sake of God, shave my hair.' Then you give me a present. Have you ever known of anyone doing a deed for the sake of God and taking payment for it?"

A thief had been hanged in Baghdad. Junayd went and kissed his feet.

"Why did you do that?" he was asked.

"A thousand compassions be upon him!" he replied. "He proved himself a true man at his trade. He did his work so perfectly, that he gave his life for it."

One night a thief entered Junayd's room. Finding nothing there but a shirt, he took that and fled. Next day Junayd was passing through the bazaars when he saw his shirt in the hands of a broker who was selling it to a customer.

"I require an acquaintance who will testify that it is your property, before I buy it," the prospective purchaser said.

"I am ready to testify that it belongs to him," said Junayd, stepping forward.

The man then bought the shirt.

An old woman came to Junayd and said, "My son is missing. Say a prayer that he may return."

"Be patient," Junayd told her.

The woman waited patiently for several days. Then she returned.

"Be patient," Junayd repeated.

This happened several times. At last the old woman came and announced, "My patience is exhausted. Pray to God."

"If you speak the truth," said Junayd, "your son has returned. God says, He who answers the constrained, when he calls unto Him."

Junayd then offered up a prayer. When the woman returned to her house, her son had come.

A disciple formed the notion that he had attained the degree of perfection.

"It is better for me to be alone," he thought.

So he withdrew into a corner and sat there for a space. It so fell out that every night he was brought a camel and told, "We will convey you to Paradise." He would sit on the camel and ride until he arrived at a pleasant and cheerful spot thronged with handsome folk and abounding in choice dishes and running water. There he would remain till dawn; then he would fall asleep, and awake to find himself in his cell. He now became proud and very conceited.

"Every night I am taken to Paradise," he would boast.

His words came to Junayd's ears. He at once arose and proceeded to his cell, where he found him putting on the greatest airs. He asked him what had happened, and he told the whole story to the shaykh.

"Tonight when you are taken there," Junayd told him, "say thrice, 'There is no strength nor power save with God, the Sublime, the Almighty.'"

That night the disciple was transported as usual. He disbelieved in his heart what the shaykh had told him, nevertheless, when he reached that place he uttered as an experiment, "There is no strength nor power." The company all screamed and fled, and he found himself on a dunghill with bones lying before him. Realising his error, he repented and repaired to Junayd's circle. He had learned that for a disciple to dwell alone is mortal poison.

A disciple of Junayd's was dwelling in seclusion in Basra. One night a sinful thought entered his mind. He looked in a mirror and saw that his face had turned black. Stupefied, he tried every device he could think of, but in vain. He was so ashamed that he showed his face to no one. Three days went by, then the blackness gradually grew less.

Unexpectedly a knock came on his door.

"Who is it?" the disciple asked.

'I have come with a letter from Junayd," said the caller.

The disciple read the letter.

"Why do you not conduct yourself becomingly in the presence of Glory? For three days and nights I have had to work as a fuller, to change your face from black to white."

There was a certain disciple of Junayd's who was taken to task one day over a small matter. Shamefaced, he fled and came no more to the convent. Several days later Junayd was passing through the market with his companions when he suddenly espied that disciple. The disciple in shame took to his heels.

"A bird of ours has flown from the snare," said Junayd, turning back his companions, and following on the disciple's heels.

Looking back, the disciple saw the shaykh coming, so he quickened his pace. Presently he reached a place where there was no exit, and in shame he turned his face to the wall. Presently the shaykh appeared on the scene.

"Where are you making for, master?" the disciple asked.

"When a disciple is up against the wall, there the shaykh can be of use," replied Junayd.

He then led the disciple back to the convent. The disciple fell at his feet and begged God's forgiveness. Those who witnessed the spectacle were deeply moved, and many repented.

The shaykh Junayd had a disciple whom he loved above all the others. The other disciples were moved to jealousy, a fact which the shaykh realised by his mystic intuition.

"He is superior to you in manners and understanding," he told them. "That is what I had in view; let us make an experiment, so that you may also realise it."

Junayd commanded twenty birds to be brought to him.

"Each of you take one," he told his disciples. "In a place where no one can see you kill it, then bring it back."

All the disciples went off and killed and brought back the birds—all, that is, except that favourite disciple. He brought his bird back alive.

"Why did you not kill it?" Junayd asked him.

"Because the master said it must be done in a place where no one can see," the disciple answered. "Wherever I went, God saw."

"You see the measure of his understanding!" Junayd exclaimed. "Compare that with that of the others."

All the other disciples begged God's forgiveness.

Junayd had eight special disciples who carried out his every thought. One day the notion occurred to them that they must go to the holy war. Next morning Junayd ordered his servant to make all preparations for the wars. He then set out to fight together with those eight disciples.

When the lines of battle were drawn up, a champion stepped forth from the ranks of the infidels and martyred all eight.

"I looked up to heaven," said Junayd, "and I saw nine litters standing by. As each of the eight was martyred his spirit was lifted up on a litter, until one remained over empty. 'That one must be meant for me,' I thought, and I joined the battle-ranks once more. Then the champion who had slain my eight companions came up and addressed me. 'Abū al-Qāsim, that ninth litter is for me. You return to Baghdad, and be the shaykh of the community. Offer me Islam.'

"So he became a Muslim. With the same sword with which he had slain the eight disciples, he slew a like number of infidels. Then he achieved martyrdom himself. His soul," Junayd concluded, "was also placed in that litter, and all vanished."

There was a sayyid called Naṣirī who was on the pilgrimage intent. When he reached Baghdad he went to visit Junayd.

"Whence comes the sayyid?" Junayd enquired when greetings had been said.

"From Gilan," he replied.

"Of whose sons are you?" asked Junayd.

"I am descended from 'Alī the Prince of the Believers, God be well pleased with him," the man answered.

"Your forefather wielded two swords," said Junayd. "One against the unbelievers, the other against himself. Now, sayyid, you who are his soṇ, which of these two do you employ?"

The sayyid wept bitterly when he heard these words and grovelled before Junayd.

"Master, my pilgrimage is here," he exclaimed. "Show me the way to God."

"Your breast is the private sanctuary of God," said Junayd. "So far as you are able, admit naught unsanctified into the private sanctuary."

"That is all I want to know," said the sayyid.

The death of Junayd

When death was near at hand Junayd bade them to lay the table and to set out a meal.

"I wish to give up the ghost whilst my companions are eating a bowl of soup."

The first agony assailed him.

"Give me the water of ablution," he said.

By chance they forgot to let the water run between his fingers. At his behest this slip was made good, and he then proceeded to the prostration, weeping.

"Chief of the Order," his disciples protested, "with all the service and obedience to God which you have sent ahead of you what time is this for prostration?"

"Never was Junayd more in need than now," he replied.

Straightway he began to recite the Qur'an, and went on reciting.

"What, you recite the Qur'an?" asked a disciple.

"Who has the better right to than I, seeing that this hour the scroll of my life will be rolled up, and I shall see my seventy years' obedience and service suspended in the air by a single thread? Then a wind will come and swing it to and fro, so that I shall not know whether it is a wind bringing separation or union. On one side of me will stretch the causeway between Heaven and Hell and on the other side the Angel of Death. The Judge whose attribute is justice will be there awaiting me, unwavering in perfect equity." Junayd continued, "A road has been laid before me, and I know not by which road I shall be taken."

He completed the whole Qur'an, then he recited seventy verses of Sūrah al-Baqarah. The second agony seized him.

"Say Allah," they prompted him.

"I have not forgotten," he replied. He grasped the rosary until four of his fingers were crooked about it, and one let it go.

"In the Name of God, the Merciful, the Compassionate," he cried.

And he closed his eyes and yielded up the ghost.

When the time for washing his body came, the one performing the rite wished to bathe his eyes in water. A voice cried from Heaven, "Withhold your hand from the eyes of My friend. His eyes were closed upon My Name, and shall not be opened save at the meeting with Me." He then tried to open Junayd's fingers. The voice cried, "The finger that has been crooked upon My Name shall not be opened save by My command."

When they lifted up his body on the bier, a white dove perched upon a corner of the bier. For all that they sought to drive it away, it would not go. At last the dove cried, "Trouble not yourselves and me. My claws have been fastened to the corner of the bier by the nail of Love. That is why I am perched here. Do not trouble yourselves; today his body passes to the care of the cherubim. Were it not for your clamour, his body would have flown with us in the sky like a white falcon.

26

‘Amr ibn ‘Uthmān

Abū ‘Abdullah ‘Amr ibn ‘Uthmān al-Makkī, a disciple of Junayd, visited Isfahan and died in Baghdad in 291 (904) or 297 (910).

‘Amr ibn ‘Uthmān al-Makkī and the Book of the Treasure

It is said that one day ‘Amr ibn ‘Uthmān al-Makkī had written down on a sheet of paper a translation of the Book of the Treasure. He had put it under his prayer rug and gone to purify himself. While he was at his ablutions report reached him, and he sent his servant to recover the script. When the servant turned up the prayer rug he could not find the paper. He told his master.

“They have taken it and gone,” said ‘Amr ibn ‘Uthmān. “The person who has taken that Book of the Treasure,” he added, “will soon have his hands and feet cut off. He will be put on the gibbet, and burned, and his ashes will be scattered to the winds. He ought to have arrived at the Treasure, whereas he has stolen the Book of the Treasure."

Now these were the contents of the Book of the Treasure.

In the time when the spirit entered the bodily frame of Adam, God commanded all the angels to prostrate themselves. All lowered their heads to the ground. Iblīs said, "I will not make prostration. I will gamble my life away, and I will see the secret, even though it may be that I shall be accursed and called rebel and sinner and hypocrite."

Iblīs did not make prostration. So he saw and knew the secret of Man. Consequently none but Iblīs is apprised of Man's secret, and none but Man knows the secret of Iblīs. So Iblīs became apprised of the secret of Man because he did not prostrate himself, so that he saw that he was preoccupied with beholding the secret. Iblīs was rejected by all, for they had exposed the Treasure to his eyes.

"We committed a Treasure to the earth," they said. "The condition attached to the Treasure is this, that one person will see it, but they will cut off his head so that he may not betray it."

"In this grant me a respite," cried Iblīs. "Do not slay me. But I am the Man of the Treasure. They exposed the Treasure to my eyes, and these eyes will not escape."

The Sword of I Care Not declared, "Thou *art among the ones that are respited.* We grant you respite, but We cause you to be held in suspicion. So if We do not destroy you,

you will be suspect and a liar, and none will hold you to be a speaker of the truth. So they will say, *He was one of the jinn, and committed ungodliness against his Lord's command.*"

He is Satan. How should he speak the truth? Therefore he is accursed and rejected and abandoned and ignored.

This was the translation of the Book of the Treasure by 'Amr ibn 'Uthmān.

'Amr ibn 'Uthmān on love

'Amr ibn 'Uthmān stated the following in his Book of Love.

Almighty God created the hearts seven thousand years before the souls, and He kept them in the Garden of Intimacy. He created the Secrets seven thousand years before the hearts, and kept them in the Degree of Union.

Every day God caused the souls to receive three hundred and sixty glances of Grace and to hear three hundred and sixty words of Love. Every day He manifested to the hearts three hundred and sixty delights of Intimacy. Every day He revealed Beauty three hundred and sixty times to the Secrets.

So they beheld every thing in the world of being, and saw none more precious than themselves. A vainglory and conceit manifested amongst them.

God therefore put them to the trial. He imprisoned the Secret in the soul. He confined the soul in the heart. He detained the heart in the body. Then He compounded in them reason.

God sent the Prophets with commandments. Then every one of them set about searching for his proper station. God commanded them to pray. So the body went into prayer; the heart attained Love; the soul achieved Propinquity; the Secret was at rest in Union.

'Amr ibn 'Uthmān writes to Junayd

When 'Amr ibn 'Uthmān was in Makkah, he wrote to Junayd, Jurayrī, and Shiblī in Iraq. This was his letter.

"Know, you who are the great ones and elders of Iraq, say to every man who yearns after the land of Ḥijāz and the beauty of the Ka'bah, *You would never reach it, excepting with great distress of spirit.* And say to every man who yearns after the Carpet of Propinquity and the Court of Glory, *You would never reach it, excepting with great distress* of soul."

At the bottom of the letter 'Amr wrote: "This is a missive from 'Amr ibn 'Uthmān al-Makkī and these elders of Ḥijāz who are all with Him and in Him and by Him. If there be any of you who entertains high aspiration, say to him, Come upon this road wherein are two thousand fiery mountains and two thousand stormy and perilous seas. If you are not of this rank, make no false pretension, for to false pretension nothing is given."

When the letter reached Junayd, he gathered the elders of Iraq together and read it to them. Then he said, "Come, say what he meant by these mountains."

"By these mountains," they replied, "he meant naughting. Until a man is naughted a thousand times and a thousand times revived, he does not attain the Court of Glory."

"Of these two thousand fiery mountains," Junayd remarked, "I have crossed only one."

"You are lucky to have crossed one," said Jurayrī. "Up to now I have gone only three steps."

Shiblī burst into tears.

"You are fortunate, Junayd, to have crossed one mountain," he cried. "And you are fortunate, Jurayrī, to have gone three steps. Up to now I have not even seen the dust from afar."

27

Abū Sa'īd al-Kharrāz

Abū Sa'īd Aḥmad ibn 'Īsā al-Kharrāz al-Baghdādī, a cobbler by trade, met Dhū al-Nūn al-Miṣrī and associated with Bishr al-Ḥāfī and Sarī al-Saqaṭī. To him is attributed the formulation of the mystical doctrine of passing-away (from human attributes) and continuance (in God). Author of several books including some which have survived, the date of his death is uncertain but probably occurred between 279 (890) and 286 (899).

The doctrine of Abū Sa'īd al-Kharrāz

Abū Sa'īd al-Kharrāz was called "the Tongue of Sufism". They gave him this nickname because no one in this community possessed a tongue of mystic truth such as he. He composed four hundred books on the theme of disassociation and detachment, and was indeed a nonpareil.

Originally of Baghdad, Abū Sa'īd met Dhū al-Nūn al-Miṣrī and associated with Bishr and Sarī al-Saqaṭī. He was the first to speak of the states of "passing-away" and "continuance" in the mystical sense, summing up his whole doctrine in these two terms. Certain of the theologians who followed the exoteric school disapproved of the subtleties of his teaching, and condemned him of blasphemy on account of certain expressions which they found in his works. In particular they criticised his *Book of the Secret,* especially a passage occurring in it which they failed to understand properly. This is where Abū Sa'īd states, "A servant of God who has returned to God and attached himself to God and has come to dwell in propinquity to God, such a man has completely forgotten himself and all other than God, so that if you were to say to him, 'Where are you from, and what do you seek?' he would have no other answer but simply 'God'."

Another passage in Abū Sa'īd's writings to which objection has been taken is where he says, "If a certain one of these mystics is asked, 'What do you want?' he replies 'God'. If he is in such a state that all the parts of his body become vocal, they all say 'God'. For his members and joints are fully bathed in the Light of God, so that he is drawn into God. So far has he reached in propinquity to God, that in his presence no one is able to say 'God'; for whatever proceeds there proceeds from Reality unto Reality and from God to God. Since here, in the state of ordinary men, nothing has resulted from God, how can anyone say 'God'? Here all reason of reasoning men ends in bewilderment."

"All men," Abū Sa'īd once said, "have been given the choice between remoteness and propinquity. I chose remoteness, because I could not support propinquity. Similarly Luqmān said, 'I was given the choice between wisdom and prophecy. I chose wisdom, because I could not support the burden of prophecy.'"

Abū Sa'īd related the following dreams.

Once I dreamed that two angels came down from Heaven and said to me, "What is truthfulness?" I replied, "Fulfilling one's covenants." "You have spoken the truth," they said, then they both departed to Heaven.

Again I dreamed that I saw the Prophet. He said to me, "Do you love me?" I replied, "Excuse me. My love for God has preoccupied me from loving you." The Prophet said, "Whoso loves God loves me."

On another occasion in a dream I saw Iblīs. I took a stick to beat him. I heard a Heavenly voice say, "He is not afraid of a stick. He is afraid of the light which is in your heart." Then I said to Iblīs, "Come!" Iblīs replied, "What can I do with you? You have cast out the thing whereby I beguile men." "What is that?" I asked. "The world," he answered. Then as he left me Iblīs looked back and said, "There is a little thing in you men by which I attain my purpose." "What is that?" I asked. "Sitting with boys," Iblīs replied.

When I was in Damascus I again saw the Prophet in a dream. He approached me leaning on Abū Bakr and 'Umar. I was reciting a verse of poetry, tapping my breast with my hunger. The Prophet said, "The evil of this is greater than its good." He meant that one should not practise audition.

Abū Sa'īd al-Kharrāz had two sons, one of whom predeceased him. One night he saw him in a dream.

"Son, what has God done with you?" Abū Sa'īd asked.

"He brought me close to Him and made much of me," his son replied.

"Son, make me testament," Abū Sa'īd begged.

"Father," his son answered, "do not entertain dark thoughts of God."

"Tell me more!"

"Father, if I speak, you will not be able to bear it."

"I ask God to assist me," said Abū Sa'īd.

"Father," said the son, "do not suffer a single shirt to come between yourself and God."

It is said that in all the thirty years which Abū Sa'īd lived after this dream he never wore a shirt again.

28

Abū al-Ḥusayn al-Nūrī

Abū al-Ḥusayn Aḥmad ibn Muḥammad al-Nūrī, a native of Baghdad of a family from Khurasan, was a pupil of Sarī al-Saqaṭī and a faithful companion of al-Junayd. A leading figure of the Baghdad circle, he composed some fine mystical poetry. He died in 295 (908).

The self-discipline of Abū al-Ḥusayn al-Nūrī

Abū al-Ḥusayn, who followed the same rules of conduct as Junayd, was called Nūrī ("the Man of Light") because whenever he spoke and the night was dark, a light would issue from his mouth so that the whole house became bright. Another explanation of his nickname is that he declared inmost secrets by the light of intuition. Yet a third version is that he had a retreat in the desert where he used to worship all the night through. People would go out to watch, and would see a light mounting from his cell and gleaming through the night.

When he first embarked on his mystical career, every morning early he would set out from his house for the shop, and pick up a few loaves. These he would distribute as alms, afterwards proceeding to mosque where he worshipped till the noon prayers, only then going on to his shop. His household imagined that he had eaten something in the shop, whilst the people in the shop supposed that he had eaten at home. He continued this practice for twenty years without anyone being aware of the true facts of his case.

Nūrī gave the following account of himself.

For years I struggled, restraining myself in prison and turning my back on other men. Despite all my austerities, the way did not become open to me.

"I must do something to mend my affairs," I said to myself. "Otherwise let me die and escape from this carnal soul."

"Body," I then said, "for many years you have followed your own lust and desire, eating and seeing and hearing, going and taking, sleeping and enjoying yourself and gratifying your passion. All this has been most harmful to you. Now enter the chamber, that I may fetter you and put as a collar round your neck all your dues to God. If you remain steadfast so, you will attain felicity; if not, at least you will die on the path of God!"

So I acted on the path of God. Now I had heard that the hearts of the mystics were delicate organs, knowing the secret of whatever they saw and heard. Not finding this in myself, I said, "The pronouncements of the prophets and the saints are true. Perhaps I have played the hypocrite in my striving, and the defect is due to myself. Here there is no room for difference of opinion. Now," I went on, "I will go around myself and see what it is."

I gazed into myself, and the fault was this, that my carnal soul and my heart were united. When the carnal soul is one with the heart, that is disastrous; for whatever shines upon the heart, the carnal soul seizes its portion of it. So I realised that this was the cause of my dilemma; all that entered my heart from the Court of God, my carnal soul seized its part of it.

Thenceforward, whatever gratified my carnal soul, that I went not about, but clutched something other. For instance, if prayer or fasting or almsgiving was agreeable to my carnal soul, or solitude or associating with my fellows, I proceeded to do the contrary, till I had cast out all those things and all gratification had been cut away. Then mystic secrets began to manifest in me.

"Who are you?" I asked.

"I am the pearl of the mine of undesire," came the answer. "Now tell the disciples, My mine is the mine of undesire, and my pearl is the pearl of the mine of unpurpose."

Then I walked down to the Tigris and stood between two skiffs.

"I will not go," I said, "until a fish falls into my net."

At last a fish fell into my net. When I drew it up I cried, "Praise be to God that my affairs have turned out well!"

I went to Junayd and told him, "A grace has been vouchsafed to me!"

"Abū al-Ḥusayn," Junayd replied, "if it had been a snake and not a fish that fell into your net, that would truly have been a sign of grace. But since you yourself intervened, it is a deception, not a grace. For the mark of a grace is that you cease to be there at all."

Nūrī before the Caliph

When Ghulām Khalīl declared hostilities against the Sufis, he went to the caliph and denounced them.

"A group have appeared on the scene," he announced, "who sing songs and dance and utter blasphemies. They parade about all day, and hide themselves in catacombs, and preach. These men are heretics. If the Prince of the Believers will issue the command for them to be slain, the doctrine of heresy will be exterminated, for they are the chief of the heretics. If this thing is done by the hand of the Prince of the Believers, I guarantee him an ample reward."

The caliph immediately ordered that they—Abū Ḥamzah, Raqqām, Shiblī, Nūrī, and Junayd—should be brought before him. This done, he commanded them to be slain. The executioner first made to slay Raqqām; Nūrī sprang up and thrust himself forward fearlessly and took Raqqām's place.

"First kill me, laughing for joy," he cried.

"Sir, this is not your time yet," the executioner said to him. "The sword is not a thing wielded in haste."

"My way is based upon preference," Nūrī explained. "I prefer my comrades above myself. The most precious thing in this world is life. I wish to devote these few remaining moments to serving my brethren, that I may have sacrificed life itself. This I do, albeit to my view one moment in this world is dearer than a thousand years in the next. For this world is an abode of service, and the other world is an abode of propinquity; and propinquity for me is in service."

They reported these words of Nūrī's to the caliph, who marvelled at his sincerity and equitableness. He ordered the execution to be stayed and referred their case to the *qāḍī* to examine.

"They cannot be proscribed without proof," said the *qāḍī*. Now he knew that Junayd was supreme in many sciences and had heard Nūrī speak. So he said, referring to Shiblī, "I will question this madman on a point of law which he will never be able to answer."

"How much is to be paid in poor-tax on twenty dinars?" he asked.

"Twenty and a half dinars," Shiblī replied.

"Whoever instituted that kind of poor-tax?" demanded the *qāḍī*.

"Abū Bakr the Great," Shiblī answered. "He gave forty thousand dinars and kept nothing back."

"Yes, but what is this half-dinar you spoke about?"

"That is a fine," replied Shiblī. "The man kept the twenty dinars to himself, so he must pay half a dinar in addition."

The *qāḍī* then questioned Nūrī on a point of law. Nūrī replied instantly, and the *qāḍī* was reduced to confusion. Nūrī then spoke.

"*Qāḍī*, you have asked all these questions, and you have asked nothing at all relevant. For God has servants who stand through Him, and move and rest through Him, who live all through Him and abide in contemplation of Him. If for a single instant they held back from contemplating Him, their souls would go out of them. Through Him they sleep, through Him they eat, through Him they take, through Him they go, through Him they see, through Him they hear and through Him they are. This is the true science, not that on which you put questions."

Bewildered, the *qāḍī* sent a message to the caliph.

"If these men are atheists and heretics, than I give judgement that on the whole face of the earth not one unitarian exists."

The caliph summoned the prisoners.

"Is there anything you want?" he asked them.

"Yes," they replied. "We want you to forget us. We want you neither to honour us with your approval nor to banish us with your rejection. For us your rejection is the same as your approval, your approval as your rejection."

The caliph wept bitterly and dismissed them with all honour.

Anecdotes of Nūrī

One day Nūrī saw a man twirling his moustaches while at prayer.

"Take your hand away from the moustaches of God," he cried.

These words were reported to the caliph. The lawyers declared unanimously that by uttering them Nūrī had lapsed into infidelity. He was haled before the caliph.

"Did you speak those words?" the caliph demanded.

"Yes," Nūrī replied.

"Why did you say them?" asked the caliph.

"To whom does the servant of God belong?" countered Nūrī.

"To God," answered the caliph.

"And to whom did the moustaches belong?" Nūrī pursued.

"To Him to whom the servant belonged," concluded the caliph. "Praise be to God, who preserved me from slaying him," he afterwards added.

"I saw a light gleaming in the Unseen," said Nūrī. "I gazed at it continually, until the time came when I had wholly become that light."

One day Junayd went to visit Nūrī. Nūrī fell to the ground before Junayd complaining of injustice.

"My battle has waxed fierce, and I have no more strength to fight," he said. "For thirty years, whenever He has appeared I have vanished, and whenever I appear He is absent. His presence is in my absence. For all that I supplicate Him, His answer is 'Either I am to be, or you.'"

"Look upon a man," said Junayd to his companions, "who has been sorely tried and bewildered by God. Such must be the state of affairs," he added, turning to Nūrī, "that whether He is veiled by you or revealed through you, you shall no more be you, and all shall be He."

A party of men went to Junayd and said, "For a number of days and nights now Nūrī has been going around with a brick in his hand, saying 'God, God.' He eats nothing and drinks nothing and does not sleep. Yet he performs the prayers at the proper times and observes all the ritual of the prayers."

"He is sober. He is not in a state of having passed away," Junayd's companions said. "That is proved by the fact that he observes the times of prayer and knows to perform the ritual. That is a mark of conscious effort, not of passing away. One who has passed away is aware of nothing."

"That is not the case," replied Junayd. "What you say is not true. Men in ecstasy are 'preserved'; God watches over them, lest they be excluded from service at the time of service."

Junayd then went to call on Nūrī.

"Abū al-Ḥusayn," he addressed him, "if you know that shouting is of profit with Him, tell me and I will also shout. If you know that satisfaction with Him is better, then practise resignation, that your heart may be at rest.'

Nūrī ceased his shouting forthwith.

"What an excellent teacher you are for us!" he exclaimed.

Shiblī was preaching, and Nūrī entered the hall and stood on one side.

"Peace be upon you, Abū Bakr," he called out.

"And upon you be peace, Prince of the Hearts," Shiblī replied.

"Almighty God," Nūrī went on, "would not be well pleased with a man of learning imparting his learning when he does not put it into practice. If you practice what you preach, keep your high station. If not, then come down!"

Shiblī considered, and finding himself not true to his preaching he came down. For four months he kept to his house and did not venture out. Then a crowd of men came and brought him out and put him in the pulpit. Nūrī heard of this and came to the hall.

"Abū Bakr," he cried, "you concealed the truth from them, so of course they set you in the pulpit. I counselled them sincerely, and they drove me away with stones and flung me on the dunghill."

"Prince of the Hearts, what was your good counselling, and what was my concealing?" asked Shiblī.

"My good counselling," Nūrī replied, "was that I let men go to their God. Your concealing was that you became a veil between God and men. Who are you, to be an intermediary between God and men? In my view, you are irrelevant."

Nūrī and another were seated together, both weeping bitterly. When the other departed, Nūrī turned to his companions.

"Did you know who that was?" he asked them.

"No," they replied.

"That was Iblīs," he told them. "He was relating the services he had performed and was telling the tale of his life, bewailing the agony of separation. As you saw, he was weeping. I too was weeping."

Ja'far al-Khuldī relates the following.

Nūrī was praying in seclusion, and I was listening to what he would say.

"Lord God," he said, "Thou punishest the denizens of Hell. They are all Thy creation, by virtue of Thy omniscience and omnipotence and pre-eternal will. If Thou wilt assuredly fill Hell with men, Thou hast the power to fill Hell with men and to transport them to Paradise."

I was amazed at his words. Then I saw in a dream one who came to me and said, "God has said, Tell Abū al-Ḥusayn, I have honoured and had compassion on thee for that prayer."

"One night," Nūrī recalled, "I found the area about the Ka'bah empty and proceeded to circumambulate. Each time I reached the Black Stone I prayed and said, 'O God, accord to me a state and an attribute from which I shall not change.' One day I heard a voice proceeding from the midst of the Ka‘bah and saying, ‘Abū al-Ḥusayn, you would make yourself equal to Me. I change not from My attribute, but I keep My servants turning about and changing. This I do, in order that Lordship may become clear from servanthood. It is I who continue in one attribute; man's attribute changes.'"

Shiblī reports: I visited Nūrī and saw him seated in meditation, not a hair of his body moving.

"From whom did you learn such excellent meditation?" I asked.

"From a cat crouching over a mouse-hole," he replied. "He was much stiller than I am."

One night report was brought to the people of Qādisiyyah.

"A friend of God has confined himself in the Valley of Lions. Go and recover him."

All the people went out to the Valley of Lions. There they found that Nūrī had dug a grave and was sitting there, surrounded by crouching lions. They interceded with him, and conducted him back to Qādisiyyah, where they asked him his story.

"For a while I had eaten nothing," he told them. "I was traversing this desert when I espied a date-tree. I had a longing for fresh dates. Then I said, 'There is still room left for desire. I will go down into this valley, that the lions may rend you, my appetite, then you will no longer desire dates.'"

"One day," Nūrī recalled, "I was washing myself in a pool when a thief came and stole my clothes. I had not yet emerged from the water when he brought them back, and his hand had become withered. I cried, 'O God, since he has brought back my clothes, give him back his hand!' At once his hand was healed."

Fire broke out in the Bazaar of Slavers in Baghdad, and many people were burnt to death. In one shop were two young Greek slaves, very handsome youths; the flames were lapping round them.

"Anyone who will fetch them out," cried their owner, "I will give a thousand gold dinars."

No one dared to attempt the rescue. All at once Nūrī arrived on the scene. He saw the two young slaves, shouting for help.

"In the Name of God, the Merciful, the Compassionate." So saying, he plunged in and brought them both to safety. The owner of the slaves offered Nūrī the thousand gold dinars.

"Keep your gold," Nūrī told him. "And give thanks to God. For this dignity that has been conferred on me has been conferred because of not accepting gold, exchanging this world for the next."

One day a blind man was crying, "God, God!" Nūrī went up to him and said, "What do you know of Him? And if you know, yet you still live?"

So saying, he lost his senses, and was so filled with mystic yearning that he went out into the desert, to freshly-harvested reedbeds. The reeds pierced his feet and sides, and the blood gushed forth. Every drop that fell, the words "God, God" appeared.

Abū Naṣr al-Sarrāj states that when they brought him from that place to his home, they said to him, "Say, There is no god but God."

"Why, I am on my way There," he replied. And thereupon he died.

29

Abū 'Uthmān al-Ḥīrī

Abū 'Uthmān Sa'īd ibn Ismā'īl al-Ḥīrī al-Nīsābūrī came originally from Rayy, where he knew Yaḥyā ibn Mu'ādh al-Rāzī and Shāh ibn Shujā' al-Kirmānī. He moved to Nishapur where he came under the influence of Abū Ḥafṣ al-Ḥaddād. He visited Junayd in Baghdad, and died at Nishapur in 298 (911).

The education of Abū 'Uthmān al-Ḥīrī

"My heart even in the days of my childhood was always seeking after something of reality," said Abū 'Uthmān al-Ḥīrī. "I had an aversion for the followers of formal religion, and I was always convinced that something else existed apart from what the general mass of the people believed in, that the Islamic way of life held mysteries other than its external manifestations."

One day Abū 'Uthmān was going to school accompanied by four slaves, an Ethiop, a Greek, a Kashmiri, and a Turk. In his hand he carried a golden pen-case; he wore on his head a muslin turban, on his back a silk robe. Passing on his way an ancient caravanserai, he peeped in and saw there an ass with sores on its back, a raven was pecking at its wounds, and the beast had not the strength to drive it away. Abū 'Uthmān was filled with compassion.

"Why are you with me?" he addressed one of the slaves.

"To assist you in every thought that passes through your mind," the slave replied.

Immediately Abū 'Uthmān took off his silken dress and covered the donkey with it, bandaging the beast with his muslin turban. With mute eloquence the ass at once communed with God Almighty. Before ever he reached home, Abū 'Uthmān was visited by a spiritual experience such as true men of God know.

Like one distraught, he found his way to the assembly of Yaḥyā ibn Mu'ādh; his preaching opened a door in his heart. Breaking away from his mother and father, Abū 'Uthmān served Yaḥyā for a while, learning the Sufi discipline. This continued until a party arrived from Shāh ibn Shujā' al-Kirmānī and told stories of that holy man. A great eagerness to see Shāh ibn Shujā' invaded Abū 'Uthmān. Having obtained permission from his spiritual preceptor he proceeded to Kirmān, to wait on the saint. Shāh ibn Shujā' declined to receive him.

"You have become habituated to hope," he told him.

"Yaḥyā's station is hope. Spiritual advancement cannot be looked for in one brought up on hope. Blind attachment to hope generates idleness. With Yaḥyā, hope is a real experience; with you it is blind imitation."

Abū 'Uthmān entreated the saint with great humility, haunting his threshold for twenty days, till at last he was admitted. He remained in his society and derived much benefit from his instruction until the time came when Shāh ibn Shujā' set out for Nishapur to visit Abū Ḥafṣ. Abū 'Uthmān accompanied him, the saint wearing a short tunic. Abū Ḥafṣ came out to receive Shāh ibn Shujā' and showered praises upon him.

Abū 'Uthmān's whole desire was to join the company of Abū Ḥafṣ, but his reverence for Shāh ibn Shujā' prevented him from broaching the matter, for Shāh ibn Shujā' was a jealous teacher. Abū 'Uthmān begged God to provide some means whereby he might remain with Abū Ḥafṣ without annoying Shāh ibn Shujā'; for he perceived that Abū Ḥafṣ was a man of great spiritual advancement.

When Shāh ibn Shujā' determined that it was time to return to Kirmān, Abū 'Uthmān busied himself with making ready provisions for the road. Then one day Abū Ḥafṣ said to Shāh ibn Shujā' very affably, "Leave this young man here. I am delighted with him."

"Obey the shaykh," said Shāh ibn Shujā', turning to Abū 'Uthmān. With that Shāh ibn Shujā' departed, and Abū 'Uthmān remained, and saw what he saw.

"I was still a young man," Abū 'Uthmān recalled, "when Abū Ḥafṣ dismissed me from his service. 'I do not wish you to come near me any more,' he told me. I said nothing, and my heart would not suffer me to turn my back on him. So I withdrew facing him as I was, weeping all the while, till I vanished from his sight. I made a place opposite him and cut out a hole through which I watched him. I firmly resolved never to leave that spot unless the shaykh ordered me. When the shaykh noticed me there and observed my sorry state, he called me out and promoted me to his favour, marrying his daughter to me."

Anecdotes of Abū 'Uthmān

"For forty years," said Abū 'Uthmān, "whatever state God has kept me in I have not resented, and to whatever state He has transferred me I have not been angry."

The following story bears out this assertion. A man who disbelieved in Abū 'Uthmān sent him an invitation. Abū 'Uthmān accepted, and got as far as the door of his house. The man then shouted at him.

"Glutton, there is nothing here for you. Go home!"

Abū 'Uthmān went home. He had gone only a little way when the man called out to him.

"Shaykh, come here!"

Abū 'Uthmān returned.

"You are very eager to eat," the man taunted him. "There is still less. Be off with you!"

The shaykh departed. The man summoned him again, and he went back.

"Eat stones, or go home!"

Abū 'Uthmān went off once more. Thirty times the man summoned him and drove him away. Thirty times the shaykh came and went, without showing the least discomposure. Then the man fell at his feet and with tears repented, becoming his disciple.

"What a man you are!" he exclaimed. "Thirty times I drove you off with contumely, and you showed not the slightest discomposure."

"This is an easy matter," Abū 'Uthmān replied. "Dogs do the same. When you drive them away they go, and when you call them they come, without showing any discomposure. A thing in which dogs equal us cannot really be accounted anything. Men's work is something quite other."

One day Abū 'Uthmān was walking along the street when someone emptied a tray of ashes on his head from the roof. His companions, infuriated, were about to abuse the offender, but Abū 'Uthmān stopped them.

"One should give thanks a thousandfold," he said, "that one who merited fire was let off with ashes!"

A dissolute young fellow was strolling along with a lute in his hand, completely drunk. Suddenly catching sight of Abū 'Uthmān, he tucked his curls under his cap and drew the lute into his sleeve, thinking that he would denounce him to the authorities. Abū 'Uthmān approached him in the kindliest manner.

"Do not be afraid. Brothers are all one," he said.

When the young man saw that, he repented and became a disciple of the shaykh. Abū 'Uthmān instructed him to be washed, invested him, and then raised his head to heaven.

"O God," he cried, "I have done my part. The rest Thou must do."

Immediately the youth was visited by such a mystical experience that Abū 'Uthmān himself was amazed.

At the time of the afternoon prayers, Abū 'Uthmān al-Maghribī arrived. Abū 'Uthmān al-Ḥīrī said to him, "Shaykh, I am consumed with envy. All that I have yearned for in a long life has been poured freely on the head of this youth, from whose belly the odour of wine still proceeds. So you know that men propose, but God disposes."

30

Ibn 'Aṭā'

Abū al-'Abbas Aḥmad ibn Muḥammad ibn Sahl ibn 'Aṭā' al-Ādamī was a close companion of Junayd. Author of mystical verses and a prominent member of the Baghdad circle, he was put to death in 309 (922).

Anecdotes of Ibn 'Aṭā'

Ibn 'Aṭā' was one of the leading disciples of Junayd. One day a party of men entered his oratory to find the whole floor drenched.

"What is this state of affairs?" they asked.

"A mystical experience came to me," he explained. "In shamefacedness I circled around the oratory, pouring tears from my eyes."

"What was it?" they enquired.

"When I was a child," he explained, "I took a dove belonging to someone. I remembered that. I gave a thousand silver dinars to compensate its owner, but my conscience could not rest. I am weeping, wondering what the consequence will be."

"How much of the Qur'an do you recite daily?" Ibn 'Aṭā' was asked.

"Formerly," he replied, "I used to complete the whole Qur'an twice every twenty-four hours. Now I have been reciting the Qur'an for fourteen years, and today I have just reached Sūrah al-Anfāl."

Ibn 'Aṭā' had ten sons, all handsome boys. They were accompanying their father on a journey when thieves fell upon them and proceeded to strike off their heads one by one. Ibn 'Aṭā' said nothing; as each son was killed, he turned his face to heaven and laughed. Nine of his sons were already executed, and the thieves were about to slay the tenth.

"A fine father you are!" the tenth son addressed him. "Nine of your sons are beheaded, and you say nothing but simply laugh."

"Soul of your father," Ibn 'Aṭā' answered him, "He who is doing this, to Him one can say nothing. He knows, and He sees; He is able, if He wills, to save them all."

The thief who was about to kill the tenth son was overcome by emotion when he heard Ibn 'Aṭā''s words.

"Old man," he cried, "if you had said this before, none of your sons would have been killed."

"How is it with you Sufis," certain theologians asked Ibn 'Aṭā', "that you have invented terms which sound strange to those who hear them, abandoning ordinary language? It can only be one of two things. Either you are practising dissimulation, and dissimulation is improper in relation to the truth, so that it is clear that your doctrine is not true; or else there is some evident flaw in your doctrine which you are concealing in your public utterances."

"We do this because it is precious to us," Ibn 'Aṭā' replied. "What we practise is precious to us, and we desired that none but we Sufis should know of it. We did not wish to employ ordinary language, so we invented a special vocabulary."

Why Ibn 'Aṭā' cursed 'Alī ibn 'Īsā

Ibn 'Aṭā' was denounced as a heretic. 'Alī ibn 'Īsā, who was then the caliph's vizier, summoned him and spoke roughly to him. Ibn 'Aṭā' replied in vigorous terms. This enraged the vizier, who ordered his servants to remove his shoes and beat his head with them until he died. In the midst of this Ibn 'Aṭā' exclaimed, "May God cut off your hands and feet!"

Some while after the caliph was angered against 'Alī ibn 'Īsā and ordered his hands and feet to be struck off

Certain of the Sufi masters have found fault with Ibn 'Aṭā' on this account. "Why," they say, "when your prayers could have effected the man's reformation, did you curse him? You ought to have blessed him." Others however have excused him, saying, "It may be that he cursed him because he was unjust to save other Muslims."

Another explanation is that Ibn 'Aṭā', being a man of intuition, foresaw what would be done to the vizier. He simply agreed with what had been Divinely destined, so that God spoke His Will by his tongue, he being not involved at all.

My own opinion is that Ibn 'Aṭā' in fact blessed him and did not curse him, so that he might attain the degree of martyrdom. He prayed that the vizier should suffer humiliation in this world and fall from his high rank and great wealth. Seen in this light, Ibn 'Aṭā' wished nothing but good for 'Alī ibn 'Īsā; for punishment in this world is light to bear, in comparison with that in the world to come.

31

Samnūn

Abū al-Ḥasan Samnūn ibn 'Abdullah (Ḥamzah) al-Khawwāṣ, a companion of Sarī al-Saqaṭī, was called "the Lover" because of his discourses and poems on the theme of mystical love. Denounced by Ghulām al-Khalīl, he died c. 300 (913).

The story of Samnūn the Lover

Samnūn commonly called the Lover (he called himself Samnūn the Liar) was a companion of Sarī al-Saqaṭī and a contemporary of Junayd. He had a special doctrine about love, which he promoted above gnosis, contrary to the view of the majority of the Sufi masters.

When Samnūn went to Ḥijāz the people of Fāyid invited him to preach. He entered the pulpit and began to hold forth, but found no one to listen to him. He therefore turned to the mosque-lamps and said, "I am going to speak to you about love." Immediately the lamps dashed upon one another and broke into pieces.

One day when he was preaching on love a bird swooped down out of the air and perched first on his head, then on his hand, then on his breast. Then it dropped from his breast on to the ground and struck its beak so violently against the ground that the blood gushed forth from it. Then the bird collapsed and died.

It is related that towards the end of his life, to accord with the Prophet's example, Samnūn married and in due course had a daughter. When the child was three years old Samnūn became very attached to her. That night he dreamed that the resurrection had come to pass. He saw that a standard had been set up for every community; one standard was so bright that its radiance filled the plains of Heaven.

"To whom does this standard belong?" Samnūn enquired.

"To the people of whom God says, He loves them and they love Him," came the answer (meaning that it was the standard of lovers).

Samnūn ranged himself among those under that banner. One came along and drove him out of their midst.

"Why do you drive me out?" Samnūn shouted.

"Because this is the standard of lovers," came the reply. "You are not one of them."

"Why not?" cried Samnūn. "After all, they call me Samnūn the Lover, and God knows what is in my heart."

"Samnūn, you were a lover," came the answer. "But

when your heart inclined towards that child, your name was expunged from the roll of lovers."

Even as he dreamed Samnūn made supplication.

"O God, if this child is to waylay me, remove her from my path."

When he awoke the cry went up, "The little girl fell from the roof and died."

It is further related that once Samnūn was reciting this couplet.

I have no joy in aught but Thee;
So, as Thou wilt, make trial of me.

Immediately his urine was blocked. He went about from school to school saying to the children, "Pray for your liar of an uncle that God may heal him!"

Samnūn and Ghulām Khalīl

Ghulām Khalīl had made himself known to the caliph as a Sufi, bartering away his eternal salvation for worldly advantage. He always maligned the Sufis before the caliph, his intention being to secure their banishment, so that none should enjoy the blessing of their presence, and to maintain himself in power and that he might not be disgraced.

When Samnūn grew to full stature and his fame spread abroad, Ghulām Khalīl occasioned him much suffering, always watching for an opportunity of bringing about his disgrace. Then one day a wealthy woman offered herself to Samnūn.

"Ask my hand in marriage," she said.

Samnūn refused. The woman then went to Junayd and begged him to intercede for her and persuade Samnūn to marry her, but Junayd rebuked her and drove her away. The woman therefore repaired to Ghūlām Khalīl and laid allegations against Samnūn. Ghulām Khalīl was delighted, and turned the caliph against Samnūn. Then the caliph ordered Samnūn to be slain. The executioner having been summoned, the caliph was about to say, "Behead him"; but he was struck dumb and he could not speak, his tongue sticking in his throat. That night he dreamed that a voice said to him, "Your kingdom is bound up with Samnūn's life." Next morning the caliph sent for Samnūn and sent him away with all honour, treating him with the highest consideration.

Thereafter Ghulām's hostility towards Samnūn increased still more. Towards the end of his life he was smitten with leprosy.

"Ghūlām Khalīl has become a leper," someone related to Samnūn.

"It would seem," Samnūn replied, "that some immature Sufi has formed designs against him and not done good. For he was an opponent of the masters, and from time to time impeded them by his actions. God grant him healing!"

These words were reported to Ghulām Khalīl. He repented of all his sins, and sent all that he possessed to the Sufis. They however refused to accept anything.

32

Al-Tirmidhī

One of the outstanding creative thinkers of Islamic mysticism, Abū 'Abdullah Muḥammad ibn 'Alī ibn al-Ḥusayn al-Ḥakīm al-Tirmidhī, was driven out of his native town of Tirmidh and took refuge in Nishapur, where he was preaching in 285 (898). His psychological writings influenced al-Ghazālī, whilst his startling theory of sainthood was taken over and developed by Ibn 'Arabī. A copious author, many of his books, including an autobiographical sketch, have been preserved and a number have been published.

The training of Ḥakīm al-Tirmidhī

At the beginning of his career, Muḥammad ibn 'Alī al-Tirmidhī arranged with two students to set out with them in quest of knowledge. When they were just ready to leave, his mother became very sorrowful.

"Soul of your mother," she addressed her son, "I am a feeble woman, and have no one in the world. You look after my affairs. To whom will you leave me, alone and feeble as I am?"

Her words pained Tirmidhī, and he abandoned his journey while his two friends went off in quest of knowledge. Some time elapsed. Then one day he was sitting in the cemetery, weeping bitterly.

"Here am I left here, neglected and ignorant. My friends will come back, perfectly trained scholars."

Suddenly there appeared a luminous elder who addressed him.

"My son, why do you weep?"

Tirmidhī told him his tale.

"Would you like me to teach you a lesson daily, so that you will soon outstrip them?" he asked.

"I would," Tirmidhī replied.

"So," Tirmidhī recalled, "every day he taught me a lesson, till three years had gone by. Then I realised that he was Khiḍr, and that I had attained this felicity because I pleased my mother."

Every Sunday (so Abū Bakr al-Warrāq reports) Khiḍr would visit Tirmidhī and they would converse on every matter. One day he said to me, "Today I will take you somewhere."

"The master knows best," I replied.

I set out with him, and within a little while I espied an arduous and harsh desert, in the midst of which a golden throne was set under a verdant tree by a spring of water.

Someone apparelled in beautiful raiment was seated on the throne. The shaykh approached him, whereupon this person rose up and set Tirmidhī on the throne. In a little while a company gathered from all directions, until forty persons were assembled. They made a signal to heaven and food appeared, and they ate. The shaykh asked that person questions which he answered, but in such language that I did not understand a single word. After a time Tirmidhī begged leave to go, and took his departure.

"Go," he said to me. "You have been blessed."

In a while we were back in Tirmidh. I then questioned the shaykh.

"What was all that? What place was it, and who was that man?"

"It was the wilderness of the Children of Isrā'īl," Tirmidhī replied. "That man was the Pole."

"How was it that we went and returned in such a short time?" I asked.

"O Abū Bakr," he answered, "when He conveys, one is able to arrive! What business is it of yours to know the why and wherefore? To arrive is your task, not to ask!"

"However hard I strove to keep my carnal soul in subjection," Tirmidhī related, "I could not prevail over it. In my despair I said, 'Haply Almighty God has created this soul for Hell. Why nurture a creature doomed to Hell?' Proceeding to the banks of the Oxus, I begged a man to bind me hand and foot. He left me thus, and I rolled over and flung myself into the water, hoping to drown myself. The impact of the water freed my hands; then a wave came and cast me up on the bank. Despairing of myself, I cried, 'Glory be to Thee, O God, who hast created a soul that is not proper either for Heaven or Hell!' In the very moment of my self-despair, by the blessing of that cry my secret heart was opened and I saw what was necessary for me. In that selfsame hour I vanished from myself. So long as I have lived, I have lived by the blessing of that hour."

Abū Bakr al-Warrāq also relates the following.

One day Tirmidhī handed over to me many volumes of his writings to cast into the Oxus. I examined them and found they were replete with mystic subtleties and truths. I could not bring myself to carry out his instructions, and instead stored them in my room. I then told him that I had thrown them in.

What did you see?" he asked.

"Nothing," I replied.

"You did not throw them in," he concluded. "Go and do so."

"I see two problems," I said to myself. "First, why does he want them flung into the water? And second, what visible proof will there be?"

However, I went back and threw the books into the Oxus. I saw the river open up, and an open chest appeared; the volumes fell into it, then the lid closed and the river subsided. I was astonished.

"Did you throw them in this time?" Tirmidhī questioned me when I returned to him.

"Master, by God's glory," I cried, "tell me the secret behind this."

"I had composed something on the science of the Sufis, the disclosing of the verification of which was difficult for human minds to grasp," he replied. "My brother Khiḍr entreated me. The chest was brought by a fish at his bidding, and Almighty God commanded the waters to convey it to him."

Anecdotes of Tirmidhī

In Tirmidhī's time lived a great ascetic who was always criticising him. Now in all the world Tirmidhī possessed nothing but a cabin. When he returned from his journey to Ḥijāz, a dog had whelped in that cabin, which had no door. Tirmidhī did not wish to drive the dog out, and he went and came eighty times in the hope that the dog would have of its own free will carried its puppies out.

That same night the ascetic saw the Prophet in a dream.

"Sirrah, you put yourself up against a man who eighty times brought succour to a dog," the Prophet said. "If you desire eternal happiness, go, bind up your loins and serve him."

The ascetic, too ashamed to answer Tirmidhī's greetings, thereafter spent the rest of his life in his service.

"When the master is angry with you, do you know?" someone asked Tirmidhī's family.

"We know," they replied. "Whenever he is vexed with

us, that day he is even kinder to us than usual. He takes neither bread nor water, and weeps and supplicates, saying, 'O God, in what did I vex Thee, that Thou hast provoked them against me? O God, I repent; restore them to rectitude.' So we know, and repent, to deliver the master out of his affliction."

For a while Tirmidhī did not see Khiḍr. Then one day a maidservant had washed the baby's clothes, filling a basin with the baby's excreta. Meanwhile the shaykh, dressed in clean robes and with a spotless turban, was proceeding to the mosque. The girl, flying into a rage over some trifle, emptied the basin over the shaykh's head. Tirmidhī said nothing, and swallowed his anger. Immediately he rediscovered Khiḍr.

In his youth a certain lovely woman invited Tirmidhī to take her, but he refused. Then one day the woman, learning that he was in a garden, arrayed herself and proceeded thither. As soon as the shaykh became aware of her approach, he fled. The woman ran after him, screaming that he was after her blood. Tirmidhī took no notice, but climbed a high wall and flung himself over.

One day in his old age Tirmidhī was reviewing his acts and sayings, and remembered that incident. The thought entered his mind, "What would it have mattered if I had gratified that woman's need? After all, I was young, and I could afterwards have repented." When he perceived this thought in his mind, he was filled with anguish.

"Foul and rebellious soul!" he exclaimed. "Forty years ago, in the first flush of youth, this thought did not occur to you. Now in old age, after so many struggles, whence has come this repining over a sin not committed?"

Very sorrowful, for three days he sat in mourning for this thought. After three days he saw the Prophet in a dream.

"Muḥammad, do not grieve," said the Prophet to him. "What happened was not due to a lapse on your part. This thought occurred to you because forty years more had passed since my death. The period of my leaving the world had become that much longer, and I was withdrawn further away. It is no sin of yours, no shortcoming in your spiritual progress. What you experienced was due to the long extension of the period of my departure from the world, not to any deficiency in your character."

The following narrative is ascribed to Tirmidhī.

When Adam and Eve came together and their repentance was accepted, one day Adam went out on business. Then Iblīs brought his child called Khannās to Eve.

"Something important has come up," he told her.

"Please look after my child till I return."

Eve consented to do so, and Iblīs went on his way.

"Who is this?" demanded Adam on his return.

"The child of Iblīs," Eve answered. "He left him in my charge."

"Why did you consent?" Adam reproved her. In a fury he slew the child and cut him into pieces, and hung each piece from the branch of a tree. Then he went off. Presently Iblīs returned.

"Where is my son?" he asked.

Eve reported to him what had happened.

"He cut him in pieces and hung each piece on the branch of a tree."

Iblīs called to his son. He reassembled and became alive and ran to his father.

"Take him," Iblīs begged Eve again. "I have another task to do."

At first Eve would not agree, but Iblīs pleaded and entreated her so earnestly that at last she consented. So Iblīs took his departure, and Adam returned to find the child there again.

"What is this?" he demanded.

Eve explained what had happened. Adam beat her severely.

"I do not know what the mystery of this is," he cried, "that you disobey me and obey that enemy of God, and are duped by his words."

He slew the child and burned his body, then scattered his ashes, half in the water and half to the winds. So he departed.

Iblīs came back again and asked for his son. Eve told him what had come to pass. Iblīs shouted to his son, and the pieces reassembled and came to life, and sat before Iblīs. Once more Iblīs spoke to Eve, and she refused him.

"Adam will kill me."

Iblīs adjured her with many oaths, until she consented. Iblīs then departed, and Adam returned to discover the child with her once more.

"God knows what will happen now," he cried out in anger. "You heed his words and not mine."

Furious, he slew Khannās and cooked him. He ate one half himself, and the other half he gave to Eve. (They also say that on the final occasion Iblīs had brought Khannās back in the form of a sheep.) Iblīs returned and demanded his son. Eve recounted what had transpired.

"He cooked him. One half I ate, and one half Adam."

"This was what I was after," Iblīs shouted. "I aimed to insinuate myself into Adam. Now that his breast has become my abode, my purpose is realised."

33

Khayr al-Nassāj

Abū al-Ḥasan Muḥammad ibn Ismā'īl (Khayr ibn 'Abdullah) al-Nassāj of Sāmarrā', a pupil of Sarī al-Saqaṭī and a member of Junayd's circle, was taken as a slave in Basra but afterwards proceeded to Makkah. He is said to have lived to the age of 120, dying in 322 (924).

The story of Khayr al-Nassāj

Khayr al-Nassāj was the chief master of his time. A pupil of Sarī al-Saqaṭī, he influenced Shiblī and Ibrāhīm al-Khawwāṣ and was greatly admired by Junayd. The following was the reason why he was called Khayr al-Nassāj. Leaving his native town Sāmarrā' bound for the pilgrimage, on the way he passed through Kūfah. He arrived at the gates of Kūfah clad in a patchwork robe, he himself being black of complexion, so that all who beheld him would cry, "The man appears a fool!" There a certain man espied him.

"I will employ him for a few days," he said to himself. Then he approached him.

"Are you a slave?" he asked.

"Yes," he replied.

"Have you run away from your master?"

"Yes."

"I will take charge of you until I can restore you to your master," the man said.

"That is what I am seeking myself," said Khayr. "All my life I have been longing to find someone who will restore me to my Master."

The man took him to his home.

"Your name is Khayr," he said.

Khayr did not gainsay him, believing firmly in the saying that "a believer does not lie". He went along with him and served him. The man taught Khayr the craft of weaving. For years he worked for the man. Whenever he called out, "Khayr!" he would reply "Here am I!" At last the man repented, having seen his sincerity, perfect behaviour and intuitive powers, and having witnessed the constancy of his devotions.

"I made a mistake," he announced. "You are not my slave. Go wherever you wish."

Khayr then departed for Makkah, where he attained such a high degree of saintliness that Junayd himself declared, "Khayr is the best of us." He preferred people to call him Khayr.

"It would not be right," he would say, "for a brother Muslim to give me a name and for me to change it."

From time to time he practised weaving. Sometimes he used to go down to the Tigris and the fishes would make advances to him and bring him various things. One day he was weaving muslin for an old woman. The old woman said, "If I bring a dirham and do not find you here, to whom shall I give it?"

"Throw it in the river," Khayr replied.

The old woman brought the dirham, and Khayr not being there she threw it into the Tigris. When Khayr returned to the bank the fishes brought that dirham to him.

It is said that Khayr lived to the age of 120. When his death drew near, it was the time of the evening prayer. 'Izrā'īl cast his shadow, and Khayr raised his head from the pillow.

"God preserve you!" he cried. "Wait a little. You are a slave under orders, and I am a slave under orders. You have been told to collect my soul. I have been told, 'When the time for prayer comes, pray.' That time has now come. You will have plenty of opportunity to carry out your orders. For me it is now or never. Please be patient until I have performed the evening prayer."

Khayr then washed himself and performed the prayer. Immediately afterwards he died.

34

Abū Bakr al-Kattānī

Abū Bakr Muḥammad ibn 'Alī ibn Ja'far al-Kattānī, a native of Baghdad, belonged to the circle of Junayd. He proceeded to Makkah on the pilgrimage, and took up residence there until his death in 322 (934).

The piety of Abū Bakr al-Kattānī

Abū Bakr al-Kattānī was called the Lamp of the Sanctuary. He was a resident in Makkah up to the day of his death. He used to pray all the night through and chant the entire Qur'an; in the course of circling the Ka'bah he completed twelve thousand recitations in all. For thirty years he was seated in the sanctuary under the waterspout, and in all those thirty years one ritual washing every twenty-four hours sufficed him. Throughout the whole period he never slept.

At the beginning of his career he sought permission from his mother to go on the pilgrimage.

"When I was proceeding into the desert," he recalled, "a state overtook me compelling me to wash for self-purification. I told myself that perhaps I had not set out under the proper auspices; so I turned back. I reached home to find my mother seated behind the door of the house, waiting for me. 'Mother,' I said, 'did you not give me leave?' 'Yes,' she replied. 'But without you I could not bear to look at the house. Since you departed I have been seated here. I resolved that I would not rise up until you came back again.' It was not until my mother died that I ventured into the desert once more."

Abū Bakr al-Kattānī tells the following story.

I was deep in the desert when I caught sight of a dead man. He was smiling.

"What, are you dead and still smiling?" I cried.

"Such is the love of God," he replied.

"I felt a little resentment in my heart towards the Prince of the Faithful, 'Alī," Abū Bakr confessed. "That was for no other reason than because the Prophet had said, 'There is no true knight but 'Alī.' It was a part of that knightliness that, although Mu'āwiyah was in the wrong and he was in the right, nevertheless 'Alī abdicated in Mu'āwiyah's favour in order that so much blood should not be spilled.

"Now I had a little house between Marwah and Ṣafā,"

he continued. "There I saw the Prophet in a dream, together with his blessed companions. He came up to me and, taking me into his embrace, pointed to Abū Bakr and said, 'Who is he?' 'Abū Bakr,' I replied. Then he pointed to 'Umar. "Umar,' I said. Then he pointed to 'Uthmān. "Uthmān,' I said. Lastly he pointed to 'Alī. I felt ashamed because of the resentment I entertained. Then the Prophet gave me to 'Alī in brotherhood and we embraced each other. After that they all departed, and only myself and 'Alī remained. 'Come,' said 'Alī to me, 'let us go to Mount Abū Qubayṣ.' We climbed to the top of the mountain and looked down on the Ka'bah. When I awoke, I found myself on Mount Abū Qubayṣ. Not a trace of that resentment remained in my heart.

"I was once in the company of a certain man," he also related, "and his society bore heavily on me. I made him a present, but still that heaviness did not go away. I took him to my house and said to him, 'Put your foot on my face.' He would not do so, but I insisted until finally he put his foot on my face and kept it there so long that the heaviness vanished and changed into love. Now I had received as a gift from a lawful source two hundred dirhams. I fetched them and placed them on the corner of his prayer rug. 'Spend these on yourself,' I told him. Looking at me out of the corner of his eye he said, 'I have purchased this occasion at a cost of seventy thousand dinars. Do you want to delude me with this?' Then he rose up, shook out his prayer rug and departed. I had never experienced anything like his dignity and my humiliation as when I was picking up those dirhams."

Abū Bakr al-Kattānī had a disciple who was in the agonies of death. He opened his eyes and gazed upon the Ka'bah. A camel came along at the moment and kicked his face, gouging out his eye.

Immediately Abū Bakr heard a voice saying within him, "In this state when authentic revelations from the Unseen were coming to him, he gazed at the Ka'bah. So he was punished. It is not right in the presence of the Lord of the House to gaze at the House."

One day a luminous elder majestically wrapped in a cloak entered by the Gate of the Banū Shaybah and went up to Kattānī, who was standing with head bowed.

"Why," he asked after the exchange of greetings, "do you not go to the Station of Ibrāhīm? A great teacher has come and is relating noble traditions. Come and listen to him."

"On whose authority is he relating, sir?" Kattānī asked.

"On the authority of 'Abdullah ibn Ma'mar, from Zuhrī, from Abū Hurayrah, from the Prophet," the elder replied.

"Master, you have produced a long chain of authorities," Kattānī remarked. "Whatever they are reporting there by authoritative chain of transmission, we are hearing here without any chain."

"From whom are you hearing?" asked the elder.

"My heart reported to me direct from my Lord ..." said Kattānī.

"Do you have any proof of your assertion?" demanded the elder.

"My proof," replied Kattānī, "is that my heart is telling me that you are Khiḍr."

"Till then," Khiḍr remarked, "I had always thought that there was no friend of God whom I did not know. That was until I saw Abū Bakr al-Kattānī. I did not know him, but he knew me. Then I realised that God has friends who know me but whom I do not know."

Kattānī also related as follows.

I saw in a dream an extremely handsome youth.

"Who are you?" I enquired.

"Piety," he replied.

"Where do you dwell?" I asked.

"In the heart," he answered, "of the sorrowful."

Then I saw a most hideous, black woman.

"Who are you?" I demanded.

"Laughter and gaiety and enjoyment," she answered.

"Where do you dwell?"

"In the hearts of the heedless and those who amuse themselves."

When I awoke, I resolved that I would never laugh again, except when I could not help myself.

35

Ibn Khafīf

One of the great saints of Persia, Abū 'Abdullah Muḥammad ibn Khafīf ibn Isfakshād, was born in Shiraz in 270 (882), it is said of a princely family. After a broad education he travelled to Baghdad, and there met al-Ḥallāj and other Sufis of the capital. He made the pilgrimage to Makkah at least six times, and is reported also to have visited Egypt, and Asia Minor. Author of a number of books, he died in his native city at a very advanced age in 371 (982).

The asceticism of Ibn Khafīf

Ibn Khafīf al-Fārisī was of royal descent. He was so called because he carried a light burden, was light of spirit and will face a light reckoning. Every night his meal on breaking his fast consisted of seven raisins, no more. One night the servitor gave him eight. He did not realise, and ate them. Finding no pleasure in his devotions, contrary to his nightly experience, he summoned the servant and interrogated him.

"I gave you eight raisins tonight," the servant admitted.

"Why?" demanded Ibn Khafīf.

"I saw that you were enfeebled, and it hurt my heart," said the servant. "I said to myself, if only you would get some strength."

"So you were not my friend but my enemy," Ibn Khafīf cried. "If you had been my friend you would have given me six, not eight."

And he dismissed him from his service and appointed another servant.

Ibn Khafīf recalled the following.

At the beginning of my career I wished to go on the pilgrimage. When I reached Baghdad, my head was filled with so much conceit that I did not go to see Junayd. As I travelled deep in the desert, carrying a rope and a bucket, thirst overcame me. I espied a well from which a deer was drinking. Just as I reached the edge of the well the water vanished into its depths.

"God," I cried, "is 'Abdullah of less worth than this deer?"

"This deer did not have a bucket and a rope," I heard a voice say. "His reliance was on Us."

Full of joy, I flung away the bucket and rope and went on my way.

"'Abdullah," I heard the voice again, "We were putting you to the test. Since you have shown fortitude, return and drink."

I returned to find the water up to the brim of the well. I performed my ablutions and drank. Then I set out once more, and all the way to Madīnah I had no need of water again because of my ritual purity.

When I was back in Baghdad, on Friday I went to mosque. Junayd there caught sight of me and addressed me.

"Had you been truly patient, the water would have gushed forth from beneath your feet."

In my youth (Ibn Khafīf also related) a certain dervish came to call on me. Observing in me the marks of hunger, he invited me to his house. Some meat had been cooking, and the smell of it pervaded the house so that I was repelled and could not eat. The dervish, noticing this disdain in me, was filled with shame. I too was overcome by confusion. So I left the table and set out with some companions.

After reaching Qādisiyyah we lost our way, and were out of provisions. We bore up for some days, till we came to the brink of destruction. Things were so bad that we bought a dog at a high price and roasted it. They gave me a morsel. I was about to eat it when I remembered the episode of the dervish and the food he had offered me.

"This," I told myself, "is in punishment for that day when the dervish was put to shame before me."

I repented, so that the way was shown to us. When I returned home, I begged that dervish's pardon.

One day I heard of an elder and a youth in Egypt who were engaged in perpetual meditation. I went to Egypt, and there saw two persons with their faces turned to Makkah. I greeted them thrice, but they did not answer me.

"God save you," I cried. "Answer my greeting!"

"Ibn Khafīf," said the youth lifting up his head, "this world is a little thing, and of this little only a little remains. Of this little take a large portion, Ibn Khafīf! Perhaps you have time to spare to trouble to greet us."

So saying, he lowered his head. Though hungry and thirsty, I forgot my hunger, so completely did they entrance me. I waited, and performed the noon and afternoon prayers with them. Then I spoke.

"Give me counsel."

"Ibn Khafīf, we are men of affliction," he replied. "We have not the tongue to offer advice. Another is needed to counsel the afflicted."

I remained there three days without eating and sleeping.

"What can I say to adjure them to counsel me?" I asked myself.

The youth lifted his head.

"Seek the company of someone, the sight of whom will

remind you of God and the awe of whom will move your heart, someone who will counsel you with the tongue of deeds, not words."

One year I was staying in Byzantium. One day I went out into the desert. They brought along a monk wasted as a shadow, burned him, and smeared his ashes on the eyes of the blind. By the omnipotent power of God they recovered their sight. The sick also partook of his ashes and were healed. I marvelled how this could be, seeing that they were following a false faith. That night I saw the Prophet in a dream.

"Messenger of God, what are you doing there?" I asked.

"I have come for your sake," the Prophet replied.

"Messenger of God, what was this miracle?" I asked.

"It was the result of sincerity and self-discipline in error," the Prophet answered. "If it had been in truth, how then would it have been!"

Ibn Khafīf and his wives

One midnight Ibn Khafīf summoned his servant.

"Bring me a woman," he said. "I want one."

"Where shall I go in the middle of the night?" the servant replied. "But I have a daughter. If the master gives me permission, I will fetch her."

"Fetch her," Ibn Khafīf ordered.

The servant brought his daughter, and Ibn Khafīf married her on the spot. Seven months later a child was born, but it died.

"Tell your daughter to divorce me," Ibn Khafīf said to his servant. "Else if she wishes, she may stay on."

"Master, what is the mystery in this?" the servant asked.

"The night of our marriage," Ibn Khafīf explained, "I dreamed that it was the resurrection. Many people were standing stupefied, up to their necks in sweat. All at once a child came along, took its mother and father by the hand and led them swift as the wind over the bridge between Hell and Heaven. I too desired to have a child. When that child came into the world and departed, my goal was attained."

It is said that thereafter Ibn Khafīf contracted four hundred marriages. For being of royal descent, when he repented and achieved perfect saintliness he received proposals from all sides. He married two or three at a time. One lady, the daughter of the vizier, was married to him for forty years.

His wives were once asked how Ibn Khafīf behaved with them privately.

"We know nothing about his company," they replied. "If anyone knows, it would be the vizier's daughter."

So they asked her.

"When I learned that the shaykh was coming that night to my apartment," she said, "I would prepare delicious dishes and adorn myself. When he arrived and saw what I had done, he would send for me and look at me for a while. Then he would contemplate the food for a while. Then one night he took my hand and drew it into his sleeve and rubbed it over his belly. I felt fifteen knots from his breast to his navel. 'Girl, ask me what these knots are,' he said. 'What are they?' I asked. 'All these,' he replied, 'are the violent flames of fortitude which I fastened knot by knot, to withstand your offering of such beauty and such delicious fare.' He then left me. That was the only time I was bold with him, so extreme was his self-discipline."

Anecdotes of Ibn Khafīf

Ibn Khafīf had two disciples, one called Aḥmad the Older and the other Aḥmad the Younger. The shaykh favoured Aḥmad the Younger the more. His companions were jealous, arguing that Aḥmad the Older had performed many tasks and endured much discipline. The shaykh, learning of this, desired to demonstrate to them that Aḥmad the Younger was the better of the two. Now a camel was sleeping at the door of the convent.

"Aḥmad the Older!" Ibn Khafīf cried out.

"Here am I," Aḥmad the Older responded.

"Carry that camel up to the roof of the convent," Ibn Khafīf ordered.

"Master," Aḥmad the Older protested, "how is it possible to carry a camel on to the roof?"

"That is enough," Ibn Khafīf said. "Aḥmad the Younger!"

"Here am I," replied Aḥmad the Younger.

"Carry that camel on to the roof of the convent!"

Aḥmad the Younger at once girded his loins, rolled up his sleeves and ran out of the convent. Putting his two hands under the camel, he tried with all his might but could not lift the beast.

"Well done! Now we know," Ibn Khafīf exclaimed. Then turning to his companions he added, "Aḥmad the Younger did his duty. He obeyed my command and offered no objection. He had regard to my command, not to whether the task could be carried out or no. Aḥmad the Older was only concerned to argue and dispute. From outward actions one can perceive the inner intention."

A traveller came to visit Ibn Khafīf wearing a black robe, a black shawl, black breeches and a black shirt. The shaykh felt inwardly a sense of jealousy. When the traveller had performed two *rak'ahs* and spoken a greeting, Ibn Khafīf addressed him.

"Brother, why are you dressed in black?"

"Because my gods are dead." (He meant the carnal soul and caprice.) "Hast thou seen him who has taken his caprice to be his god?"

"Put him out!" cried Ibn Khafīf.

They drove him out with contumely.

"Now bring him back!"

They brought him back. Forty times the same treatment was repeated. Then Ibn Khafīf arose and kissed his head and begged his pardon.

"You have every right to wear black," he said. "In all the forty times they insulted you, you never lost your composure."

Two Sufis came from a far distance to visit Ibn Khafīf. Not finding him in the convent, they enquired where he might be.

"In the palace of 'Aḍud al-Dawlah," came the answer.

"What business has the shaykh with the palace of princes?" they demanded. "Alas for our high opinion of him! "Then they added, "Well, we will make a tour of the city."

They proceeded to the bazaars, and made their way to a tailor's shop to have a stitch put in the front of their gown. The tailor's scissors were missing.

"You took the scissors!" the crowd shouted, and they handed them over to a policeman. The two Sufis were hustled to the palace.

"Strike off their hands!" ordered 'Aḍud al-Dawlah.

"Wait!" exclaimed Ibn Khafīf who was present in the court. "This is not their doing."

So the two were set free.

"Good sirs," Ibn Khafīf addressed them, "what you thought was perfectly just. But our resorting to the palace of princes is precisely for such purposes."

The Sufis thereupon became his disciples.

36

Al-Ḥallāj

The most controversial figure in the history of Islamic mysticism, Abū al-Mughīth al-Ḥusayn ibn Manṣūr al-Ḥallāj was born c. 244 (858) near al-Bayḍā' in the province of Fāris. He travelled very widely, first to Tostar and Baghdad, then to Makkah, and afterwards to Khuzestan, Khurasan, Transoxiana, Sistan, India and Turkestan. Eventually he returned to Baghdad, where his bold preaching of union with God caused him to be arrested on a charge of incarnationism. He was condemned to death and cruelly executed on 29 Dhū al-Qa'dah 309 (28 March 913). Author of a number of books and a considerable volume of poetry, he passed into Muslim legend as the prototype of the intoxicated lover of God.

The wanderings of Ḥallāj

Ḥusayn al-Manṣūr, called Ḥallāj ("the Woolcarder") first

came to Tostar, where he served Sahl ibn 'Abdullah for two years; then he set out for Baghdad. He made his first journey at the age of eighteen.

Thereafter he went to Basra and joined 'Amr ibn 'Uthmān, passing eighteen months in his company. Ya'qūb al-Aqṭa' gave him his daughter in marriage, after which 'Amr ibn 'Uthmān became displeased with him. So he left Basra and came to Baghdad where he called on Junayd. Junayd prescribed for him silence and solitude. He endured Junayd's company for a while, then he made for Ḥijāz. He took up residence in Makkah for one year, after which he returned to Baghdad. With a group of Sufis he attended on Junayd and put a number of questions to him to which Junayd gave no reply.

"The time will soon come," Junayd told him, "when you will incarnadine a piece of wood."

"The day when I incarnadine that piece of wood," Ḥallāj replied, "you will be wearing the garb of the formalists."

So it turned out. On the day when the leading scholars pronounced the verdict that Ḥallāj must be executed, Junayd was wearing the Sufi robe and did not sign the warrant. The caliph said that Junayd's signature was necessary. So Junayd put on the academic turban and gown, went to the *madrasah* and endorsed the warrant. "We judge according to externals," he wrote. "As for the inward truth, that God alone knows."

When Junayd declined to answer his questions, Ḥallāj was vexed and without asking leave departed to Tostar.

There he remained for a year, widely acclaimed. But because he attached no weight to the prevailing doctrine, the theologians turned envious against him. Meanwhile 'Amr ibn 'Uthmān wrote letters regarding him to the people of Khuzestan, blackening him in their eyes. He too had grown weary of that place. Casting aside the Sufi garb, he donned tunic and passed his time in the company of worldly folk. That made no difference to him, however, and for five years he vanished. Part of that period he spent in Khurasan and Transoxiana, part in Sistan.

Ḥallāj then returned to Ahwaz, where his preaching won the approval of the elite and the public alike. He would speak of men's secrets, so that he was dubbed "Ḥallāj of the Secrets". After that he dressed himself in the ragged dervish robes and set out for the Sacred Territory, accompanied by many in like attire. When he reached Makkah, Ya'qūb al-Nahrajūrī denounced him as a magician. So he returned to Basra, then to Ahwaz.

"Now I am going to the lands of polytheism, to call men to God," he announced.

So he went to India, then to Transoxiana, then to China, calling men to God and composing works for them. When he returned from the distant parts of the world, the peoples of those regions wrote him letters. The Indians addressed him as Abū al-Mughīth, the Chinese as Abū al-Mi'īn, the Khurasanians as Abū al-Muhr, the Parisians as Abū 'Abdullah, the Khuzestanis as Ḥallāj of the Secrets. In Baghdad he was called Mustalim, in Basra Mukhabbar.

The passion of Ḥallāj

After that many tales about Ḥallāj began to circulate. So he set out for Makkah where he resided for two years. On his return, his circumstances were much changed. He was a different man, calling people to the "truth" in terms which no one understood. It is said that he was expelled from fifty cities.

In their bewilderment the people were divided concerning him. His detractors were countless, his supporters innumerable. They witnessed many wonders performed by him. Tongues wagged, and his words were carried to the caliph. Finally all were united in the view that he should be put to death because of his saying, "I am the Truth."

"Say, He is the Truth," they cried out to him.

"Yes. He is All," he replied. "You say that He is lost. On the contrary, it is Ḥusayn that is lost. The Ocean does not vanish or grow less."

"These words which Ḥallāj speaks have an esoteric meaning," they told Junayd.

"Let him be killed," he answered. "This is not the time for esoteric meanings."

Then a group of the theologians made common cause against Ḥallāj and carried a garbled version of his words to Mu'taṣim; they also turned his vizier 'Alī ibn 'Īsā against him. The caliph ordered that he should be thrown into prison. There he was held for a year. But people would come and consult him on their problems. So then they were prevented from visiting him, and for five months no one came near him, except Ibn 'Aṭā' once and Ibn Khafīf once. On one occasion Ibn 'Aṭā' sent him a message.

"Master, ask pardon for the words you have spoken, that you may be set free."

"Tell him who said this to ask pardon," Ḥallāj replied.

Ibn "Aṭā' wept when he heard this answer.

"We are not even a fraction of Ḥallāj," he said.

It is said that on the first night of his imprisonment the gaolers came to his cell but could not find him in the prison. They searched through all the prison, but could not discover a soul. On the second night they found neither him nor the prison, for all their hunting. On the third night they discovered him in the prison.

"Where were you on the first night, and where were you and the prison on the second night?" they demanded. "Now you have both reappeared. What phenomenon is this?"

"On the first night," he replied, "I was in the Presence, therefore I was not here. On the second night the Presence was here, so that both of us were absent. On the third night I was sent back, that the Law might be preserved. Come and do your work!"

When Ḥallāj was first confined there were three hundred souls in the prison. That night he addressed them.

"Prisoners, shall I set you free?"

"Why do you not free yourself?" they replied.

"I am God's captive. I am the sentinel of salvation," he answered. "If I so wish, with one signal I can loose all bonds."

Ḥallāj made a sign with his finger, and all their bonds burst asunder.

"Now where are we to go?" the prisoners demanded. "The gate of the prison is locked."

Ḥallāj signalled again, and cracks appeared in the walls.

"Now go on your way," he cried.

"Are you not coming too?" they asked.

"No," he replied. "I have a secret with Him which cannot be told save on the gallows."

"Where have the prisoners gone?" the warders asked him next morning.

"I set them free," Ḥallāj answered.

"Why did you not go?" they enquired.

"God has cause to chide me, so I did not go," he replied.

This story was carried to the caliph.

"There will be a riot," he cried. "Kill him, or beat him with sticks until he retracts."

They beat him with sticks three hundred times. At every blow a clear voice was heard to say, "Fear not, son of Manṣūr!"

Then they led him out to be crucified.

Loaded with thirteen heavy chains, Ḥallāj strode out proudly along the way waving his arms like a very vagabond.

"Why do you strut so proudly?" they asked him.

"Because I am going to the slaughterhouse," he replied. And he recited in clear tones,

My boon-companion's not to be
Accused of mean inequity.
He made me drink like him the best,
As does the generous host his guest;
And when the round was quite complete
He called for sword and winding-sheet.
Such is his fate, who drinks past reason
With Draco in the summer season.

When they brought him to the base of the gallows at Bāb al-Ṭāq, he kissed the wood and set his foot upon the ladder.

"How do you feel?" they taunted him.

"The ascension of true men is the top of the gallows," he answered.

He was wearing a loincloth about his middle and a mantle on his shoulders. Turning towards Makkah, he lifted up his hands and communed with God.

"What He knows, no man knows," he said. Then he climbed the gibbet.

"What do you say," asked a group of his followers, "concerning us who are your disciples, and these who condemn you and would stone you?"

"They have a double reward, and you a single," he answered. "You merely think well of me. They are moved by the strength of their belief in One God to maintain the rigour of the Law."

Shiblī came and stood facing him.

"*Have we not forbidden thee all beings?*" he cried. Then he asked, "What is Sufism, Ḥallāj?"

"The least part of it is this that you see," Ḥallāj replied.

"What is the loftier part?" asked Shiblī.

"That you cannot reach," Ḥallāj answered.

Then all the spectators began to throw stones. Shiblī, to conform, cast a clod. Ḥallāj sighed.

"You did not sigh when struck by all these stones. Why did you sigh because of a clod?" they asked.

"Because those who cast stones do not know what they are doing. They have an excuse. From him it comes hard to me, for he knows that he ought not to fling at me."

Then they cut off his hands. He laughed.

"Why do you laugh?" they cried.

"It is an easy matter to strike off the hands of a man who is bound," he answered. "He is a true man, who cuts off the hands of attributes which remove the crown of aspiration from the brow of the Throne."

They hacked off his feet. He smiled.

"With these feet I made an earthly journey," he said. "Other feet I have, which even now are journeying through both the worlds. If you are able, hack off those feet!"

Then he rubbed his bloody, amputated hands over his face, so that both his arms and his face were stained with blood.

"Why did you do that?" they enquired.

"Much blood has gone out of me," he replied. "I realise that my face will have grown pale. You suppose that my pallor is because I am afraid. I rubbed blood over my face so that I might appear rose-cheeked in your eyes. The cosmetic of heroes is their blood."

"Even if you bloodied your face, why did you stain your arms?"

"I was making ablution."

"What ablution?"

"When one prays two *rak'ahs* in love," Ḥallāj replied, "the ablution is not perfect unless performed with blood."

Next they plucked out his eyes. A roar went up from the crowd. Some wept, some flung stones. Then they made to cut out his tongue.

"Be patient a little, give me time to speak one word," he entreated. "O God," he cried, lifting his face to heaven, "do not exclude them for the suffering they are bringing on me for Thy sake, neither deprive them of this felicity. Praise be to God, for that they have cut off my feet as I trod Thy way. And if they strike off my head from my body, they have raised me up to the head of the gallows, contemplating Thy majesty."

Then they cut off his ears and nose. An old woman carrying a pitcher happened along. Seeing Ḥallāj, she cried, "Strike, and strike hard and true. What business has this pretty little Woolcarder to speak of God?"

The last words Ḥallāj spoke were these. "Love of the One is isolation of the One." Then he chanted this verse: "*Those that believe not therein seek to hasten it; but those who believe in it go in fear of it, knowing that it is the truth.*"

This was his final utterance. They then cut out his tongue. It was the time of the evening prayer when they cut off his head. Even as they were cutting off his head, Ḥallāj smiled. Then he gave up the ghost.

A great cry went up from the people. Ḥallāj had carried the ball of destiny to the boundary of the field of resignation. From each one of his members came the declaration, "I am the Truth."

Next day they declared, "This scandal will be even greater than while he was alive." So they burned his limbs. From his ashes came the cry, "I am the Truth," even as in the time of his slaying every drop of blood as it trickled formed the word Allah. Dumbfounded, they cast his ashes into the Tigris. As they floated on the surface of the water, they continued to cry, "I am the Truth."

Now Ḥallāj had said, "When they cast my ashes into the Tigris, Baghdad will be in peril of drowning under the water. Lay my robe in front of the water, or Baghdad will be destroyed." His servant, when he saw what had happened, brought the master's robe and laid it on the bank of the Tigris. The waters subsided, and his ashes became silent. Then they gathered his ashes and buried them.

37

Ibrāhīm al-Khawwāṣ

Abū Isḥāq Ibrāhīm ibn Aḥmad al-Khawwāṣ of Sāmarrā', a companion of al-Junayd, is famous for his long journeys in the desert. He died at Rayy in 291 (904).

Ibrāhīm al-Khawwāṣ in the desert

Ibrāhīm al-Khawwāṣ, a contemporary of Junayd and Nūrī, was known as the Chief of the Trustful. So complete was his trust in God, that he would cross the desert on the scent of an apple. For all that he was unique in his trustfulness, he was never without a needle, a thread, a flask and a pair of scissors. Asked why he carried these, he answered, "That much does not impair trust." He told the following stories of the marvels he had seen on his journeys.

I was once travelling through the desert when I espied a maiden in the throes of ecstasy, wandering distraught with her head uncovered.

"Maiden, cover your head," I cried.

"Khawwāṣ, close your eyes!" she retorted.

"I am in love," I said, "and the lover does not cover his eyes. But my eyes involuntarily fell upon you."

"I am intoxicated," she answered, "and the drunkard does not cover his head."

"At which tavern did you become intoxicated?" I asked.

"Have a care, Khawwāṣ," she cried. "You are impeding me. Is there any in the two abodes but God?"

"Maiden, would you have my company?" I asked.

"You are callow, Khawwāṣ," she answered. "I am not the sort that is looking for a man!"

Once I beheld Khiḍr in the desert in the form of a flying bird. When I espied him so, I lowered my head that my trust might not become void. Immediately he approached me and said, 'If you had looked at me, I would not have descended on you." I did not greet him, lest my trust should be impaired.

One day in the desert I came upon a tree where there was water. I beheld a huge lion making for me, and committed myself to God. When he came near I noticed that he was limping. He laid down before me and groaned.

I looked and saw that his paw was swollen and gangrenous. So I look a stick and cut open the paw, till all the pus was drained; then I bandaged the paw with a rag. The lion arose and went away. Presently the lion returned bringing his cub. They circled around me wagging their tails, and brought a round bread and laid it before me.

Once I had lost my way in the desert. I pushed on some distance, but could not find the way. For several days I went on like that, till at last I heard a cock crowing. I rejoiced, and hastened in that direction. I sighted a person who promptly ran up and struck me on the neck. The blow hurt, and I cried out.

"O God, that is how they treat one who puts his trust in Thee!"

"So long as you put your trust in Me," I heard a voice say, "you were precious in My sight. Now that you have put your trust in a cockcrow, you have been beaten in consequence."

Still in pain, I continued on my way. Then I heard a voice which said, "Khawwāṣ, that pained you. Now look yonder!"

I looked, and saw lying before me the head of the man who had struck me.

I had made a vow that I would cross the desert without provisions and mount. As I entered the desert a young man came after me and hailed me.

"Peace be upon you, O shaykh!"

I halted and answered his greeting. Then I saw that the youth was a Christian.

"Do you allow me to accompany you?" he asked.

"Where I am going you may not come, so what advantage will you gain in my company?" I replied.

"All the same I will come," he answered. "It may bring a blessing."

For a week we journeyed together. On the eighth day my companion said, "Good Ḥanifite ascetic, be bold with your God, for I am hungry. Ask for something."

"My God," I prayed, "by the merits of Muḥammad, peace be upon him, do not put me to shame before this stranger, but manifest something out of the Unseen."

Immediately I beheld a dish appear filled with bread and roast fish and dates, and a jug of water. We both sat down and applied ourselves to the fare.

We pushed on for another week. Then on the eighth day I said to my companion, "Monk, now display your power too. I am hungry."

Leaning on his staff, the young man moved his lips. Two tables appeared covered with *ḥalwā*, fish and dates, and two jugs of water. I was amazed.

"Ascetic, eat!" the Christian cried.

I was too shamefaced to eat anything.

"Eat," he repeated, "then I will give you some good news."

"I will not eat until you tell me your good news," I replied.

"The first piece of good news is this, that I am cutting my girdle."

With that he cut his girdle.

"I testify that there is no god but God, and I testify that Muḥammad is the Messenger of God," he said. "The other piece of good news is this, that I said, 'O God, by the merits of this elder who is of value in Thy sight and whose religion is true, send Thou food that I may not be put to shame before him.' This too was by your blessing."

So we ate, and proceeded on our way till we came to Makkah. There he resided in the Holy Territory till his term drew nigh.

I was passing one day through the parts of Syria when I espied some pomegranate-trees. My appetite was whetted, but I controlled myself and did not eat any because the pomegranates were sour, and I wanted sweet ones. Presently I entered a valley where I saw a man lying exhausted and helpless. The worms had fallen on him, and hornets buzzed around him stinging him. My compassion was moved by his pitiful condition.

"Would you like me to pray," I said when I reached him, "that haply you may be delivered out of this affliction?"

"No," he replied.

"Why not?" I asked.

"Because healing is what I would choose, and affliction is what He chooses," he answered. "I do not prefer my choice above His choice."

"At least let me drive these hornets away from you," I said.

"Khawwāṣ," he answered, "drive away from yourself that hankering for sweet pomegranates. Why do you trouble me? Pray for your own heart's healing. Why do you pray that my body may be made whole?"

"How did you know that I am Khawwāṣ?" I asked.

"Whoever knows Him," he replied, "from him nothing remains hidden."

"How do you feel with these hornets?" I enquired.

"So long as these hornets sting me and the worms devour me," he answered, "I am happy."

Once I heard that in Byzantium there was a monk who had been living for seventy years in a monastery in the state of celibacy.

"Amazing!" I exclaimed. "Forty years is the qualification for being a monk."

So I set forth to call on him. When I came near he opened a little wicket.

"Ibrāhīm, why have you come?" he enquired. "I am not seated here as a celibate. I have a dog which falls upon people. Now I am seated here keeping watch over the dog and preventing it from doing mischief to people. But for that, I am not what you supposed."

"O God," I exclaimed on hearing this answer, "Thou art able to guide Thy servant aright even when he is in very error!"

"Ibrāhīm," the monk said to me, "how long will you search for men? Search for yourself, and when you have found yourself, sit in watch over yourself. For every day this wayward desire puts on three hundred and sixty various guises of divinity and invites a man to error."

38

Al-Shiblī

Abū Bakr Dulaf ibn Jaḥdar (Ja'far ibn Yūnus) al-Shiblī, of Khurasan by origin but born in Baghdad or Sāmarrā', son of a court official and himself promoted in the imperial service, as Governor of Demavend was summoned to Baghdad to be invested and there experienced conversion. Joining the circle of Junayd, he became a leading figure in the stormy history of al-Ḥallāj, notorious for his eccentric behaviour which led to his committal to an asylum. He died in 334 (846) at the age of 87.

The calling of Shiblī

Abū Bakr al-Shiblī was originally Governor of Demavend. A dispatch came to him from Baghdad, and he set out with the Governor of Rayy and a retinue to present himself before the caliph. Having been invested by the caliph with robes of honour, they returned homewards. By chance the Governor of Rayy suddenly sneezed. He wiped his mouth and nose in his robe of honour. This being reported to the caliph, he commanded that he should be stripped of his robe, soundly cuffed and dismissed from his office of governor. This opened Shiblī's eyes.

"One who uses as a handkerchief a robe conferred by a mortal being," he mused, "is accounted deserving to be deposed and slighted. He forfeits his robe of office. What then of him who uses as a handkerchief the robe conferred by the King of the world—what will be done to him?"

At once he went to the caliph.

"Prince," he addressed the caliph, "you, a mortal being, do not approve that the robe conferred by you should be treated disrespectfully, and it is well known what your robe is worth. The King of the world has given me a robe of honour, even the love and knowledge of Him. How shall He ever approve my using it as a handkerchief in the service of a mortal?"

And he left the court and proceeded to the assembly of Khayr al-Nassāj. There a miracle happened to him, and Khayr sent him to Junayd. So Shiblī came before Junayd.

"You are recommended as an expert on pearls," he said. "Either give me one, or sell one to me."

"If I sell you one, you will not have the price of it, and if I give you one, having so easily come by it you will not realise its value," Junayd replied. "Do like me; plunge head first into this Sea, and if you wait patiently you will obtain your pearl."

"Now what shall I do?" asked Shiblī.

"Go and sell sulphur for a year," said Junayd.

Shiblī did so. When the year was up, Junayd gave him new instructions.

"This work brings notoriety and commerce. Go and beg for a year, so that you be not busied with aught else."

For a whole year Shiblī wandered throughout Baghdad. No one gave him anything. He returned and reported to Junayd.

"Now realise your own worth, for you count for nothing in the eyes of your fellows," said Junayd. "Fasten not your heart on them, neither have any regard of them. For some days you were a chamberlain and for some days you acted as governor. Now repair to your former province and seek quittance of the inhabitants there."

Shiblī returned to Demavend and went from house to house, till only one victim of oppression remained. That man he could not trace.

"With him in mind," Shiblī recalled, "I distributed a hundred thousand dirhams, but still my heart did not find rest."

Four years went by in this way. Then he returned to Junayd.

"Some fragment of pomp and pride still lingers in you," said Junayd. "Beg for another year."

"Every day I went begging," Shiblī recalled. 'I brought him all I got, and he would give it to the poor. At night he kept me hungry. When a year had gone by, he said to me, 'Now I admit you to my companionship, but on one condition, that you shall be the servant of my companions.' So for a year I served the companions. Then Junayd said to me, 'Abū Bakr, what is your view of yourself now?' 'I regard myself as the least of God's creatures,' I replied. 'Now,' remarked Junayd, 'your faith is whole."'

By then Shiblī had progressed to the point that he would fill his sleeve with sugar, and every boy he saw he would put a piece in his mouth.

"Say Allah!" he would say.

After that he filled his sleeve with dirhams and dinars.

"Every one who says Allah once, I will fill his mouth with gold."

Thereafter the spirit of jealousy stirred in him, and he unsheathed a sword.

"Every one who mentions the name of Allah, I will strike off his head with this sword," he cried.

"Hitherto," they said, "you used to give sugar and gold. Now you will strike off heads?"

"Then I supposed that they pronounced His name out of true experience and knowledge," he explained. "Now I realise that they speak it unheeding and merely out of habit. I cannot permit Him to be named by an impure tongue."

After that on every place he could find he inscribed the name of God. Suddenly a voice addressed him.

"How long will you go about the name? If you are truly a seeker, stride forth on the quest of the Named!"

These words affected him deeply. Peace and composure altogether deserted him. So powerful was the love possessing him, so completely was he overwhelmed by mystical tumult, that he went and flung himself into the Tigris. The river surged and cast him up on the bank. Then he hurled himself into the fire, but the flames affected him not. He sought a place where hungry lions were gathered and cast himself before them; the lions all fled away from him. He threw himself down from the summit of a mountain; the wind picked him up and deposited him on the ground. His disquiet increased a thousandfold.

"Woe to him," he cried, "whom neither water nor fire will accept, neither the wild beasts nor the mountains!"

"He who is accepted of God," came a voice, "is accepted of no other."

Then they loaded him with chains and fetters and carried him to the asylum.

"This man is mad," some shouted.

"In your eyes I am mad and you are sane," he replied. "May God augment my madness and your sanity, that by reason of that madness I may be admitted nearer and nearer, and because of that sanity you may be driven farther and farther!"

The caliph sent one to care for him. The attendants came and by force thrust the medicine in his throat.

"Do not put yourself to such pains," Shiblī cried. "This sickness is not such as will yield to healing by medicine."

Anecdotes of Shiblī

When Shiblī was confined in chains a group of his companions one day went to visit him.

"Who are you?" he cried.

"Your friends," they told him.

He at once began to throw stones at them, and they all fled.

"Liars!" he shouted. "Do friends run away from their friend because of a few stones? This proves that you are friends of yourselves, not of me!"

Once Shiblī was observed running with a burning coal in his hand.

"Where are you going?" they asked.

"I am running to set fire to the Ka'bah," he answered, "so that men may henceforward care only for the Lord of the Ka'bah."

On another occasion he was holding in his hand a piece of wood alight at both ends.

"What are you going to do?" he was asked.

"I am going to set Hell on fire with one end and Paradise with the other," he replied, "so that men may concern themselves only with God."

Shiblī danced once for several days and nights beneath a certain tree crying, "Hoo, Hoo."

"What is all this?" his friends demanded.

"This ringdove in yonder tree is saying Coo Coo," he explained. "I am accompanying it with Hoo Hoo."

It is said that the ringdove did not stop cooing until Shiblī ceased hooing.

It is said that when Shiblī first began his self-mortification, for many long years he used to rub salt in his eyes so that he should not sleep. It is stated that he put seven maunds of salt in his eyes in this way.

"Almighty God is watching me," he would say. "The man who sleeps is heedless," he added, "and the heedless man is veiled."

One day Junayd visited him to find him pulling up the skin of his eyebrows with tweezers.

"Why are you doing that?" he asked.

"Truth has become manifest, and I cannot endure it," Shiblī answered. "I am pricking myself that haply He may grant me one glance."

Shiblī had a grotto where he used to go, carrying with him a bundle of sticks. Any time his heart was invaded by inattention he would beat himself with those sticks. Once it happened that he had broken all the sticks, so he beat his hands and feet against the wall.

Overpowered by mystic ecstasy, Shiblī began to preach, and proclaimed before the people the secret. Junayd reproached him.

"We utter these words in grottos," he said. "Now you have come and declare them in the market-place."

"I am speaking and I am listening," Shiblī replied. "In both worlds who is there but I? Nay rather, these are words proceeding from God to God, and Shiblī is not there at all."

"If that is the case, you have dispensation," Junayd said.

One day Shiblī was repeatedly uttering the word God, God. An earnest young disciple addressed him.

"Why do you not say, There is no god but God?" Shiblī sighed.

"I am afraid," he explained, "that if I say 'no god' my breath may be stopped before I reach 'but God' and I shall be utterly desolated."

These words made such an impression on the youth that he trembled and expired. His friends came and haled Shiblī to the caliph's palace. He, being still in the throes of ecstasy, walked along like one drunk. They accused him of murder,

"Shiblī, what do you say?" demanded the caliph.

"It was a soul wholly consumed by the flame of the fire of love, in eager expectancy of confronting the majesty of God," Shiblī replied. "It was a soul severed from all connections, passed away from all carnal corruption. It was a soul come to the end of its tether that could endure no longer, visited successively inwardly by the importunate envoys of the Presence Divine. A lightning-flash of the beauty of the contemplation of this visitation leaped upon the very core of his soul. His soul bird-like flew out of the cage of the body. What was Shiblī's offence or crime in this?"

"Send Shiblī home immediately," ordered the caliph. "His words have produced such a state in me inwardly that there is danger that I may fall from this throne!"

Once Shiblī was in Baghdad. He said, "We require a thousand dirhams, to buy shoes for the poor and despatch them on the pilgrimage."

A Christian jumped up and said, "I will give them, only on one condition, that you take me with you."

"Young sir, you are not qualified for the pilgrimage," said

"There is no mule in your caravan," the youth replied. "Take me along as your mule."

The dervishes set out, the Christian along with them loins girded to the trail.

"How are you faring, young man?" asked Shiblī.

'I am so happy at the thought of accompanying you that I cannot sleep," he replied.

On the road the Christian took a brush and at every halting place he swept the floor for the pilgrims and plucked out the thorns. When the time came for putting on the white robes, he saw what the rest were doing and followed their example. At last the party arrived at the Ka'bah.

"With your girdle I cannot let you enter the Holy House," Shiblī told the Christian.

"O God," the Christian cried, laying his head on the threshold, "Shiblī says he will not allow me into Thy House."

"Shiblī," came a voice out of heaven, "We have brought him here from Baghdad. Kindling the fire of love in his heart, We have dragged him to Our House with the chains of loving kindness. Shiblī, get out of the way! You, friend, come in!"

The Christian entered the Holy House and performed the visitation. The rest of the party then entered and in due course emerged, but the youth still did not come out.

"Young man, come out!" Shiblī called.

"He will not let me out," the youth replied. "Every time I make for the door of the House I find it shut. What will become of me?"

Once Junayd and Shiblī both fell sick. A Christian physician visited Shiblī.

"What pains are you feeling?" he asked.

"None," Shiblī replied.

"What do you say?" the doctor repeated.

"I have no pain," Shiblī told him.

The physician then visited Junayd.

"What pains do you have?" he enquired.

Junayd described his symptoms in detail, enumerating each pain in turn. The Christian treated him, and departed. Later the two friends came together.

"Why did you expose all your pains to a Christian?" Shiblī asked.

"So that he might realise," Junayd answered, "if His friend is treated so, what He will do to His foe! And you," he added, "why did you not describe your pains?"

'I was ashamed," Shiblī replied, "to complain to an enemy of the Friend!"

One day as Shiblī was going along he encountered two

boys quarrelling over a walnut they had found. He took the walnut from them.

'Be patient, till I divide it between you!" he told them.

When he broke it open, the nut proved to be empty. A voice proclaimed, "Go on, divide it, if you are the Divider!"

"All that quarrelling over an empty nut," Shiblī commented shamefaced. "And all that pretension to be a divider over nothing!"

The death of Shiblī

When the hour of his death drew near, Shiblī's eyes were shrouded in darkness. He asked for ashes and sprinkled them over his head, and was possessed of an indescribable restlessness.

"Why all this agitation?" his friends asked him.

"My soul is filled with envy and jealousy of Iblīs," he answered. "Here I sit athirst, and He gives of His own to another. Upon thee shall rest My curse till the Day of Doom. I cannot bear to see that attribution of the Divine curse to Iblīs. I wish it to be mine; for even though it is a curse, yet is it not His, and is it not of His attribution? What does that accursed one know of its worth? Why did He not vouchsafe to the princes of the Community to set their feet on the crown of the Throne? The jeweller knows the value of the jewel. If a king sets a glass bead or a crystal on his hand, it appears as a jewel; but if a greengrocer makes a seal-ring of a jewel and puts it on his finger, it appears as a bead of glass."

Thereafter Shiblī was composed for a while. Then his agitation returned.

"What is it?" they asked.

"Two winds are blowing," he answered. "One is the wind of loving kindness, the other the wind of wrath. Upon whomsoever the wind of loving kindness blows, he attains his goal; upon whomsoever the wind of wrath blows, he is imprisoned in the veil. Upon whom shall that wind alight? If the wind of loving kindness is to light on me, in that fond hope I can endure all this hardship and suffering. If the wind of wrath is to light on me, this my present suffering shall be naught in comparison with what will then befall me. Nothing," he added, "weighs more heavily on my heart than the one dirham of oppression I have been guilty of, though I have given a thousand dirhams in expiation thereof. My heart will not rest. Give me the water of purification."

They brought him water, but forgot to let it run through his beard till he reminded them.

All that night Shiblī recited these verses.

Whatever house Thou tak'st for thine
No lamp is needed there to shine.
Upon the day that men shall bring
Their proofs before the Judge and King,
Our proof shall be, in that dread place,
The longed-for beauty of Thy face.

A company then gathered around him to say the funeral prayers. His end had come, and he realised what was passing.

"How marvellous!" he exclaimed. "A throng of dead men came to pray over one living."

"Say, There is no god but God," they said.

"Since there is no other than He," he replied, "how can I utter a negative?"

"There is no help. Say the words of attestation," they urged him.

"The King of Love says, I will not accept a bribe," Shiblī retorted.

Then one present raised his voice to prompt him.

"Here is a dead man come, to awaken the living!" Shiblī exclaimed.

A little while passed. Then they said, "How are you?"

"I have rejoined the Beloved," he answered. Then he expired.

Bibliography

- R.A. Nicholson, The *Tadhkirat'l-Awliya of Shaykh Faridu'd-din 'Attar*. 2 vols. (London, 1905-1907). Critical edition of text with remarks on the language and conspectus of parallel passages in the *Risālah* of Abū al-Qāsim al-Qushayrī. Preface on the biography of 'Aṭṭār by Mirza Muḥammad Qazwīnī.
- Sa'id Nafisi, *Jostoju dar ahwal u athar-e Farid al-Din 'Attar-e Nishaburi* (Tehran, 1320 [1942]). Scholarly examination of the biography and writings of 'Aṭṭār.
- H. Ritter. *Das Meer der Seele* (Leiden, 1955). Contains much valuable information on the life and works of 'Aṭṭār. See also the same scholar's articles "Philologika X" in *Der Islam,* XXVI (1942), and in *Encyclopaedia of Islam,* (new edition), I, 752-755.
- F. Rouhani, *Le Livre divin* (Paris, 1961). This translation of the *Elahi-nama* of 'Aṭṭār contains in the preface a critical study of the life and works of the poet.

- Badi' al-Zaman Foruzanfar, *Sharh-i ahwal o naqd o tahlil-e athar-e Farid al-Din Muḥammad-e 'Attar-e Nishaburi* (Tehran, 1340 [1962)]). Erudite study of the life and works of 'Aṭṭār.
- C.A. Storey, *Persian Literature* (London, 1953). A very valuable bibliography, listing the manuscripts of the text, editions, translations and studies.

Other books helpful to the study of the text and to the persons mentioned in it are listed above under several entries. The relevant entries on 'Aṭṭār in the standard histories of Persian literature should also be consulted.

Index